P9-DCI-849

We've Had a Hundred Years of Psychotherapy
—And the World's Getting Worse

By James Hillman

The Dream and the Underworld

Interviews

Freud's Own Cookbook (with Charles Boer)

Anima: An Anatomy of a Personified Notion

Healing Fiction

A Blue Fire (edited by Thomas Moore)

Re-Visioning Psychology

Emotion: A Comprehensive Phenomenology of Theories and Their Meanings for Therapy

Suicide and the Soul

Insearch: Psychology and Religion

The Myth of Analysis: Three Essays in Archetypal Psychology

The Feeling Function

An Essay on Pan

"Psychological Commentary" to Gopi Krishna's Kundalini

Loose Ends: Primary Papers in Archetypal Psychology

By Michael Ventura

Shadow Dancing in the U.S.A.

Night Time, Losing Time

We've Had a Hundred Years of Psychotherapy —And the World's Getting Worse

James Hillman and Michael Ventura

HarperSanFrancisco
A Division of HarperCollins*Publishers*

Portions of "The First Dialogue" originally appeared in the July 1, 1990, issue of *L.A. Weekly.* Portions of the letters "On Being Practical" and "Talking" by James Hillman were printed in *Stirrings of Culture: Essays from the Dallas Institute,* ed. Robert Sardello and Gail Thomas, Dallas, 1986. An expanded version of the letter "Recovery" appeared in *Spring 52: A Journal of Archetype and Culture,* Dallas, 1992. Excerpts from *Crow with No Moth: Ikkyu, 15th Century Zen Master* copyright © 1989 by Stephen Berg. Reprinted by permission of Copper Canyon Press, P.O. Box 271, Port Townsend, WA 98368.

FIRST EDITION

Library of Congress Cataloging-in-Publication Data

Hillman, James.
We've had a hundred years of psychotherapy—and the world's getting worse / James Hillman and Michael Ventura.—1st ed.
p. cm.
ISBN 0-06-250409-6 (alk. paper)
1. Psychotherapy—Philosophy. 2. Psychotherapy—Social aspects—United States. 3. Civilization, Modern—20th century—Psychological aspects. 4. Psychoanalysts—United States—Interviews. 5. Hillman, James—Interviews. I. Ventura, Michael. II. Title.
RC437.5.H55 1992
150′.1—dc20 91.55294
CIP

---

92 93 94 95 96 HAD 10 9 8 7 6 5 4 3 2 1
This edition is printed on acid-free paper that meets the American National Standards Institute Z39.48 Standard.

Contents

Preface
vii

Part I
The First Dialogue
A Cell of Revolution
1

Part II
The Letters
Life Lived Backwards,
Frontwards, and Sideways
49

Part III
The Second Dialogue
"Pick Up If You're There"
161

Preface

The genesis of this book can be told in a short series of *thats:* that the psychologist James Hillman's work (especially his book *The Dream and the Underworld*) influenced, instigated, and haunted my thought long before we started crossing paths at various conferences and lectures; that one day I was talking about Hillman to Kit Rachlis, the editor of the *L. A. Weekly,* and that Kit was so intrigued he suggested I do a cover-story interview with Jim; that the cover-story (which, in extended form, is now Part One of this book) was widely and strenuously discussed up and down the town; and that, on the strength of this reaction, we decided to make a book.

We wanted an informal, wild, even funny book about therapy, a book that takes chances, breaks rules, runs red lights. To do this, we decided to stick to spoken, friendly (and hence irreverent) speech, and the conversational prose of letters. Why? Because psychotherapy wants and demands to be questioned, even attacked, in the form it prefers: staid, contained, well-behaved—in other words, like any established institution, the psychotherapy industry wants to be addressed in a manner that accepts its basic codes of conduct, and therefore, by implication, its basic *goals,* of conduct. But if you fall for that, then instead of questioning those codes and goals, perhaps you're accepting them more than you know, reinforcing them by playing by their rules.

That's no way to begin a breakthrough—the breakthrough in which, as James Hillman suggests here, the consulting room becomes a cell of revolution, a means to change not only oneself but one's world. So we chose another route, and made the book you hold.

Michael Ventura
Los Angeles
1991

Part I

The First Dialogue: A Cell of Revolution

Two men are on an afternoon walk in Santa Monica, on the Pacific Palisades. They are walking in a direction Californians always call north because it follows the coastline "up" on the map; actually, the coast bends sharply here and they're heading due west. That's worth mentioning only because it's the sort of detail that would interest these men, and, if it catches their attention, they'll talk about it, digress about it, and even attach a great deal of significance to it—partly just for fun and partly because that's how they are.

The two men began their walk on the Santa Monica Pier, with its rundown carnival air, where the affluent and the homeless pass among each other—and among Latinos from East L.A. and the new Central American ghettos; blacks from South Central; Asians from Chinatown, Koreatown, and the Japanese enclaves; pale whites from Culver City and North Hollywood; tan, svelte whites from West L.A.; old people of all descriptions and accents; and tourists from everywhere. The poor fish for food off the pier, though signs in English and Spanish tell them it's dangerous to eat their catch. The beach is often closed from sewage spills. But the ocean doesn't show its filth, it looks as lovely as always, and it's anywhere from ten to thirty degrees cooler at the Pacific than even just a few miles inland—so everybody comes.

The two men have walked the steady incline up the Palisades, along the cliffs overlooking the Pacific Coast Highway and the sea, and, at the far end of the park, where the cliffs are highest and there aren't so many people, they've sat down on a bench.

The men are James Hillman and Michael Ventura. Hillman is in his midsixties, tall and slender. Though born Jewish in Atlantic City he carries himself like an old-timey New Englander, with that Yankee sense of tolerant but no-nonsense authority—softened somewhat by the eagerness of his interest in whatever and, usually, whoever's around him. Ventura is in his midforties, shorter, darker, and scruffier than Hillman. He wears the kind of hat men wore in 1940s movies and a good but battered set of cowboy boots, and he gives the impression of trying to balance between these incongruities. Hillman is a psychoanalyst, author, and lecturer; Ventura is a newspaper columnist, novelist, and screenwriter.

Ventura carries a small tape recorder, and when he's with Hillman these days it's almost always on, even when they're walking or driving. Their conversation has a theme: psychotherapy. And it has something like a form: each man is to push the other not to make more sense but to get further out in his thinking. And their conversation has an ambition: that their talks and, later, their letters will make a book, an informal but (they hope) fierce polemic to give psychotherapy a shake. For they share the conviction that psychotherapy needs desperately to push past the boundaries of its accepted ideas; it needs a new wildness before it's co-opted entirely as just another device for compressing (shrinking) people into a forced, and false, normality.

They sit on the bench, Ventura puts the tape recorder between them, and Hillman takes off on what, these days, is his favorite theme.

JAMES HILLMAN: We've had a hundred years of analysis, and people are getting more and more sensitive, and the world is getting worse and worse. Maybe it's time to look at that. We still locate the psyche inside the skin. You go *inside* to locate the psyche, you examine *your* feelings and *your* dreams, they belong to you. Or it's interrelations, interpsyche, between your psyche and mine. That's been extended a little bit into family systems and office groups—but the psyche, the soul, is still only *within* and *between* people. We're working on our relationships constantly, and our feelings and reflections, but look what's left out of that.

Hillman makes a wide gesture that includes the oil tanker on the horizon, the gang graffiti on a park sign, and the fat homeless woman with swollen ankles and cracked skin asleep on the grass about fifteen yards away.

What's left out is a deteriorating world.

So why hasn't therapy noticed that? Because psychotherapy is only working on that "inside" soul. By removing the soul from the world and not recognizing that the soul is also *in* the world, psychotherapy can't do its job anymore. The buildings are sick, the institutions are sick, the banking system's sick, the schools, the streets—the sickness is out *there*.

You know, the soul is always being rediscovered through pathology. In the nineteenth century people didn't talk about psyche, until Freud came along and discovered psychopathology. Now we're beginning to say, "The furniture has stuff in it that's poisoning us, the microwave gives off dangerous rays." The world has become toxic.

Both men, watching the sun flash on the sea, seem to be thinking the same thing.

MICHAEL VENTURA: That sea out there is diseased. We can't eat the fish.

HILLMAN: The world has become full of symptoms. Isn't that the beginning of recognizing what used to be called animism?

The world's alive—my god! It's having effects on us. "I've got to get rid of those fluorocarbon cans." "I've got to get rid of the furniture because underneath it's formaldehyde." "I've got to watch out for this and that and *that*." So there's pathology in the world, and through that we're beginning to treat the world with more respect.

VENTURA: As though having denied the spirit in things, the spirit—offended—comes back as a threat. Having denied the soul in things, having said to things, with Descartes, "You don't have souls," things have turned around and said, "Just you *watch* what kind of a soul I have, muthafucka."

HILLMAN: "Just watch what I can do, man! You're gonna have that ugly lamp in your room, that lamp is going to make you suffer every single day you look at it. It's going to produce fluorescent light, and it's going to drive you slowly crazy sitting in your office. And then you're going to see a psychotherapist, and you're going to try to work it out in your relationships, but you don't know I'm really the one that's got you. It's that fluorescent tube over your head all day long, coming right down on your skull like a KGB man putting a light on you, straight down on you—shadowless, ruthless, cruel."

VENTURA: And yet we sense this in all we do and say now, all of us, but we're caught in a double bind: on the one hand this is "progress," a value that's been ingrained in us—and if you think it's not ingrained in you, take a drive down to Mexico and see if even poor Americans would want to live the way most of those people have to live (the life of the American poor seems rich to them, that's why they keep coming); but on the other hand, we know that the things of our lives are increasingly harmful, but we haven't got Idea One about what to do. Our sense of politics has atrophied into the sort of nonsense that goes on in presidential elections.

HILLMAN: There is a decline in political sense. No sensitivity to the real issues. Why are the intelligent people—at least among the white middle class—so passive now? Why? Because the sensitive, intelligent people are in therapy! They've been in therapy in the United States for thirty, forty years, and during that time there's been a tremendous political decline in this country.

VENTURA: How do you think that works?

HILLMAN: Every time we try to deal with our outrage over the freeway, our misery over the office and the lighting and the crappy furniture, the crime on the streets, whatever—every time we try to deal with that by going to therapy with our rage and fear, we're depriving the political world of something. And therapy, in its crazy way, by emphasizing the inner soul and ignoring the outer soul, supports the decline of the actual world. Yet therapy goes on blindly believing that it's curing the outer world by making better people. We've had that for years and years and years: "If everybody went into therapy we'd have better buildings, we'd have better people, we'd have more consciousness." It's not the case.

VENTURA: I'm not sure it's causal, but it's definitely a pattern. Our inner knowledge has gotten more subtle while our ability to deal with the world around us has, well, *deteriorated* is almost not a strong enough word. *Disintegrated* is more like it.

HILLMAN: The vogue today, in psychotherapy, is the "inner child." That's the therapy thing—you go back to your childhood. But if you're looking backward, you're not looking around. This trip backward constellates what Jung called the "child archetype." Now, the child archetype is by nature apolitical and disempowered—it has no connection with the political world. And so the adult says, "Well, what can I do about the world? This thing's bigger than me." That's the child archetype talking. "All I can do is go into myself, work on my growth, my development, find good parenting, support groups." This is a disaster for our political world, for our democracy. Democracy depends on intensely active citizens, not children.

By emphasizing the child archetype, by making our therapeutic hours rituals of evoking childhood and reconstructing childhood, we're blocking ourselves from political life. Twenty or thirty years of therapy have removed the most sensitive and the most intelligent, and some of the most affluent people in our society into child cult worship. It's going on insidiously, all through therapy, all through the country. So *of course* our politics are in disarray and nobody's voting—we're disempowering ourselves through therapy.

VENTURA: The assumption people are working out of is that inner growth translates into worldly power, and many don't realize that they go to therapy with that assumption.

HILLMAN: If personal growth did lead into the world, wouldn't our political situation be different today, considering all the especially intelligent people who have been in therapy? What you learn in therapy is mainly feeling skills, how to really remember, how to let fantasy come, how to find words for invisible things, how to go deep and face things—

VENTURA: Good stuff to know—

HILLMAN: Yes, but you don't learn political skills or find out anything about the way the world works. Personal growth doesn't automatically lead to political results. Look at Eastern Europe and the Soviet Union. Psychoanalysis was banned for decades, and look at the political changes that have come up and startled everybody. Not the result of therapy, their revolutions.

VENTURA: So you're making a kind of opposition between power, political power or political intelligence, and therapeutic intelligence. Many who are therapeutically sensitive are also dumb and fucked up politically; and if you look at the people who wield the most power in almost any sphere of life, they are often people whose inner growth has been severely stunted.

HILLMAN: You think people undertake therapy to grow?

VENTURA: Isn't growth a huge part of the project of therapy? Everybody uses the word, therapists and clients alike.

HILLMAN: But the very word *grow* is a word appropriate to children. After a certain age you do not grow. You don't grow teeth, you don't grow muscles. If you start growing after that age, it's cancer.

VENTURA: Aw, Jim, can't I grow *inside* all my life?

HILLMAN: Grow what? Corn? Tomatoes? New archetypes? What am I growing, what do you grow? The standard therapeutic answer is: you're growing yourself.

VENTURA: But the philosopher Kierkegaard would come back and say, "The deeper natures don't change, they become more and more themselves."

HILLMAN: Jung says individuation is becoming more and more oneself.

VENTURA: And becoming more and more oneself involves a lot of unpleasantness. As Jung also says, the most terrifying thing is to know yourself.

HILLMAN: And becoming more and more oneself—the actual experience of it is a shrinking, in that very often it's a dehydration, a loss of inflations, a loss of illusions.

VENTURA: That doesn't sound like a good time. Why would anybody want to do it?

HILLMAN: Because shedding is a beautiful thing. It's of course not what consumerism tells you, but shedding feels good. It's a lightening up.

VENTURA: Shedding what?

HILLMAN: Shedding pseudoskins, crusted stuff that you've accumulated. Shedding dead wood. That's one of the big sheddings. Things that don't work anymore, things that don't keep you—keep you alive. Sets of ideas that you've had too long. People that you don't *really* like to be with, habits of thought, habits of sexuality. That's a very big one, 'cause if you keep on making love at forty the way you did at eighteen you're missing something, and if you make love at sixty the way you did at forty you're missing something. All that changes. The imagination changes.

Or put it another way: *Growth is always loss.*

Anytime you're gonna grow, you're gonna lose something. You're losing what you're hanging onto to keep safe. You're losing habits that you're comfortable with, you're losing familiarity. That's a big one, when you begin to move into the unfamiliar.

You know, in the organic world when anything begins to grow it's moving constantly into unfamiliar movements and unfamiliar things. Watch birds grow—they fall down, they can't quite do it. Their growing is all awkwardness. Watch a fourteen-year-old kid tripping over his own feet.

VENTURA: The fantasy of growth that you find in therapy, and also in New Age thought, doesn't include this awkwardness, which *can* be terrible and can go on for years. And when we look at people going through that, we usually don't say they're growing, we usually consider them out of it. And during such a time one certainly doesn't feel more powerful in the world.

HILLMAN: The fantasy of growth is a romantic, harmonious fantasy of an ever-expanding, ever-developing, ever-creating, ever-larger person—and ever integrating, getting it all together.

VENTURA: And if you don't fulfill that fantasy you see yourself as failing.

HILLMAN: Absolutely.

VENTURA: So this idea of growth can put you into a constant state of failure!

HILLMAN: "I ought to be over that by now, I'm not together, I can't get it together, and if I were really growing I would have grown out of my mess long ago."

VENTURA: It sets you up to fail. That's really cute.

HILLMAN: It's an idealization that sets you up to fail.

VENTURA: Because you're constantly comparing yourself to the fantasy of where you *should* be on some ideal growth scale.

HILLMAN: It sets up something worse. It sets up not just failure but anomaly: "I'm peculiar." And it does this by showing no respect for sameness, for consistency, in a person. Sameness is a very important part of life—to be consistently the same in certain areas that don't change, don't grow.

You've been in therapy six years and you go back home on Thanksgiving and you open the front door and you see your family *and you are right back where you were.* You feel the same as you always did! Or you've been divorced for years, haven't seen the wife though there's been some communication on the phone, but you walk into the same room and *within four minutes* there's a flare-up, the same flare-up that was there long ago.

Some things stay the same. They're like rocks. There's rocks in the psyche. There are crystals, there's iron ore, there's a metallic level where *some* things don't change.

VENTURA: And if those elements did change, could change, you would be so fluid that you would not, could not, be you. You would be dangerously fluid. Where would that thing that is you reside, if the psyche didn't depend on some things not changing? And this dependence on the changeless is far below the level of the ego's control or consent.

HILLMAN: This changeless aspect, if you go all the way back in philosophy even before Aristotle, was called Being. "Real Being doesn't change." That was one fantasy. Other people would say, "Real Being is always changing." I'm not arguing which one is right, I'm arguing that both are fundamental categories of life, of being. You can look at your life with the eye of sameness and say, "My god, nothing's really changed." Then you can look at it with the other eye: "My god, what a difference. Two years ago, nine years ago, I was thus and so, but now all that's gone, it's changed completely!"

This is one of the great riddles that Lao Tse talked about, the changing and the changeless. The job in therapy is, not to try and make the changeless change, but how to separate the two. If you try to work on what's called a character neurosis, if you try to take someone who is very deeply emotionally whatever-it-is, and try to change that person into something else, what are you doing? Because there are parts of the psyche that are changeless.

VENTURA: And that has to be respected.

HILLMAN: It has to be respected, because the psyche knows more why it resists change than you do. Every complex, every psychic figure in your dreams knows more about itself and what it's doing and what it's there for than you do. So you may as well respect it.

VENTURA: And if you, as a therapist, don't respect that, then you're not respecting that person.

HILLMAN: And it has nothing to do with *wanting* to change. Like the joke, "How many psychiatrists does it take to change a light bulb?" "It only takes one, but the light bulb has to really want to change." This light bulb that really wants to change still can't change those areas of changelessness.

VENTURA: The fantasy of growth, the fantasy of the ever-expanding, ever-developing person—which is a very strong fantasy out there right now, especially among the educated, and among all those buyers of self-help books—doesn't take changelessness into account at all, doesn't set up a dialectic between change and changelessness. So (bringing this all back to the relation of therapy to politics) this fantasy, fed by many sorts of therapies, can't help but make people feel more like failures in the long run. Which, in turn, can't help but increase the general feeling of powerlessness.

That's a pretty vicious circle.

HILLMAN: There's another thing therapy does that I think is vicious. It internalizes emotions.

Hillman looks down at the Pacific Coast Highway packed with cars going as fast as they can bumper to bumper.

I'm outraged after having driven to my analyst on the freeway. The fucking trucks almost ran me off the road. I'm terrified, I'm in my little car, and I get to my therapist's and I'm shaking. My therapist says, "We've gotta talk about this."

So we begin to talk about it. And we discover that my father was a son-of-a-bitch brute and this whole truck thing reminds me of him. Or we discover that I've always felt frail and vulnerable, there've always been bigger guys with bigger dicks, so this car that I'm in is a typical example of my thin skin and my frailty and vulnerability. Or we talk about my power drive, that I really wish to be a truck driver. We convert my fear into anxiety—an inner state. We convert the present into the past, into a discussion of my father and my childhood. And we convert my outrage—at the pollution or the chaos or whatever my outrage is about—into rage and hostility. Again, an internal condition, whereas it starts in *out*rage, an emotion. Emotions are mainly social. The word comes from the Latin *ex movere,* to move out. Emotions connect to the world. Therapy introverts the emotions, calls fear "anxiety." You take it back, and you work on it inside yourself. You don't work psychologically on what that outrage is telling you about potholes, about trucks, about Florida strawberries in Vermont in March, about burning up oil, about energy policies, nuclear waste, that homeless woman over there with the sores on her feet—the whole thing.

VENTURA: You're not saying that we don't need introspection, an introspective guy like you?

HILLMAN: Put this in italics so that nobody can just pass over it: *This is not to deny that you do need to go inside*—but we have to see what we're doing when we do that. By going inside we're maintaining the Cartesian view that the world out there is dead matter and the world inside is living.

VENTURA: A therapist told me that my grief at seeing a homeless man my age was really a feeling of sorrow for myself.

HILLMAN: And dealing with it means going home and working on it in reflection. That's what dealing with it has come to mean. And by that time you've walked past the homeless man in the street.

VENTURA: It's also, in part, a way to cut off what you would call Eros, the part of my heart that seeks to touch others. Theoretically this is something therapy tries to liberate, but here's a person on the street that I'm feeling for and I'm supposed to deal with that feeling as though it has nothing to do with another person.

HILLMAN: Could the thing that we all believe in most—that psychology is the one good thing left in a hypocritical world—be not true? Psychology, working with yourself, could that be part of the disease, not part of the cure? I think therapy has made a philosophical mistake, which is that cognition precedes conation—that knowing precedes doing or action. I don't think that's the case. I think reflection has always been after the event.

They reflect on that a bit.

HILLMAN: The thing that therapy pushes is relationship, yet work may matter just as much as relationship. You think you're going to die if you're not in a good relationship. You feel that not being in a significant, long-lasting, deep relationship is going to cripple you or that you're crazy or neurotic or something. You feel intense bouts of longing and loneliness. But those feelings are not only due to poor relationship; they come also because you're not in any kind of political community that makes sense, that matters. Therapy pushes the relationship issues, but what intensifies those issues is that we don't have (a) satisfactory work or (b), even more important perhaps, we don't have a satisfactory political community.

You just can't make up for the loss of passion and purpose in your daily work by intensifying your personal relationships. I think we talk so much about inner growth and development because we are so boxed in to petty, private concerns on our jobs.

VENTURA: In a world where most people do work that is not only unsatisfying but also, with its pressures, deeply unsettling; and in a world where there's nothing more rare than a place that feels like a community, we load all our needs onto a relationship or expect them to be met by our family. And then we wonder why our relationships and family crack under the load.

HILLMAN: It's extraordinary to see psychotherapy, that came out of those nuts from Vienna and Zurich, and out of the insane asylums of Europe, talking the same language today as the Republican right wing about the virtues of family. The government and therapy are in symbiotic, happy agreement on the propaganda that we had from Ronald Reagan for so many years about family. Yet family, we know sociologically, doesn't exist anymore. The statistics are astounding. And the actual patterns of family life, how people feel and act in the families that still exist, have changed radically. People don't live in families in the same way; people *won't* live in families. There are broken families, half-families, multiple families, all kinds of crazy families. The idea of family only exists in the bourgeois patient population that serves psychotherapy. In fact, the family is largely today a white therapist's fantasy.

Why do we need this Norman Rockwell family, this make-believe ideal, that's so rampant now in politics and in therapy? I don't know what it's doing for the body politic, but I know what it's doing for therapy. For therapy, it is keeping an ideal in place so that we can show how dysfunctional we all are. It keeps the trade going; this would be Ivan Illich's view. We need clients.*

VENTURA: But even the Norman Rockwell ideal of the happy, self-sufficient family is a distortion of what families were for thousands, probably tens of thousands, of years. During that time, no family was self-sufficient. Each family was a working unit that was part of the larger working unit, which was the community—the tribe or the village. Tribes and villages were self-sufficient, not families. It's not only that everyone worked togther, everyone also played and prayed together, so that the burden of relationship, and of meaning, wasn't confined to the family, much less to a romantic relationship, but was spread out into the community. Until the Industrial Revolution, family always existed in that context.

HILLMAN: And family always existed in the context of one's ancestors. Our bones are not in this ground. Now our families don't carry the ancestors with them. First of all, we Americans left our homelands in order to come here, and we let go of the ancestors. Second, we're all now first-name people. I was just at a psychotherapists' conference with seven thousand people, and everybody had on their name tags. Everybody's first name was in large caps and the last name was in small letters below it.

VENTURA: And in the last name are the ancestors, the country, the residue of the past.

HILLMAN: It's all in the last name. The first name is fashion, social drift. One generation you have a lot of Tracys and

---

* Illich is such a beautifully radical thinker! I love his idea that therapy is an industry that has to find new sources of ores to exploit. Ordinary neurotics won't fill the practices, so therapy has to find new "mines"—geriatric cases, corporate offices, little children, whole families.

Kimberlys, Maxes and Sams, another generation you have Ediths and Doras, Michaels and Davids. You've got your ancestors with you in your psyche when you use your last name. You've got your brothers and sisters with you, they have the same name. When I'm called Jim, I'm just plain Jim, it has no characteristics.

To have only a first name is a sign of being a peasant, a slave, an oppressed person. Throughout history slaves had only first names. Now our entire nation has only first names. At this conference, the only people who had last names were the faculty—the twenty-five people that these other seven thousand had paid to see and hear. We had our last names in big letters and our first names in small letters. I asked about this and was told, "We don't want you people called James or Jim or Bob or Bill, we want you addressed as Mr. Hillman."

Therapy's no different here; it complies with the convention, too. The early cases of analysis, Freud's, Jung's, had only first names—Anna, Babette. It's supposed to show intimacy and equality—

VENTURA: —and anonymity—

HILLMAN: What it actually does is strip down your dignity, the roots of your individuality, because it covers over the ancestors, who are in the consulting room too. Worse, this way of talking concentrates all attention on me, Jim, my little apple, ignoring the whole complexity of my social bag, my racial roots. We ought to have three or four last names, all hyphenated, like in Switzerland or Spain, with my mother's family name in there too, and my wife's and my exwife's and so on and so on. No one is just plain Jim.

VENTURA: I'm too American for that, I *like* being able to leave some of that behind. Still, we should carry both our parents' names, at least—but not hyphenated.

You know, speaking of slaves: bosses and owners are almost always called Mister, but they have the freedom to address their employees by their first names. And among workers of equal or supposedly equal status, it's not unusual for a man to be called by his last name while women are almost always called by their first names unless they're really heavy-duty. So we're also dealing with power when we use names. We're reinforcing certain kinds of authority and inequality.

But I want to get back to something: that to tout the ideal family is a way of *making* ourselves dysfunctional, because that ideal makes anything outside it, by definition, not ideal, i.e., dysfunctional. Without that ideal, we're just who we are.

HILLMAN: The ideal of growth makes us feel stunted; the ideal family makes us feel crazy.

VENTURA: We have these idealizations that make us feel crazy, even though we don't see any of these ideals in life. I feel crazy that I can't be in one relationship all my life, even though I look around and where do I see anybody in one relationship all their lives?

HILLMAN: I know people who've been married fifty years and more.

VENTURA: So do I, and one partner's an alcoholic, or one's played around a lot or been away a lot, they haven't made love in decades (literally), or one is a closet gay. These aren't abstract examples, these are people I know. Most fifty-year wedding anniversaries would look very different if you knew what everybody's covering up. Yet we keep measuring ourselves against these ideals.

HILLMAN: And psychology idealizes family in another, perhaps even more destructive, way: psychology assumes that your personality and behavior are determined by your family relationships during childhood.

VENTURA: Well, people grow up somehow, some way, and how they grow up determines their life, doesn't it?

There's an uncomfortably long silence between them. The oil tanker has gone over the horizon, but traffic is still backed up on the Pacific Coast Highway. A single-engine plane flying low over the Santa Monica Pier pulls a yellow banner wishing somebody named Eliza a happy birthday. Farther down the coast, 747s take off from LAX one after another and do a slow banking turn far out at sea. The homeless woman has woken up (her eyes are open), but she hasn't moved.

Hillman clears his throat.

HILLMAN: The principal content of American psychology is developmental psychology: what happened to you earlier is the cause of what happened to you later. That's the basic theory: our history is our causality. We don't even separate history as a story from history as cause. So you have to go back to childhood to get at why you are the way you are. And so when people are out of their minds or disturbed or fucked up or whatever, in our culture, in our psychotherapeutic world, we go back to our mothers and our fathers and our childhoods.

No other culture would do that. If you're out of your mind in another culture or quite disturbed or impotent or anorexic, you look at what you've been eating, who's been casting spells on you, what taboo you've crossed, what you haven't done right, when you last missed reverence to the Gods or didn't take part in the dance, broke some tribal custom. Whatever. It could be thousands of other things—the plants, the water, the curses, the demons, the Gods, being out of touch with the Great Spirit. It would never, *never* be what happened to you with your mother and your father forty years ago. Only our culture uses that model, that myth.

VENTURA *(appalled and confused)***:** Well, why wouldn't that be true? Because people will say . . . okay, *I'll* say, "That *is* why I am as I am."

HILLMAN: Because that's the myth you believe.

VENTURA: What other myth can there be? That's not a myth, that's what happened!

HILLMAN: "That's not a myth, that's what happened." The moment we say something is "what happened" we're announcing, "This is the myth I no longer see as a myth. This is the myth that I can't see through." "That's not a myth, that's what happened" suggests that myths are the things we *don't* believe. The myths we believe and are in the middle of, we call them "fact," "reality," "science."

But let's say somebody looked at it differently. Let's say that what matters is that you have an acorn in you, you are a certain person, and that person begins to appear early in your life, but it's there all the way through your life. Winston Churchill, for example, when he was a schoolboy, had a lot of trouble with language and didn't speak well. He was put in what we would call the remedial reading class. He had problems about writing, speaking, and spelling. Of course he did! This little boy was a Nobel Prize winner in literature and had to save the Western world through his speech. Of course he had a speech defect, of course he couldn't speak easily when he was eleven or fourteen—it was too much to carry.

Or take Manolete who, when he was nine years old, was supposedly a very frightened little skinny boy who hung around his mother in the kitchen. So he becomes the greatest bullfighter of our age. Psychology will say, "Yes, he became a great bullfighter because he was such a puny little kid that he compensated by being a macho hero." That would be Adlerian psychology—you take your deficiency, your inferiority, and you convert it to superiority.

VENTURA: That notion has seeped in everywhere—feminism and the men's movement both depend on it more than they know.

HILLMAN: But suppose you take it the other way and read a person's life backwards. Then you say, Manolete was the greatest bullfighter, and he *knew* that. Inside, his psyche sensed at the age of nine that his fate was to meet thousand-pound black bulls with great horns. Of course he fucking well held onto his mother! Because he couldn't hold that capacity—at nine years old your fate is all there and you can't handle it. It's too big. It's not that he was inferior; he had a great destiny.

Now, suppose we look at all our patients that way. Suppose we look at the kids who are odd or stuttering or afraid, and instead of seeing these as developmental problems we see them as having some great thing inside them, some destiny that they're not yet able to handle. It's bigger than they are and their psyche knows that. So that's a way of reading your own life differently. Instead of reading your life today as the result of fuck-ups as a child, you read your childhood as a miniature example of your life, as a cameo of your life—and recognize that you don't really know your whole life until you're about eighty—and then you're too old to get it in focus, or even care to!

VENTURA: But that's crazy. How can a child know what's going to happen?

HILLMAN: Our children *can't* know what's going to happen, because *our* children are not imagined as being Platonic children who are born into this world knowing everything. "The soul knows who we are from the beginning," say other theories of childhood. We're locked in our own special theory of childhood. According to us, a baby comes into the world with a few innate mechanisms, but not a destiny.

VENTURA: What you're saying rings a bell for me. There's a book of photographs called *As They Were,* of famous people when they were kids, and it's amazing how, at four or six or nine, Abbie Hoffman and J. Edgar Hoover and Franz Kafka and Joan Baez and Adolf Hitler looked just like—well, like their destinies.

HILLMAN: Why not? I mean, a tree is the same tree all the way through. A zebra is a zebra from the very first day.

VENTURA: Yeah, yeah, I like all that, I like it a lot, but—Hillman, how does a child know what's going to happen?

HILLMAN: Ventura—I don't think a child does know what's going to happen, I think that's far too literal. I think a child feels—

No, there *are* children who know what's going to happen. There was this great cellist, a woman who died recently—she was quite young. Jaqueline du Pré. I don't know what she died of, but she was one of the greatest cellists in the world. When she was five years old she heard a cello on the radio and said, "I want what makes noise like that," or "sounds like that." She knew. It was there. And that's sometimes the case in genius musicians. They often know.

VENTURA: Actually, now that I think of it, it's not that uncommon with artists. I'm no genius, but from the age of nine I knew I was going to be a writer and I never made the least effort to be anything else.

HILLMAN: But let's not use those examples, they're too clear. Most people don't have those feelings; at the age of twenty they're still groping. But I do believe there are inklings, like little nubs on the edge of a tree. As the tree is growing—a young tree, let's say a little beech tree—it makes a little nub as it grows, and those nubs become branches, and eventually they become huge branches. I think a child has those little nubs. It doesn't know what it's going to be, but it has its inklings, it has its tendencies, it has its little pushes, its little obsessions.

VENTURA: And not only are these obsessions usually not honored, but many parents perceive them as frightening. "He should go out more, he's not seeing any friends." "She shouldn't be so serious." "How's he gonna earn a living if all he does is draw?" "That kid's not normal"—which usually means, "That kid's not easy."

I know a woman who barely went to any of her classes in high school, didn't deserve to graduate on marks, graduated purely on the force of her personality and because she was such an incredible leader and organizer. In her senior year she became head of the student council, organized practically everything that went on in the school. The first job she got after high school was a waitress in a restaurant. A year later she was the manager of that restaurant, a year after that the co-owner. By the time she was thirty she'd produced two movies and become an executive at one of the major film studios. The education being offered in high school was useless to her, but she got her own education there by exercising her business and political talents as a leader and organizer. So it's not only artists.

The more I consider it, this kind of thing happens a lot.

HILLMAN: Our culture doesn't see it because not only do we have no theories to see it with, but these phenomena (which, as you say, aren't uncommon) undermine the theories we do have—theories we've built a very profitable industry out of and are part of our religious faith in history.

VENTURA: The more I think of it, you do have an image of what your face will look like. You do feel other people in you, who are older, and they talk to you—they talk to me, at any rate. I have a much older man inside me who talks to me every day, quietly, usually kindly, tolerantly, sometimes sternly when I'm really fucking up, always with humor. I like him enormously; he seems very much the best part of me. I never thought about him in this light before.

Hillman starts to speak.

VENTURA: No, let me go on while I'm thinking of it, another aspect of what I think you're getting at. I know several men who are, like me, in their forties, and they're starting to feel middle-aged in the flesh, and they say, "My body is betraying me." They even dye their hair and lie about their age. And I know women the same age, not Beverly Hills housewives or movie stars but women whom I never thought would do this, getting breast implants, tucks, that kind of thing—and I'm afraid for them, because they are deeply insulting the older people in them. And those insults are weakening the older people in them.

So when they finally turn sixty-five, when it's their sixty-five-year-old's turn to *be,* that sixty-five-year-old has been so insulted and weakened that he or she may not be able to do the job.

HILLMAN: You're saying it's not just nubs, that there's a cast of characters given. I think so too. I saw a drawing of a woman—she was about forty-four. It was a pencil drawing, very touching. She didn't like it because it made her look too old. I said, "That drawing, that's the old woman who is waiting for you at the end of the corridor." They're there. Those figures are our companions, they're always around, and they need strengthening all the way down the line.

Michelangelo called that "the image in the heart."

I mean, how is it that we can become thirty-five when we are twenty-five? There has to be a form of being thirty-five that we put on.

VENTURA: So we are saying, "You don't know what's going to happen but you feel the people in you. That's how you're designed, if the culture or your family hasn't demolished that way of feeling when you're very young."

HILLMAN: The form of those people, the figures, are already there. You want to strengthen those figures as you go along.

Hillman pauses.

There's a lot of fear that there's nobody there. I think that's one of the great fears behind dyeing your hair or removing the lines around your eyes. "When I hit fifty I'm going to be empty, there's nobody there." Because what is that sense of being empty? It's because there's nobody there.

VENTURA: And if we've insulted the older people in us sufficiently and attacked them every time we, say, cursed an older driver—

HILLMAN: —or the person in front of you in the supermarket who doesn't put her money away quickly enough—

VENTURA: Every time we've done that we've frightened and diminished the old ones in us, and those figures shrink until maybe there *isn't* anybody there.

HILLMAN: There's another way we do it. Every time you go, "I haven't got time for the pain," every time you cover up your illness. Your illnesses are partly ways of developing the older people. They're the ways of developing the knowledge of your own body. The illnesses tell you tremendous things about what you can eat and when you can eat it, what goes on with your bowels, what goes on with your balls, what goes on with your skin. The illnesses are your teachers, especially about aging. Devaluing the illnesses and suppressing them removes you from these figures.

We insult the inner people by what we do with our own weaknesses.

VENTURA: And as we get older we turn that around and we dislike young people.

HILLMAN: Oh yeah.

VENTURA: And when we attack young people, in the same impatient way we've attacked old people, we weaken our young selves *who are still in us,* the way the older selves were in us when we were young.

HILLMAN: Absolutely. We attack the younger people in us. As you say, the young ones who give us urges, send us fantasies. And so we no longer allow ourselves to feel or to imagine sexuality, we no longer allow ourselves to imagine risk—the incredible risks that young people take! They just do it! We don't allow ourselves to risk in the sense of abandon, letting go.

The great old people that you know were once masters of letting go, tremendous courage—and some still are, fearless in crossing the street, in walking out at night.

VENTURA: We especially reject and attack adolescents, can't stand being around them, because our own adolescence is so painful.

HILLMAN: The falling in love, the romance, the suicidal fantasies of adolescence—

VENTURA: And all those dreams you didn't live up to. And you can't say anything worse to somebody than, "You're being adolescent."

HILLMAN: Try, "You're just getting old."

VENTURA: When you're in your forties and you hit what they call midlife crisis, when you're going through a kind of adolescence again, because you're breaking a bunch of crusts —that's belittled. "Whataya goin' through, a midlife crisis?"

HILLMAN: You hit another at sixty.

VENTURA: And if you turn around and say, "You're goddamn right I am, and you'd better stay out of its way," then you're seen as nuts: "Boy, Ventura's losin' it." But what you're really saying is, "I'm molting."

HILLMAN: "I'm molting, and I'm at the beginning of something, and when I'm at the beginning of something I am a fool."

VENTURA: "The changeless thing in me is sitting quiet in the center of everything that's changing, and much is dropping away."

They sit quietly a moment. The people walking past their bench for a stroll, the drivers inching up and down the Pacific Coast Highway, the swimmers and sunners on the beach, the crew of another oil tanker now in view, and the Saturday sailors out in small boats are outside the little circle of their quiet. For the moment, these two men aren't even noticing.

VENTURA: Okay, so developmental psychology, the idea that everything I am now was caused in my childhood, at the very least leaves out far too much and may be misleading altogether. Yeah, but what about all that time and money I spent in therapy about being sexually molested and all that? It seemed important at the time!

HILLMAN *(laughs)*: Yes, it does seem important at the time. Well, what's all that about? If we're going to be vicious we're going to say, as Ivan Illich would say, it's a way of maintaining

VENTURA: Therapy, in effect, aggravates *and* profits from the abuse by the way it thinks about it. But what does that mean, "remembering traumatically"?

HILLMAN: Well, let's say my father took the belt or the brush to me, or maybe he fucked me or beat the shit out of me again and again. Sometimes he was drunk when he did it, sometimes he just did it because he was a mean son of a bitch, sometimes he beat me because he didn't know who else to beat. And I go on remembering those violations. I remain a victim in my memory. My memory continues to make me a victim. Secondly, it continues to keep me in the position of the child, because my memory is locked into the child's view, and I haven't moved my memory. It isn't that the abuse didn't happen—I'm not denying that it happened or that I need to believe that it did concretely happen. But I may be able to think about the brutality—reframe it, as they say—as an initiatory experience. These wounds that he caused have done something to me to make me understand punishment, make me understand vengeance, make me understand submission, make me understand the depth of rage between fathers and sons, which is a universal theme—and I took part in that. I was *in* that. And so I've moved the memory, somehow, from just being a child victim of a mean father. I've entered fairy tales and I've entered myths, literature, movies. With my suffering I've entered an imaginal, not just a traumatic, world.

VENTURA: You've entered what tribal people might call the Dreamtime.

HILLMAN: Yes. Part of the Dreamtime.

VENTURA: That this happened to you not only in the day-to-day but in the Dreamtime, for all things that happen in one place happen in the other. "As above, so below," as the ancients taught. That this happened to you in the Dreamtime means: (a) that it's a mythological act, and (b) that it didn't happen twenty years ago; it's happening now, it always happened, it always will happen. Which isn't as depressing as it sounds.

the psychotherapy trade, which is a large business needing new raw material such as abuse, trauma, childhood molestation. And if you're a believer—which we are, unconsciously—in the myth of development rather than a believer in acorns and nubs, structure, or essence, then what happened back then must be overwhelmingly important. Now what about the fact that children have been abandoned, molested, and abused for centuries—and it wasn't considered important?

VENTURA: What about that? Weren't those cultures as advanced as ours?

HILLMAN: Come on, you don't believe that.

VENTURA: You're right, I don't. But a lot of folks do, and they go further to say that a significant part of the explanation for the socially, economically, and ecologically ravaged planet we inhabit is child abuse, hundreds of years of it. (Which doesn't wash historically, by the way. Forced sexual relationships have been with us since the dawn of time, if we can judge by ancient myths and fairy tales, and the ravaging of the planet has only been going on since the beginning of the Industrial Age two hundred years ago.)

HILLMAN: The fact that everybody is upset about the child is exactly the point I made before, that the archetype of the child dominates our culture's therapeutic thinking. Maintaining that abuse is the most important thing in our culture, that our nation is going to the dogs because of abuse, or that it's the root of why we exploit and victimize the earth, as some are saying, that is the viewpoint of the child.

VENTURA: And it's to be stuck in that viewpoint.

HILLMAN: I'm not saying that children aren't molested or abused. They *are* molested, and they *are* abused, and in many cases it's absolutely devastating. But therapy makes it even more devastating *by the way it thinks about it.* It isn't just the trauma that does the damage, it's remembering traumatically.

This means its significance can always change. It's a place where literal life and mythical life meet. That's what wounds are.

And then there's: (c) the abuse is in the Dreamtime context of many, many mythological acts, some brutal and some beautiful, instead of being just the major myth of *your* act.

So there's a sense in which—

HILLMAN: It becomes more intense when it becomes less personal.

VENTURA: Right.

HILLMAN: More intense in the sense of how tremendously important it is. It's more important than *me,* in a strange way.

VENTURA: Because in the Dreamtime, in the mythological way of thought, it's joined with so many other events that are more important than me.

HILLMAN: Therapy tends to confuse the importance of the event with the importance of me.

VENTURA: I can hear a voice in me saying, "But this thing *happened,* it's not mythological, goddammit!" At the same time, as any journalist or cop can tell you, if you talk to several different people about an event they all witnessed or participated in, you'll have several different events. I know in my own family, if you ask me and my sister to describe our mother, you'll get two totally different mothers, and neither one of us is lying. Memory is a form of fiction, and we can't help that. So we are very much the creation of the stories we tell ourselves. And we don't know we're telling stories.

HILLMAN: We're not conscious we're telling stories.

I think Freud was getting at that when he said, "It's how you remember, not what actually happened." That the memory is what really creates the trauma. And everybody's been attacking Freud recently, saying that Freud was covering up, that he wasn't admitting these childhood abuses really happened. Whether they really happened or not, Freud's point, which is so tremendous, is that it's what memory does with them that's important.

We don't know we're telling stories. And that's part of the trouble in the training of psychotherapy, that psychotherapists don't learn enough literature, enough drama, or enough biography. The trainee learns cases and diagnostics—things that do not necessarily open the imagination. So the trainees don't realize that they're dealing in fictions. That's not to say that things aren't literally real too—

VENTURA: —but that what you get in the consulting room is, has to be, someone telling a story. The form is a story. You're right, it's weird that people whose work will largely consist of listening to stories aren't taught anything, from literature and from journalism and even from court records, about how people tell stories.

HILLMAN: Regarding the abuse, the actual abuse in *early* childhood—what does the damage, besides the shock and the horror and all those other things, is that early abuse tends to literalize the imagination. It either literalizes the imagination or dissociates it into multiple personality, so that it's split off. And that *is* damage. But kids from thirteen to seventeen, say, seduced by their stepfathers (or who seduce them) that's a different quality of abuse, different from that of a three-year-old or two-year-old. There are different levels to this, but it's all been grouped into one thing, so that we get all sorts of people claiming themselves victims of molestation and identifying themselves as hurt children. Seduction in families, as you said, is a pretty old thing. It is not the same as brutally violating an infant. We have to keep some gradations distinct—

VENTURA: —because if we don't, we can't think well about it.

When those memories of sexual abuse started coming up for me—which happened like clockwork on my fortieth birthday—after about a month of car crashes and black holes, I went to a therapist. He was an old man, a Jungian. I was going on and on about the abuse and about my mother, and he sort of smiled and said, "You know, what happened to you, it forged your connection with the soul's mysteries, didn't it? And that's what you write about, isn't it? Would you rather have been writing about something else?"

I was absolutely stunned that he said that. It didn't lessen my anger or my fear about my mother, but it jolted me out of looking at the experience as a child. I had to look at it from the point of view of how I've lived my life as an adult. Not that I've finished dealing with the great anger that came up toward my mother or toward the other people of my childhood and adolescence who tried to do the same thing to me, but—

HILLMAN: When you say, "I haven't dealt with," there's an assumption that that anger toward your mother is *supposed* to go somewhere. And I'm not going to assume that.

VENTURA: Well, this is an enormous assumption in our culture now, that this anger and rage and heartbreak are supposed to be *processed.* A word I hate, by the way—processed psyche, like processed food.

HILLMAN: Yeah, nice thin slices of yellow cheese. Put it in a package and label it.

VENTURA: But what are you supposed to do with this stuff if not process it? How the fuck are you going to "individuate," or even grow up, if you don't process it?

HILLMAN: Well now, what did Jonathan Swift do? He wrote the most incredible satires. What did people do in the Elizabethan and Jacobean vengeance plays? I mean, this stuff is tremendously powerful. What did Joyce do with his feelings about Ireland? What did Faulkner do with his feelings about the South? This kind of processing is really hard. This is the stuff of art. Rilke said about therapy, "I don't want the demons taken away because they're going to take my angels too." Wounds and scars are the stuff of character. The word *character* means, at root, "marked or etched with sharp lines," like initiation cuts.

VENTURA: Hey, we can't all be artists. We are not all Joyce or Jonathan Swift. Most of us are just working stiffs of one sort or another. What are *we* supposed to do?

HILLMAN: It isn't to be literal about artists. It is that there's a way the imagination can work with these powerful things. Artists are simply models of people who turn to the imagination to work with things. That's why one needs to read the biographies of artists, because biographies show what they did with their traumas; they show what can be done—not what they did but what can be done—by the imagination with hatred, with resentment, with bitterness, with feelings of being useless and inferior and worthless. Artists found modes in the imagination to process it, if you like.

Second thing is, you assume again with your question that you can't carry around unprocessed ore. Suppose you see these lumps as ore.

VENTURA: There's rocks in the psyche—"I got rocks in my head."

HILLMAN: Ore, rocks, that make for character, for the peculiar idiosyncrasy that you are. Just as you have physical scars, so you have soul blemishes. And they're rocks. And they are what you are. It's peculiar in our culture to believe that this stuff all gets ironed out. Is it a melting pot fantasy? Do we all try to be nice? In the service of this fantasy we abuse our own raw material.

I mean, you go to another culture and the people who are suffering, they're suffering from the facts of their existence. And by "another culture" I mean our own street culture—African American, Latino, and the rural poor, and that woman on the grass over there.

VENTURA: Yes, if you're an artist you *know* that stuff is your ore—you know that, and that's why many artists steer clear of therapy. They don't want that ore processed in the wrong way.

HILLMAN: The obsession that prevents it from being valued as ore is the obsession with processing, the obsession with smoothing it out. It doesn't become as damaging unless you think it shouldn't be there. That's what I mean about the therapeutic attitude hurting the actual potential of people. Because, as Ivan Illich would say, therapy wants to ameliorate the suffering in the ore. And our culture accepts the proposition that it must be ameliorated.

VENTURA: So if we're saying this is what therapy cannot, or should not, do, what *can* therapy do?

HILLMAN: Make—those—things—be—felt.

That used to be called lifting repression and bringing to consciousness. I'd rather say, Make those things be felt.

I see it as a kind of building of doorways, opening conduits, and making channels, like a giant bypass operation, throwing in all kinds of new tubings so that things flow into each other. Memories, events, images, all become enlivened. And our feelings about this ore become more subtle. Learn to appreciate it. That's one thing therapy can do.

VENTURA: So you're not saying to people, "Don't go to therapy."

HILLMAN: I'm saying to people, "*If* you go to therapy, watch out for the collusion between the therapist and the part of you that doesn't want to feel the ore." There are many ways to repress feeling the ore, one of which is processing it. The different schools of therapy have different processing systems, but *all* of them are fixers. From my angle, fixing what's wrong represses the ore.

VENTURA: "Processing" is often "repression" in disguise! That's really cute.

HILLMAN: "This hurts, goddammit, this hurts!" And the first move away from the hurt is, "What do I do about it? What do I take for it?"

VENTURA: "What clinical name can I call it?"

HILLMAN: "What's the treatment?" Those are all ways of dealing with "This hurts." But until one has been in the hurt, explored the hurt, you don't know anything about it. You don't know why it's there. Why did the psyche put it there?

VENTURA: "Exploring the hurt" sounds suspiciously like processing. "Working through"—

HILLMAN: —is the term that processing usually goes by. That's not what I mean by exploring the hurt. The question to be asked is, "How does therapy really work?" I'm not sure that therapy itself—that is, insight, understanding, recollection, owning your part of it, how you brought it about, seeing patterns, abreacting—

VENTURA: What does that mean, *abreacting,* in English?

HILLMAN: It means "getting it out"—I'm not sure that any of these working-through modes, which are supposed to be the modes of psychological processing, really do it. What I think does it is the six months, or six years, of grief. The mourning. The long ritual of therapy.

VENTURA: Ahhhhh.

HILLMAN: The dumb hours.

VENTURA: Going back and back and back, talking about this shit over and over, no matter what you happen to be saying or thinking, just going back and back to it.

HILLMAN: And one day it doesn't feel the same. The body has absorbed the punch. But I'm not sure that's because you processed it or got insights or understanding. I think that could happen also to the woman weeping in the church at the altar of Joseph.

VENTURA: Because you're sitting with it.

HILLMAN: Sitting *in* it.

VENTURA: In it. And being *in* it, in whatever form, is the exploration.

HILLMAN: You're in it for a while, then you're with it for a while, and then you visit it.

VENTURA: And then it walks with you instead of on you.

HILLMAN: And it may even go its own way.

VENTURA: And why isn't that processing?

Hillman is silent.

VENTURA: I'll tell you why it's not processing. Because you're not taking it and purifying it and making it into something else.

HILLMAN: You're not transforming.

VENTURA: Processing implies, "I can take this ore and make it into a plow. I can make it into a tool by which I can live more efficiently." And it implies that somehow, magically, if I do that then the ore isn't there anymore.

HILLMAN: "Either I can use it or I can get rid of it, but it's fucking inefficient to have it around where it's not usable but it's still there." This is what makes us, Americans, white Americans, psychological amateurs and innocents. We don't have enough stuff in the psyche, we keep getting rid of the ore! We're not psychologically sophisticated people.

I'd rather not say is it or isn't it processing. I'd rather say, "What happens if you call it processing?" And you described what happens, you either try to get rid of it or make it useful. So it's exploitative. The notion of transformation that dominates therapy: transform something useless into something useful.

VENTURA: A consumer's ideology. You're consuming your psyche, as both a consumer and as a carnivore.

HILLMAN: And also as an industrialist: you're making a profit out of it.

VENTURA: And the psyche doesn't like that. So what it says is, "Okay! I'll make you *boring*."

HILLMAN *(laughs)*: I was waiting for you to say something very different; I was waiting for you to say, "Okay, I'll send you another complaint!"

VENTURA: That's only if it still likes you—then the psyche gives you another chance with something new to deal with. If it's really disgusted with you it says, "I'll make you boring."

HILLMAN: So that you become processed cheese.

VENTURA: And you will be very well adjusted and even tempered, you won't "lose it," you won't have any extremes. And maybe you can even have a successful marriage with somebody as boring as you are.

HILLMAN: Usually, fortunately, that doesn't work, because the God of marriage doesn't allow that.

VENTURA: Right. The God of marriage is a very crazy God.

HILLMAN: The God of marriage wants a lot more.

VENTURA: And the psyche says to therapists especially, "I'll make you boring." That's what the therapists I know complain about.

HILLMAN: Oh, yes. The repressive atmosphere of therapy—

VENTURA: —repressive to the therapist—

HILLMAN: —that dictates psychology has to be respectable. This produces a terrible repression to the actual psychologist. We're not allowed in the street. We have to be careful, pretty correct, not extreme or radical, and not mix it up with our clients and patients out in the world. And this slants our thinking toward white, middle-class psychology. As one good friend of mine told me, "The trouble with getting old as a therapist is that I can't grow into my eccentricity." Because what's expected of a therapist is regular hours, being on time, being a kind of square, reasonable person. *The therapist is unconsciously modeling the goal of therapy.*

VENTURA: The therapist is unconsciously modeling the *unconscious* goal of therapy.

HILLMAN: Well, that isn't my goal. The goal of my therapy is eccentricity, which grows out of the Jungian notion of individuation. Jung says, "You become what you are." And nobody is square. We all have, as the Swiss say, a corner knocked off.

VENTURA: It's not processing and it's not growth, 'cause that's the same thing, that's a consumer attitude toward life. So what the fuck is it?

HILLMAN: I think it's *life.* That's what it is. Meaning: going through life. Rousseau said, "The man among you is the most educated who can carry the joys and sorrows of life." Education meant the joys and sorrows of life. So do you want to call it education? That's pretty boring too.

VENTURA: Then there are all the words that the New Agers have made unpalatable, like *journey.*

HILLMAN: I tell you what I feel about it. I feel it's service. I feel it's devotion.

VENTURA: To what?

HILLMAN: To the Gods. I feel that these things occur, and they are what the psyche wants or sends me. What the Gods send me. There's a lovely passage from Marcus Aurelius: "What I do I do always with the community in mind. What happens to me, what befalls me, comes from the Gods." And *befall* is a very important word, because that's where the word *case* comes from: *cadere,* to fall. And in German the word for a case is *fall.* So what falls on you is what happens to you, is the origins of the Greek word *pathos* too—what drops on you, what wounds you, what happens to you, what falls on you, how you fall, the way the dice fall.

VENTURA: You know, we keep circling the basic premise of American life, which has infected therapy, namely, "Everything is supposed to be all right. If things are not all right, then they're very, very wrong."

HILLMAN: So what happens to the pathos, the pathology of our lives, "that which can't be accepted, can't be changed, and won't go away."

VENTURA: You live it out.

HILLMAN: That becomes a devotion. A service. What else can you do?

A long pause.

What else can you do?

And that's human limitation. That's what the Greeks mean by being mortal: it's to be tragic.

VENTURA: So we haven't got a word to stick in here in place of *process,* and maybe we don't want one!

They laugh.

HILLMAN: Right. That's much better. We have no word to replace *process—*

HILLMAN AND VENTURA: —and we don't want one.

HILLMAN: This isn't about a process to do that.

VENTURA: Because it's part of the concept of process to find a word to replace it, and to hell with that. And we have no word to replace *growth,* either, and maybe we don't want one.

We're talking about living it out.

HILLMAN: Taking it on, too.

VENTURA: Taking the weight.

HILLMAN: Wait. Taking the weight is not taking the weight of the Man. That's been a big mistake. "I did my time." I'm not talking about serving the Man. That's where rebellion and subversion are important. I'm talking about serving the Gods.

VENTURA: How do you tell the difference?

HILLMAN: You can quit the Man. You can tell the Man to stuff it.

VENTURA: But the Gods don't go away.

HILLMAN: You can move to nirvana, but the Gods find out where you go.

I don't know if the Gods love you as the Christians are told, or even if they are very interested in what you decide to do and worry about, but they sure don't let you off easy. In Italy, editors called one of my books *The Vain Flight from the Gods.* You see, they get to us through our pathology, and that's why pathology is so important. It's the window in the wall through which the demons and the angels come in.

VENTURA: They don't love you but they don't let you get away. Sounds a little like family.

HILLMAN: "Called or not, the Gods will be present." Jung had that saying in Latin over his front door. Carved in stone. So we may as well serve. Willingly. That's how I understand the human will, it just means to do the stuff you have to go through willingly.

VENTURA: They don't love you but they keep on your case. Butch Hancock has a song where he sings, "She was a model of mercy, she never cut me no slack." If they love you, that's how they love you.

He pauses a moment.

By "serving the Man" you mean that being reconciled to the system, to authority, is very different from what you call serving the Gods. You can't rebel against the Gods—or you can, but that's just another step in the dance; but you'd *better* rebel against authority.

At least, that's what I mean. What do you mean?

HILLMAN: Look. Our assumption, our fantasy, in psychoanalysis has been that we're going to process, we're going to grow, and we're going to level things out so that we don't have these very strong, disturbing emotions and events.

VENTURA: Which is probably not a human possibility.

HILLMAN: But could analysis have new fantasies of itself, so that the consulting room is a cell in which revolution is prepared?

VENTURA: What?

HILLMAN: Could—

VENTURA: —could the consulting room be a cell in which *revolution* is prepared? Jesus. Could it?

HILLMAN: By *revolution* I mean turning over. Not development or unfolding, but turning over the system that has made you go to analysis to begin with—the system being government by minority and conspiracy, official secrets, national security, corporate power, *et cetera*. Therapy might imagine itself investigating the immediate social causes, even while keeping its vocabulary of abuse and victimization—that we are abused and victimized less by our personal lives of the past than by a present system.

It's like, you want your father to love you. The desire to be loved by your father is enormously important. But you can't get that love fulfilled by your father. You don't want to get rid of the desire to be loved, but you want to stop asking your father; he's the wrong object. So we don't want to get rid of the feeling of being abused—maybe that's very important, the feeling of being abused, the feeling of being without power. But maybe we shouldn't imagine that we are abused by the past as much as we are by the actual situation of "my job," "my finances," "my government"—all the things that we live with. Then the consulting room becomes a cell of revolution, because we would be talking also about, "What is actually abusing me right now?" That would be a great venture, for therapy to talk that way.

VENTURA: Let's double back a second. You said, "Could analysis have new fantasies about itself?" What do you mean by *fantasy?* For most people that word's associated with "unreal."

HILLMAN: Oh, no, no. Fantasy is the natural activity of the mind. Jung says, "The primary activity of psychic life is the creation of fantasy." Fantasy is how you perceive something, how you think about it, react to it.

VENTURA: So *any* perception, in that sense, is fantasy.

HILLMAN: Is there a reality that is not framed or formed? No. Reality is always coming through a pair of glasses, a point of view, a language—a fantasy.

VENTURA: But if therapy is to take this new direction, have this new perception or fantasy about itself, it seems we need some basic redefinition of some basic concepts.

Hillman smiles, looks out into the distance. The light has changed, the sun will be down soon, and the breeze off the sea is suddenly cool. The homeless woman is wrapping herself in plastic garbage bags, muttering something. The highway traffic below is moving smoothly again. The oil tanker's lights are on, and in a few moments it will be out of sight. And the lights of the Santa Monica Pier have come on, too, as sad as forced cheer.

HILLMAN: Maybe the idea of self has to be redefined.

VENTURA: *That* would be revolutionary. That would eventually change the entire culture, if it caught on.

HILLMAN: The idea of self has to be redefined. Therapy's definition comes from the Protestant and Oriental tradition: self is the interiorization of the invisible God beyond. The inner divine. Even if this inner divine is disguised as a self-steering, autonomous, homeostatic, balancing mechanism; or even if the divine is disguised as the integrating deeper intention of the whole personality, it's still a transcendent notion, with theological implications if not roots. I would rather define self as *the interiorization of community.* And if you make that little move, then you're going to feel very different about things. If the self were defined as the interiorization of community, then the boundaries between me and another would be much less sure. I would be with myself when I'm with others. I would not be with myself when I'm walking alone or meditating or in my room imagining or working on my dreams. In fact, I would be estranged from myself.

And "others" would not include just other people, because community, as I see it, is something more ecological, or at least animistic. A psychic field. And if I'm not in a psychic field with others—with people, buildings, animals, trees—I *am* not.

So it wouldn't be, "I am because I think." (*Cogito ergo sum,* as Descartes said.) It would be, as somebody said to me the other night, "I am because I party." *Convivo ergo sum.*

VENTURA: That's a redefinition of self, all right.

HILLMAN: Look, a great deal of our life is manic. I can watch thirty-four channels of TV, I can get on the fax and communicate with people anywhere, I can be everywhere at once, I can fly across the country, I've got call waiting, so I can take two calls at once. I live everywhere and nowhere. But I don't know who lives next door to me. Who's in the next flat? Who's in 14–B?

I don't know who they are, but, boy, I'm on the phone, car phone, toilet phone, plane phone, my mistress is in Chicago, the other woman I'm with is in D.C., my exwife is in Phoenix, my mother in Hawaii, and I have four children living all over the country. I have faxes coming in day and night, I can plug into all the world's stock prices, commodity exchanges, I am everywhere, man—but I don't know who's in 14–B.

You see, this hyper communication and information is part of what's keeping the soul at bay.

VENTURA: Oh yeah. Very much so. But—maybe it's because I'm a writer, maybe it's the way I've trained myself—but I feel most myself when I'm alone.

HILLMAN: It's not because you're a writer or because you've trained yourself. That training began two thousand years ago.

VENTURA: How?

HILLMAN: That training is the emphasis upon withdrawal, innerness—in Augustine's sense of confessions, in Jerome's sense of hiding out in the desert. This is the result of a long discipline to sever a person from the natural world of community. It's a monkish notion. A saintly notion.

And there's a second reason you are convinced that you're more yourself when you're alone: because it's more familiar. You are in a habitual, repetitious rut. "This is me, because I'm in the same pattern"; it's recognizable. When you're with another person you're out of yourself because the other person is flowing into you and you are flowing into them, there are surprises, you're a little out of control, and then you think you're not your real true self. The out of control—that's the community acting through you. It's the locus that you're in, acting through you.

VENTURA: But if you let that go too much, then you're in Nuremburg Square with your arm up in the air. Or, closer to home, you're waving flags and yellow ribbons for reasons you don't even care about understanding. That's the community acting through you too. If the community acts through you too much, you don't exist. And when you don't exist, in this way, you open yourself up to possession by whatever force or idea or demagogue that seeks to possess you.

HILLMAN: Why do we use the image of the mob or of fascist conformity when we give up the self?

VENTURA: Because we've suffered so much in this century, and we're suffering now, from people giving up their individuality.

HILLMAN: That's true. Still, it's interesting that that's the only image we use. We don't use the image of a tribal society, where I still remain John-of-the-One-Leg.

VENTURA: That's true. It's an interesting, very significant detail that in the tribal societies, which we think have the least individuality, people have the most individual names. One-of-a-kind names that come from their dreams or their actions, which are rarely repeated or handed down because they're so individual. It's as though, because the community shares so much and because so much is handed down through the community, individuality is treated with more respect.

HILLMAN: In tribal life and religion there was often a place for people who were different—homosexuals, visionaries, hermits, people with special qualities or powers. This wasn't unknown in village life, either. Nor in the city life of the ancient Greeks. Not that these were perfect societies—

VENTURA: —since perfection is not a human possibility—

HILLMAN: —but we do have examples of the self-as-community that aren't totalitarian and in which individuality is respected.

I won't accept these simple opposites—either individual self in control or a totalitarian, mindless mob. This kind of fantasy keeps us afraid of community. It locks us up inside our separate selves all alone and longing for connection. In fact, the idea of surrendering to the fascist mob is the result of the separated self. It's the old Apollonian ego, aloof and clear, panicked by the Dionysian flow.

We have to think about community as a different category altogether. It's not individuals coming together and connecting, and it's not a crowd. Community to me means simply the actual little system in which you are situated, sometimes in your office, sometimes at home with your furniture and your food and your cat, sometimes talking in the hall with the people in 14–B. In each case your self is a little different, and your true self is your actual self, just as it is in each situation, a self *among,* not a self apart.

VENTURA: And when you ask, "What about the person in 14–B?" are you or I respecting that person as part of the community or as an individual? Neither, if we choose to be totally cut off from them. And if they accept being cut off from us, they're not respecting us either, in any of our roles. We're talking about *neighbors,* after all. Yes, to ignore the fact that one is or has a neighbor is a profound form of disrespect, both to the other and to ourselves, and it's completely taken for granted now in our cities and suburbs. I take it for granted; I ignore my neighbors and I bet you do too.

HILLMAN: I think it's absolutely necessary for our spiritual life today to have community where we actually live. Of course, we have dear friends from thirty years ago who are living in Burma or Brazil now. And they're there for you when you're busted—in an emergency. But is that sufficient? For the maintenance of the world? It's definitely not. I think for the maintenance of the world that other kind of local community requires regular servicing. And that's a very unpleasant, hard thing to stay with, to realize how much service one needs to perform—not for an old, distant friend, but for the people in 14–B.

VENTURA: How can therapy possibly deal with that? I mean, nuts and bolts.

HILLMAN: Part of the treatment of these difficulties is to look at a person's schedule, his notebook, her calendar. Because your schedule is one of your biggest defenses.

VENTURA: Treat my schedule?

HILLMAN: Treat your schedule. And I'll tell you, I have had more resistance in trying to treat people's schedules and change their schedules than you can ever imagine.

VENTURA: You'd get a shitload of resistance out of me.

HILLMAN: Do you ever ask your soul questions when you make your schedule?

VENTURA *(groaning)*: My soul just went, *"He fucking-a doesn't!"*

HILLMAN: The job then becomes how the soul finds accommodations within your day. Regarding dreams, regarding persons, regarding time off. Because the manic defense against depression is to keep extremely busy—and to be very irritated when interrupted. That's part of the sign of the manic condition.

VENTURA: Me and many of the people I know are often too busy to be anything but busy. Yes, it's manic, and we sort of know that. You're saying it's a defense against depression. If we go back to what we were talking about before and assume that the source of our depression is in the present rather than twenty or thirty years ago, then the question is, What chronic depression are we—as individuals, as a city, as a culture—trying to avoid by being so chronically manic?

HILLMAN: The depression we're all trying to avoid could very well be a prolonged chronic reaction to what we've been doing to the world, a mourning and grieving for what we're doing to nature and to cities and to whole peoples—the destruction of a lot of our world. We may be depressed partly because this is the soul's reaction to the mourning and grieving that we're not consciously doing. The grief over neighborhoods destroyed where I grew up, the loss of agricultural land that I knew as a kid—

VENTURA: —or the sense, in younger people, that those things are in the past, you've never known them and you're never going to—

HILLMAN: —all those things that are lost and gone. Because that's what depression feels like.

We paint our national history rosy and white and paint our personal history gray. We're so willing to admit that we're trapped in our personal history, but we never hear that said of our national history.

VENTURA: Or our civilization's history. Which in a reverse way is an indication of how much we *really* believe in the self as interiorization-of-community, because there's so much denial about the importance and the darkness of our national and cultural history. We wouldn't need to deny it so much if it wasn't so incredibly important to us. The strength of that denial measures a tremendous fear and loss.

HILLMAN: I think we've also lost shame. We talk about our parents having shamed us when we were little, but we've lost our shame in relation to the world and to the oppressed, the shame of being wrong, of messing up the world. We've mutated this shame into personal guilt.

Perhaps the way to begin the revolution is to stand up for your depression.

VENTURA: That *is* depressing. And there's so much to revolt against. All that ugly, money-driven, bottom-line thinking that's the excuse for so much stupidity and cruelty. But you began by saying that things, objects, are not passive—that, through things, the world is fighting back. So?

HILLMAN: Look, any major change needs a breakdown. Chernobyl—it didn't seem to affect us in America, but in Europe people couldn't eat vegetables, couldn't drink milk; all the reindeer meat in Scandinavia was contaminated. This changes values immensely. Suddenly certain things are life giving and others are death giving. Money no longer matters to the same extent; there's no price tag on Chernobyl. So the change of financial bottom-line thinking comes about through symptoms. It comes about through poison. Valdez, Bhopal, Chernobyl have made everything there toxic, bad, poisonous—and it's beyond money. The threat of death gets us past the determination of value by finance. After catastrophes money no longer carries value. The nature or quality of soul of a thing would be the ultimate value. We would ask, Is this a good thing, is this a helpful thing, is this a beautiful thing? instead of, What's its price?

VENTURA: *That* would certainly be revolutionary. Changing the nature of that fundamental question—What's its price? —would change everything. And the consulting room *could* become a cell of revolution if therapy located our troubles more in the present and directed our attention to the world instead of only inside, because ultimately the question would have to be, What's its price? What's the real price we pay for how we live?

Ventura laughs suddenly.

HILLMAN: What?

VENTURA: Immediately my greedy little private self, the part that only cares about my relationships and would just as soon the people in 14–B mind their own damn business, that self leaps to the question: In this new revolutionary therapy, what about l-o-v-e?

HILLMAN: You know, there's a feeling about a good day —it's slow, and very much like being with a lover. Having a good moment at breakfast, tasting something—it has to do with beauty, this matter of love. And I think all the "work" at personal relationships fucks that up. That "work" is not aesthetic and sensuous, which is really what love, for me, is about. Aesthetic and sensuous, and a kind of joy. Love doesn't result from working at something. So the therapeutic approach to love, of clearing up the relationship, may clear up communication disorders, expression inhibitions, insensitive habits, may even improve sex, but I don't think it releases love; I don't think love can be worked at.

VENTURA: That's a distinction that our culture seems to have been busy forgetting for the last several decades—the distinction between "the relationship" and "love." To apply the word *aesthetic* to "the relationship"—that would make a lot of us blink hard.

HILLMAN: That's what love is about—aesthetic and sensuous. And when that aspect isn't functioning, the other person becomes a little bit of a camel, carrying so much weight through the desert of the relationship—your baggage, the other person's baggage. No wonder camels spit.

Part II

The Letters: Life Lived Backwards, Frontwards, and Sideways

Soul-Making

Dear Michael,

Surprise! I want to defend therapy, your basic kind—inward-searching, long-term, insight therapy—and its goal of individuation.

To my mind, there is clearly a place for the skills and knowledge acquired during the one hundred years of solitude—knowledge about the solitude, its significance, its imaginative richness, its relation to death, and its education in love. Also, the value of staying with tough stuff in a time of the fast fix and quick buck. There is a place for the strength of character and subtlety of insight that the investigation of interiority produces. I've called this psychological engagement "soul-making," a term and an idea taken from the Romantics: Keats, Blake, and D. H. Lawrence. A long-term, soul-focused, depth analysis provides a discipline—a religious devotion with rituals, symbols, teachings, kind submissions, obediences, sacrifices—that is truly a care of soul. There are individual patients and individual therapists whose work, whose love, whose calling is clearly in this area, but—and this is crucial—the calling does not have to be away from the world or rest upon a theory of self-enclosed individuals. Soul-making and care of soul do not have to be identified with introversion and the spiritual denial of the world of matter, objects, things.

Keats said, "Call the world if you please, 'the vale of Soul-making.' Then you will find out the use of the world." This was my motto for therapy for fifteen years, longer.

The motto imagines the tribulations of life as contributions to soul. I found Wallace Stevens saying something similar: "The way through the world/Is more difficult to find than the way beyond it." Simply said, you make soul by living life, not by retreating from the world into "inner work" or beyond the world in spiritual disciplines and meditation removes.

This way through the world was a hugely satisfying insight, a great step for me. No longer was I trapped in the usual program of, first, retreat into deep inner work and, then, return to the world. Instead, I began to value every ongoing engagement for the sake of soul. It doesn't matter where the stimulus or distraction comes from, how lofty or how cheap, one simply feels it and reflects on it in terms of soul. You ask yourself: How does this event bear on soul-making? This insight from Keats—a puer, by the way, who died before he was twenty-six—also separated me from my classical colleagues who, I believe, never really left the Cartesian split between inner and outer—good soul inside and the world, the flesh, and the devil outside—reformulated as introversion and extraversion.

Horribile dictu, now I see that even the Keatsian solution is inadequate. Why? Because it is still self-centered. It still focuses on one's personal destiny or, as they now call it, "journey." The exterior world's value is simply utilitarian, for the sake of soul-making. It provides obstacles, pitfalls, monsters to be met in order to make one's interior soul.

So, I want to clear this up here, because Keats's phrase, which has sustained my therapy for so long, contains a major mistake! It actually neglects the world, even while finding a soul use for it. You go through the world for your own sake, making your own soul. But what about the world's soul, Michael? What about the *anima mundi* and making that? The plight of the world, the suffering of its oceans and its rivers, its air and its forests, the ugliness of its cities and depletion of its soils have certainly forced us to feel that we cannot go through the world for our own benefit and that we are actually destroying our souls by an attitude that pretends to save them. The ship of death Lawrence says we must each build is no longer a private ark that can take the storms; the ship of death is the world soul sinking like an overloaded garbage barge. That's why I say therapy—even the best deep therapy—contributes to the world's destruction.

We have to have new thinking—or much older thinking than Lawrence, Blake, and Keats—to find roots for therapy's deep interiorizing work. Soul-making must be reimagined. We have to go back before Romanticism, back to medieval alchemy and Renaissance Neoplatonism, back to Plato, back to Egypt, and also especially out of Western history to tribal animistic psychologies that are always mainly concerned, not with individualities, but with the soul of things ("environmental concerns," "deep ecology," as it's now called) and propitiatory acts that keep the world on its course.

As Sendivogius, an alchemist, said, "The greater part of the soul lies outside the body." *Mens sana in corpore sano* (Galen's medical motto of a healthy mind in a healthy body) today means "the body of the world"; if it is not kept healthy, we go insane. The neglect of the environment, the body of the world, is part and parcel of our personal "insanity." The world's body must be restored to health, for in that body is also the world's soul. I don't think spiritual disciplines take the world enough into account; they're always set on transcending, that is, denying it with spiritual practices. That's why therapy is still so important—once it makes the effort of rethinking its base—because therapy stays here on earth, in the mess of life, truly concerned with soul.

The only way I can justify still using the term *individuation* today is by extending it to mean the individuation of each moment in life, each action, each relationship, and each thing. The individuation of things. Not merely my individuation with its belief in an interior self that draws my care from the world to my "process," my "journey."

Our focus could be on the soul potential of the object—as we are trying to do with this book we are writing. *Aren't we trying for a well-made book rather than trying to express or realize our subjective personalities?* This means individuating each act we do and thing we live with, actualizing *its* potential (the human potential movement turned outward beyond the human) so that the innate dignity, beauty, and integrity of any act and any thing from doorknob to desk chair to bed sheet may become fully present in its uniqueness. I am inviting us to think again of the morality of craft, the value of rhetoric, and the truth of the body's gestures. Let's make things "well"—which means both well made and also healthy. For this, we need the individuating eye that can see what Wallace Stevens called "the poem in the heart of things," that innate imaginal essence I called an acorn. So, individuating begins with noticing, paying attention to the specifics of what is actually there so that it can become fully what it is. This is simply what therapy has been doing all along, only that its attention has been held exclusively to humans.

Curiously, just as humans show the first inklings of their uniqueness in their pathologies, so a thing's *pathology* may show its specific essence, its *raison d'être.* The hard light from a fluorescent tube says that light is not "well," but it also says that the tube's essential purpose is light making. The tear-off tab on an aluminum can says that its job is to make the contents easily available, yet that tab cuts our fingers. Like with human pathology, the pathology of things is where the noticing eye first alights, despite glossy cover-up ads.

Michael, if we don't begin speculating and experimenting with extending individuation into the world of things, the idea remains captured by private capitalism, an enterprise of developing my own private property, "myself," my very own soul, my personal journey, and my locked-away journal, the gesture for which points away from the world and toward the recesses of the chest. Me oh my.

The Neoplatonic idea I am pursuing in this book and everywhere I go to talk cannot separate soul in me from soul in others—others being not just people but environment. You could also say what I am reaching for by bringing in doorknobs and beer cans is shifting the idea of depth from the psychology of the inner person to a psychology of things, a depth psychology of extraversion.

I look forward to your answer to this essay. Fondly, as usual,

Jim

What Am I Doing Here?

Dear Jim,

You're right, I was surprised to see you defend "your basic kind" of therapy. Don't worry about therapy, man. Therapy's all grown up now, powerful and autonomous; it can take care of itself. Everyone likely to read this book has had some experience with therapy, been in it, done it, had friends and families in it and doing it. Plenty of their experience has been beneficial. There's a sense in which *they* are therapy, and their experience is all the defense therapy needs.

We're not attacking therapy so much as trying to extend it, reveal its blind spots, and begin the enormous task of redefining its premises. It's not the idea of doing therapy (in-depth introspective therapy, family systems therapy, whatever)

that is wrong; there are many who need such therapy, even need it desperately, and who may never truly know themselves without it. But, as you've said, therapy's theoretical base has not gone far enough, has not connected with the world, and without that connection it's incapable of treating the whole individual.

This is something I've been writing in one form or other since 1975: If more than half the marriages in America end in divorce; if most of the not-yet-divorced marriages one sees are not, to say the least, wonderful; and if most of the relationships around you are falling apart, and/or haunted, boring, or miserable, then clearly the fundamental cause *can't* be individual. If it's happening (as it is) across every level of class, ethnicity, and region, then the cause can't be found solely in the study of families, either. *Doesn't something that happens no matter what kind of family you come from cancel out family as the prime source?* Obviously the family as a form is being subjected to pressure on a massive, collective scale. Thus your family is just one wrinkle of a collective event, important for you to know, perhaps, but not to be confused or treated as a cause. It should seem self-evident to say this, but in Western thought it's a radical idea: *There must be something collective in the cause of a collective phenomenon.* Therefore, if a cure is possible, the collective has to be addressed for and in and by that cure. Getting in touch with your inner life and figuring out your family system is, at best, no more than part of the job.

Surely pointing this out is not an "attack."

To change the subject: something that's occurred to me as I've transcribed and edited the interviews is . . .

People know who you are and why you're doing this and by what right, and if they don't the book jacket will tell them: James "Big Jim" "Tapdance" Hillman, chock-full of degrees, major-domo of Jung's own Jung Institute, theorist, author, and practicing therapist extraordinaire. But who's the other guy—the one who ain't got no degrees? What's he got to do with therapy? I don't even think *you* know; you've just kind of taken me on faith and on my rap. So I'll tell you.

Therapy's been a part of my life since I was seven, when my mother had her first psychotic episodes (the first, at least, that were noticed by the grown-ups). We're a family of two biological parents, a stepparent, and five children. My mother and one of my siblings spent years and years and years in every conceivable kind of state hospital (we're a poor family), receiving every conceivable kind of diagnosis and treatment. Some of their stays lasted two and three years at a time. Another sibling spent a shorter time in that system and later was in couple's counseling. Still another sibling and I have spent god knows how many years and how much money on the receiving end of the consulting room.

Let's see. When I was eleven I started, went for three years. Then two or three more in my early twenties, then about four and a half more in my late thirties and early forties. That's roughly ten years in therapy! My first long-term girlfriend and two of my first four close male friends became therapists. I spent my late twenties and most of my thirties mainly writing and honky-tonking in Texas, L.A., and on the road, a life you know about from my novel *Night Time Losing Time.* Dig it, wild as that life was, *four* dear friends from those years (three of whom I had, as the M.D.'s say, "relations" with) have become therapists. During my marriage, it was our largest expense by far. Then I put my now-exwife through shrink school, she's a therapist now. I made another good therapist friend over the last year.

Shouldn't I receive some sort of degree for all this? Couldn't you arrange it? Or is mine a common experience? Is America crawling with therapists? Has therapy saturated everything? You'd say yes, I think—both to the saturation and to my degree: Master of Talking to, Paying for, Sleeping with, and/or Befriending Therapists-and-Therapists-to-Be. That's all the Ph.D. I need.

To change subjects again:

I remember a few years ago in Santa Barbara, you were giving a lecture and I was invited to be on the panel commenting on and questioning you. The panel consisted of me and three shrinks. (That's another odd connection. I've never directly written about therapy in my *L.A. Weekly* column, never, but for years shrink schools and institutes have invited me to speak and be on panels, which I usually turn down because it feels so strange to me.) Anyway, you and I went out for a drink afterward, and you said, "We come from very different backgrounds but we have the same enemy."

Enemy meaning puritanism, with all its subtle and not-so-subtle warpings of the culture, and the monotheism in *thought,* rather than religion, that has infected and determined Western life.

The fascinating thing as I transcribe and edit the tapes is that it's not our very different life-styles that are evident, but what I would call (without sentimentality, I hope) our brotherhood. By which I mean, the facing of our common enemy. Two things seem to have happened. The first is that what started off as me interviewing you ended up as the two of us goading each other into deeper, or at least wilder, thought. Pushing it, pushing it, like two jazz musicians trading riffs back and forth. And that caused the second thing to happen: the voices start to blend. Which happens when musicians duet intensely too, especially if they're two guitarists or trumpet players or saxophone players. If you're listening to such an exchange on records it can be hard to tell them apart even if you know their individual styles very well. Something happens in the act of playing the music together, going in the same direction and basing individual improvisation on the same chords and theme. And in that way our voices sometimes turn into a kind of mutual voice, so that, as much as our deliveries are different on the tape, in the transcript if you deleted our names it's sometimes hard to tell who's talking.

It has to do with where individuality starts and stops and with whether ideas are merely passive, *thought of,* or rather have a kind of life, which is to say, a kind of will. These issues are linked and are part of what has become our book's theme. Bear with me, Jim, I'm about to go very far afield.

For some historical context, let's go back to the 1940s. Fundamental changes occurred in science and the arts at the same time (and mostly in the same area). In science, IBM and Howard Aiken built the first major computer, the Mark I, in Massachusetts in 1939. Then in Pennsylvania in 1946, John Mauchly and J. Presper Eckert made the ENIAC, a computer one thousand times faster than its predecessors. The new pattern and sheer speed of calculation would change and intensify patterns of thought, influencing what we researched, how we researched, and the form (and therefore the data) of the results.

During this same period, 1939 to 1946, musician-composers were coming up with comparable structural changes in music. Trumpeter Dizzy Gillespie, saxophonist Charlie Parker, pianists Thelonius Monk and Bud Powell, and drummers Kenny Clarke and Max Roach worked with sounds, patterns, and speeds of music that had never been attempted before. They were as unaware of the invention of the computer as the scientists were of what came to be called Bebop. But the complexity and speed of a Parker, Gillespie, or Powell solo; the new harmonic spaces of Monk's chords; the freedom, explosiveness, and subtlety of Clarke's and Roach's drumming—here was music paralleling in its form what was going on in the new field of electronics. The different mediums were hit at the same time with previously unheard-of forms of speed and complexity.

Also at the same time, and in the same area, painters achieved something very similar. Abstract Expressionism and Thelonius Monk go hand in hand, or ear in hand. Space is to painting what motion is to other mediums, and the painting of this era created impressions of vast inner spaces while playing as freely with shape as Bebop did with melody. If you did a film cutting back and forth from Jackson Pollock's "action" paintings to those loud flashing computers with their whirling reels and added a Dizzy Gillespie or Bud Powell sound track, the conceptual unities of the era would announce themselves with no equivocation.

No, you can't translate exactly from science to music to art; but you can see that workers in each medium, scientists and musicians and painters, simultaneously felt the need to work with the qualities of speed and space, and greatly increased their form's complexity.

But see all this in the light of another art, the art of behavior: acting. While scientists changed the speed and pattern of certain kinds of thought, and jazz musicians and painters did the same to sound and vision, theater people clustering around Lee Strasberg and Elia Kazan transformed how human behavior would be interpreted on stage and screen. The new Actors Studio method expressed moods and realms of the psyche that had been off-limits to the more traditional acting of England and Hollywood, but those moods and realms were right at home with what was being expressed in the new painting and jazz.

Again the quality of speed was key, but the Actors Studio method of people like Marlon Brando slowed down reactions, doing with pace what many Abstract Expressionists were doing with space. It's fascinating that while science and music responded to their era by increasing the qualities of speed and density, in order to express the same density and complexity in terms of human motivation actors made more use of silence and pauses. There is an air of being knocked off center, of having to regain your balance in every new moment, in the Actors Studio style as it was practiced in the forties and fifties—as though portraying the motivation of any character had to take into account that character's being a bit dazed at the speed and intensity of the changes surrounding him. When you think of artists like Marlon Brando, Montgomery Clift, and Gena Rowlands, a kind of suspicious bewilderment is taken for granted in their style.

But if you read studies of the science, jazz, art, or theater of this era, they will mention each other, if at all, only in passing. The innovations will be ascribed to this or that person—J. Presper Eckert or Lee Strasberg. The story is told purely in terms of the traditions of the medium they worked in and the personal history of the innovators. If there's a sociological or political slant, economics or concepts like the patriarchy will figure, but still in terms of the particular art or artist. The fact that parallel innovations were being made in disciplines as socially separate as nightclub jazz and advanced electronics; and that the personal histories of the innovators often have little in common (although they innovated with the same qualities at the same time and, for the most part, within three hundred miles of each other)—this is ignored.

I think of what Doris Lessing wrote in *The Four-Gated City:* "In any situation anywhere there is always a key fact, the essence. But it is usually every other fact, thousands of facts, that are seen, discussed, dealt with. The central fact is usually ignored, or not seen." And a sentence of Yukia Mishima's in *Spring Snow:* "To live in the midst of an era is to be oblivious to its style."

What Lessing would call a key fact of the 1940s is that parallel revolutionary innovations were made in different mediums by very different individuals from different backgrounds. Obviously something is going on here that doesn't have to do with individuals or individuality or anything that would be presented in a psychological personal history, indicating that, yes, even the precious ideal that we call creativity has crucial collective elements that we haven't begun to think about.

Only Carl Jung has explored the concept of collective psychology seriously, but his path-breaking concepts of synchronicity and the collective unconscious are more descriptions of the phenomena than tools for thought and change. The proof of this is that the concepts are so rarely employed in *practice* by Jungian therapists.

Artists and scientists sometimes speak of these concerns. Einstein, who dreamed parts of his theories, felt his ideas came from outside himself. Dizzy Gillespie said, "All the music is out there in the first place, all of it. From the beginning of time, the music was there. All you have to do is try to get a little piece of it. I don't care how great you are, you only get a little piece of it." The phenomenon gets alluded to, mentioned, sometimes joked about, but, Jung aside, the West is a long way from thinking about it, much less incorporating it into its sense of history, criticism, or psychology.

We could say that something courses through the collective and is picked up and expressed in different mediums by different individuals, and that that expression constellates a kind of subcollective around it, a style of music or a school of painting or a branch of science, to articulate back to the collective this impulse that came, originally, from or through the collective. This something, this impulse, this idea, hasn't a will so much as a force—a force so strong that it's felt by individuals (individual scientists or artists or thinkers) as a compulsion, as something they *must* express. Western thought has taken that expression to be personal, the result of Charlie Parker's or Jackson Pollock's creativity, but I am suggesting that it's far less personal than it seems. In *The Education* Henry Adams said, "Susceptibility to the highest forces is the highest genius." The genius of a Parker or a Pollock or a Jung is not what they originate but what they're susceptible to—how open or susceptible they remain to these impulses and the technique and determination with which they follow and express that susceptibility. It's not that there isn't deep personal originality and courage in what we do individually; it's that what we work with as individuals is an impulse or wave or force that courses through the collective we belong to. Talents, you remember, used to be referred to as gifts.

What has this got to do with therapy? Only everything. Until therapy finds better ways to think about the collective and to differentiate among collective and individual impulses and forces and to look at how they interact, how can it fully address the world *or* the individual? Because if what I'm saying has any validity, then therapy is only treating a part of the individual, and therapy is not even sure which part. How that individual expresses or denies, acts out or resists, a collective impulse—isn't even on the table for consideration.

For psychotherapy, what Lessing would call the key fact is that even the most obvious forms of collective behavior (a grass-roots totalitarian movement, a teen gang, or a fashion fad) are beyond the range of insight. And you can't treat or change what you don't know how to think about.

Okay, Jim, now let's wheel all this around to you and me and how our individual voices sometimes, in the transcripts, blend into a kind of mutual voice like jazzmen riffing a duet. I would say that what we're tuned into, what's coming through us, is, at least in part, the beginning of the articulation of a new theoretical framework that would extend psychotherapy in particular and Western thought in general into the realms of the collective. We're not the people who are going to build the new theoretical superstructure. That's the work of the next century, and, anyway, the building of superstructures isn't a job either one of us would choose. We're instigators, goaders, conceptual adventurers, if you like, through whom the new theoretical framework is putting out feelers, announcing itself, whispering in the ear of psychotherapy, leaving cryptic notes in strange places, singing under its window. And that impulse, that new constellation of ideas, draws our voices toward it and makes them, in this particular moment and this particular work, more alike than not when we speak together, because in that moment we're engaging, invoking the impulse at the same time, it's finding us at the same time. As we write, all our distinctions will come out again.

Which is where I leave off tonight, hoping this reaches you in good health. One more thing: because these letters too are part of that impulse, I don't think we should bother to answer each other, particularly. We should instead take jazz for a model and consider each letter as a sort of solo; sometimes one soloist picks up phrases from the other and answers them, sometimes the first soloist is "answered" by the next going off on his own track with nothing but their common intent (the chords, the theme) to connect them. Jazz is the best metaphor for what we're doing, in form at least, because it's art consciously built upon the interplay between the collective and the individual.

Enough.

Michael

Life Lived Backwards

Dear Michael,

There is a painting by Picasso done when he was ninety-one, the year before he died. It is titled *Le jeune peintre* (the young painter). It is a freely drawn, broad-brushed sketch in oils—whites, grays, slate blues, and black—of a dark-, sharp-, and hollow-eyed, small, boyish face, a little impish, staring out at you under a wide floppy hat, a palette board and brush in hand. The white on white gives it the feeling of a ghost, of a clown, of an angel, and also of an innocent, though lively and intensely concentrated, observer, whose mercurial alertness has just been caught by the painter.

When I first saw this painting—and it is a big one, nearly a yard tall—I had that *frisson* André Malraux says leaps from one work of art to another via the human person. This haunting, simple image turned out to be the initiatory experience for my theory of life lived backwards. Here is the invisible Picasso caught on the canvas, a self-portrait of the daimon that inhabited him all his life. At the end, it emerges and shows itself.

"Here," it says, "this is who you are, Picasso, you are me, the ever-young painter. I am the clown, the innocent, fresh eye, the dark eye, the quick-moving Mercurius, the sentimental, bluish melancholy, the little boy. I am your ghost. Now you see who drives you, what has kept you fresh and eager, and now you can die."

It was as if Picasso had been realizing and actualizing and individuating this figure all his life, ever since he was an exceptionally talented, teenage painter—even before Paris and his youth of the blue and rose periods, when he was *le jeune peintre.* Here was a portrait of the acorn painted by the oak.

Picasso's image confirms Henry Corbin's theory that it is not my individuation but the individuation of the angel that is the main task: the materialization with paint, brush, and canvas of Picasso's daimon. This image also presents Corbin's basic premise about *ta'wil,* or the art of interpretative reading, how to read life itself: we must "read things back to their origins and principle, their archetype." "In *ta'wil* one must carry sensible forms back to imaginative forms and then rise to still higher meanings; to proceed in the opposite direction (to carry imaginative forms back to sensible forms . . .) is to destroy the virtualities of the imagination." This idea is applicable to how we read our lives: we must begin with the angel, the young painter, who is attempting to enter the sensible world and individuate through the life of Picasso.

How so? Because the primary activity of the psyche is imagining.

My point here is that we humans are primarily acts of imagination, images. Jung says, "The psyche consists essentially of images." And what is an image? Not only the depiction of something there on the canvas in oil paint. Jung says: "When I speak of image . . . I do not mean the psychic reflections of an external object, but a concept derived from poetic usage, namely, a figure of fancy or *fantasy image,* which is related only indirectly to . . . an external object." Or, put it my way, what we are *really,* and the reality we live, is our psychic reality, which is nothing but—get that demeaning *nothing but*—the poetic imagination going on day and night. We really do live in dream time; we really are such stuff as dreams are made of.

If at the soul's core we are images, then we must define life as the actualization over time (for Keats twenty-six years, for Picasso ninety-two) of that originating seed image, what Michelangelo called the *imagine del cuor,* or the image in the heart, and that image—not the time that actualized it—is the primary determinant of your life.

Do you see what this means?

It means that our history is secondary or contingent, and that the image in the heart is primary and essential. If our history is contingent and not the primary determinant, then the things that befall us in the course of time (which we call development) are various actualizations of the image, manifestations of it, and not causes of who we are. I am not caused by my history—my parents, my childhood and development. These are mirrors in which I may catch glimpses of my image.

Picasso says, "When I hear people talk of the development of the artist, it seems to me as if they were seeing the artist between two opposed mirrors which were endlessly reflecting his mirror image, and as if they saw the series of images in one mirror as his past and the images in the other mirror as his future. . . . They do not realize that all are the same images." He goes on, "I am astounded over the way people let the word *development* be misused; I don't develop; I am."

Do you notice here that when he speaks of who he is, he speaks of himself *as an image?* "I am an image," he says. That's what I mean by the acorn, and that's why I use artists like Picasso and Wallace Stevens instead of psychologists to say it for me. They realize that they are imagination before they are history. In a poem called "The Plain Sense of Things," Stevens says we can't get beyond imagination: ". . . the absence of the imagination had / Itself to be imagined." So your life is the ongoing operation of imagination; you imagine yourself into existence, or let's say, an image is continuing to shape itself into the oak tree you consider your reality.

In Picasso's case, *le jeune peintre* was always there, is always there. As the historical Picasso of the flesh falls away, the daimonic ghost stands forth. The white figure in the hat is like an image of the "free soul," also called "dream soul," "ghost soul," and "death soul." (I take these terms from writers on

Native American Indians and on Inuits [Eskimos].) This usually hidden ghost in the machine is our angel, our underworld, our fateful image and seed that is our death. The key to your life and my life, Michael, is not locked away in childhood to be recovered by remembering and analyzing; it is found in your death and who you are then—and the moment of death is any moment.

I may die in a veterans' hospital with Alzheimer's or gasping with tubes and wires and oxygen or smashed and tangled against a tree in a car crash, or I may drop dead at a corporate board of directors meeting. These are not, however, literally any more revelations of my image than this moment now. In other words, we have to take care we don't take death too literally, as we take childhood. Time is not the primary factor; *an image is not cumulative, and the late stages of life are not the fullest and finest presentation of one's seed.* The oak tree is not any more itself after four hundred years and at the moment of its felling. It is always itself, like Picasso in the mirror. Camus's death against a tree on a French roadside fits his image of *The Stranger,* of the existentially absurd, of the *acte gratuit,* of his statement that suicide is the only truly serious question. Each of these events and thoughts and ideas mirrors his angel.

The job of life becomes one of making its moments accord with the image, or what might once have been called "being guided by your genius" ([or daimon or angel]). The Catholics at the end want absolution, so that the free soul or death soul, one's essence, may be freed of those historical contingencies called sins, which impede the immortality of the soul, fastening it to its mortal errancy. Another way we can make life accord with the angel is when, each morning, we return from the dream soul trying to adjust to the day world, that moment when the two souls exchange places in the driver's seat. And another way we try to keep life essential, in accord with the seed, is by sensitive responses in the daily round. How well we do this, I think, doesn't matter so much as living life with this sense of image in mind. It gives one an aesthetic and ethical sensitivity about rightness and trueness, and it functions like a gyroscope, which doesn't mean that we are not for the most part lost in a fog or becalmed and drifting. The genius is pretty tricky; it keeps quiet often when you need it most!

Sometimes, the genius seems to show only in symptoms and disorders, as a kind of preventive medicine, holding you back from a false route. Do you know how many extraordinary people were runaways, school dropouts, hated school, could not fit in? My source for this data (Goertzel and Goertzel, *Cradles of Eminence*) lists Pearl Buck, Isadora Duncan, Willa Cather, Sigrid Undset, Susan B. Anthony—to name some of the women only. William Randolph Hearst, Paderewski, Brendan Behan, Stalin, William Osler, Sarah Bernhardt, and Orville Wright were all expelled from school. The power of the acorn does not allow compromises with standard norms—and remember, school for teachers was once called "normal" school, and the Goddess of school is the Roman Minerva, the great normalizer, the great weaver into the social fabric. Cezanne was rejected from the Beaux Arts academy. Grieg at age thirteen was completing his opus one ("Variations on a German Melody") in a school classroom; his teacher shook him to put a stop to it. Proust's teachers thought his compositions disorganized. Zola got a zero in literature at his high school and also failed rhetoric. Eugene O'Neill, Faulkner, and F. Scott Fitzgerald all had failures in college. Edison says, "I was always at the foot of the class." And Einstein was considered dull by his teachers. As for Picasso, my data says he was taken out of school at age ten because "he stubbornly refused to do anything but paint."

I'm saying, among twenty other things, that we have to take a new look not only at childhood, but at psychopathology too. Did you know that when Lindbergh was a boy he had tremendous nightmares about falling from a high place, and he even tried to meet this fear by jumping from a tree? Did his interior imagination already know that he had to fly over the Atlantic alone? The Mexican social revolutionary painter Diego Rivera, at the age of six, mounted the pulpit in his local church and gave such a violent anticlerical speech that the priest fled and the congregation was frightened. Salvador Dali was a real weirdo child: he stomped a classmate's violin, kicked his sister's head as if it were a football, and—get this—bit into a rotting bat. By adolescence he was considered so strange that he was pelted with stones going to the movies. (All this good stuff from the Goertzels.) Isn't Dali's behavior "surrealism" in acorn?

For another sort of kinkiness, take Baden-Powell, the founder of the Boy Scouts. At his school he was overeager, "ready to assume a father-role, to keep his fellow students amused, to be useful to his teachers," though his classmates thought him odd. He was in all the committees, too. Wasn't he already a Boy Scout before there were Boy Scouts?

These exceptional people reveal the thesis of looking at life backwards because exceptional people can't keep from letting it all show. I've picked peculiar behaviors rather than the usual examples of early talent—Mozart, Yehudi Menuhin, Marie Curie. Since the peculiar genius can appear in the guise of dysfunctional behavior, we have to pay attention and revise our thinking about children and their pathology in terms of the nascent possibilities exemplified in these biographies of eminence.

You see, we need biographies of the Great to understand the rest of us. Psychology starts the wrong way around. It plots statistical norms, and what deviates are deviants. I follow Corbin. I want to start from the top down, because to start the regular way, to extrapolate from the usual to the unusual, doesn't account for the remarkable determining force of the acorn. We cannot grasp Leonardo da Vinci by examining his distorted relationship with his mother, as Freud tried. Thousands of us, millions and millions of us, have had every sort of mother trouble, but there is only one Leonardo. And Leonardo's exceptionality may provide better images, a better, more interesting approach to my mother troubles than understanding mother troubles will help grasp Leonardo.

Edgar Wind has a little excursion on method in his incredible book, *Pagan Mysteries in the Renaissance,* where he writes, "A method that fits the small work but not the great has obviously started at the wrong end. . . . It seems to be a lesson of history that the commonplace may be understood as a reduction of the exceptional, but that the exceptional cannot be understood by amplifying the commonplace." No matter how much you blow up the symptom of timidity in the bullfighter Manolete or the explorer Stefansson, you never will reach their exceptional genius. You will never discover the angel. But if you start with the angel of their destinies appearing in their childhood fears, you can begin to grasp what was most deeply going on. As Wind says, "Both logically and causally the exceptional is crucial, because it introduces (however strange it may sound) the more comprehensive category." I would add that the exceptional is crucial also because it gives a wholly new understanding of psychopathology and why it is so obdurately hard to change.

So, Michael, this letter is expanding upon the earlier remarks about Manolete and Churchill and those other biographies of childhood I cited. I am elaborating the idea of the acorn and the value of this idea for imagining life in reverse, lived backwards, not in time from birth to death, but backwards in significance. For this suggests a completely different method for psychotherapy. It means *what is fatefully effective in our lives is what is truly significant, that is, the character of the guiding ghost, whose idiosyncrasies—call them symptoms—limit life to the only possibilities that are actually yours.*

Hindus speak of karma; Romans would have called this ghost your *genius* and, probably, tied it with Saturn. In our century Saturn has reappeared as Jung's "Wise Old Man" and "Wise Old Woman" who, he says, are configurations of the guiding Self. The guiding ghost is like the God Saturn in that Saturn binds and limits and acts like the daimon of Socrates, a voice that never told Socrates what to do, only what not to do—a cautionary, inhibiting voice. You recognize your seed by its husk and shell, by the hard impediments, forebodings, naysayings that keep you inside your unique shape.

I said that this way of thinking suggests a completely different method for psychotherapy. Instead of starting with the small (childhood) and going toward the large (maturity), instead of starting with causal traumas and external blames that determine what is to come, we start with the fullness of maturity, who and where and what you are in your communal world now, and read from the tree's leaves and branches and dead wood backwards to younger phases as foreshadowings, as smaller mirrors of the larger person. For instance, when I was in third grade, I got the lowest marks in the class in penmanship. I had to stay after school again and again to practice writing. Of course I couldn't write! My hand, maybe like Manolete's, was afraid of its life task that pen and ink implied, and that my acorn "knew." A lifelong task, unable to be mastered in third grade. But make it less speculative, just turn around any of the major psychological stories you tell about your own life. Read them backwards. You picked your wife because she was very different from (or very much like) your mother. This is an old saw in psychology. But suppose your soul gained practice with your mother for the life later lived with your wife. Or suppose a person conceives of her childhood illness (that kept her bedridden and out of touch during crucial socializing years) to have been early practice at the work she does now, like writing in solitude or inventing electronic devices or becoming a therapist. She had to be isolated for those years in order to follow her seed.

This way of seeing removes the burden from these early years as having been a mistake and yourself a victim of handicaps or cruelties; instead, it's all the acorn in the mirror, the soul endlessly repeating in different guises the fundamental pattern of your karma.

Psychology starts with an upside-down premise, that childhood is primary and determining, that development is cumulative, a kind of organic evolution, reaching a peak and declining. The early scars become suppurating wounds or healed-over strengths, but not necessary prunings for the shape of the tree, a shape ordained by the seed itself. Not only is childhood thus overvalued, but aging is trapped in an organic, and melancholy, model.

Rather than *developmental* psychology, we should study *essential* psychology, the structure of character, the innate endowment of talent, the unalterable psychopathologies. I suspect that's what the MMPI personality test, in its American way of making lists, tries to do: get at the essential inventory of the seed. I also believe that the old phrenologies, which examined the skull to see what its bumps and dents indicated about a person's gifts and weaknesses, as well as hand reading and astrology—all these Saturnian disciplines—offer a view of human nature that starts in the heavens and in the ancestors, reading downwards from essences and principles into contingencies. If we began with Saturn, we would be far more reconciled with our *givens,* including everything that doesn't work and is imagined to be a trauma, a curse and bad luck, and we would be far less impatient about our growth. Maybe a human life is organic but in Goethe's sense of negative form. The shape of a leaf, he said, is determined by the absent spaces (like the shape of an Oriental jar is shaped around and by the emptiness inside). Maybe all the missing bits and the misfortunes are actually the blessings that make us the peculiar people that we are.

As I've grown older, I've come to realize that the curses, the frustrations, and the character faults visited on me by Saturn mean something completely different than what I thought when I was younger. I took them literally as curses, and I cursed my stars for not giving me what I believed I needed and wanted. That is, I cursed Saturn, to use the old language. But it isn't Saturn who curses us; we curse him. We make him into that poor, shunned, limping old God because we don't understand his mode of blessing. What a curse it must be to keep giving gifts that are received as punishments! The faults and frustrations he visits on us are his way of keeping us true to our particular image. No way out. The old lore attributed the last years of life to Saturn. That makes sense. Only now can I begin to reconcile myself with and not rebel against what I am and what I am not.

This is turning into a long, long letter, and heavy. It's late at night. I feel Saturn's weight. Perhaps the ghost is writing this letter, and that's why it feels "way out." But life—this planet, this galaxy—is an extraordinary mystery, and our human lives can certainly not be encompassed by college psychology departments or therapeutic training programs. Yet these departments and these programs produce the people who counsel the soul. To stay way out may be a better way to start. We can let our imaginations roam beyond the humanistic confines of therapeutic ideology. Is it so hard to believe that artists, mystics, and visionary speculators might have better notions about life and the soul than conclusions drawn from data assembled on college campuses from experiments with a random sample of sophomores?

I want theories that blow the mind, as art can, not settle our minds. And the value of a psychological theory lies in its capacity to open the mind, take the top of your head off like a good poem or voice in song. The childhood developmental theory, life lived forwards, reduces us to our lowest capacity, to the infantile state and its ineptitudes. Then we need the idea of growth and development to be delivered from the root image we ourselves propagated by our emphasis on childhood: growth offers salvation from what developmental theory has dogmatically declared to be our basic nature, the helpless and hope-filled state called "my inner child." Growth equals secular salvation. The overriding importance of childhood in contemporary American culture I believe to be a direct consequence of the importance psychology gives to childhood, psychology's lack of theoretical imagination. Maybe you would take it further, contending that the overriding importance of childhood in American culture has historical roots in our separation from parental Europe and that psychology is merely one more expression of the domination of the child archetype throughout the culture. Whatever . . . I want to insist only on psychology's part in this, that if we imagine differently, childhood itself looks different, feels different.

Life lived backwards, from top down with its roots in heaven (an image, by the way, from the mysticism of Jewish Kabbala), sees in the mirror of childhood the traits, the wounds, and the wonders, but it sees them as fundamentally *uncaused,* even if they are performed by actors like parents and siblings and teachers (and violators) in the drama I call my life. That these traits become more enunciated and more skilled, or in some cases more obliterated and clumsy, through time is no mystery. The development of one's essential traits depends indeed on circumstances that allow for practice and risk taking. Development is no mystery; but the acorn is. Picasso said, "I don't develop; I am." *And the puzzle in therapy is not how did I get this way, but what does my angel want with me?* Good night, Michael, sleep well.

Jim

Little Demons, Little Daimons

Dear Jim,

One problem with the inner child concept is that it's precious, delicate, utterly vulnerable. Where, for instance, in this inner child they speak of, is the stubbornness of children? Fed food she hated, my friend Zanne (age about five) held that food in her mouth for hours without swallowing it, until her family just gave up. We could all tell a dozen stories like this about our own childhoods and the children we actually know (instead of those we "visualize"), yet they don't figure in what you would call psychology's fantasy of children.

At age eleven I hated my Brooklyn grade school teacher. (And this word *hate* is very real with children; they're capable of passionate hates.) This teacher thought I was strange and made fun of me. Her favorite form of punishment was to make students copy out of the encyclopedia or an American history textbook; if you misbehaved on Monday morning you did nothing but copy until Friday afternoon. Well, I loved the encyclopedia and American history, so I often misbehaved on Monday or Tuesday in order to copy all week and not have to deal with this teacher. It was a thick history text; I still remember its faded and frayed blue cover, and I got all the way from Columbus's voyage to the beginning of World War Two and I was proud of that, perhaps sensing that not only had I avoided that teacher, I'd begun the discipline of self-education on which my future would depend.

Where is the inner child as survivor? The child is seen not only as marvelous vessel of creativity or vulnerable, wounded beauty, but also as impish presence, scanning a room from the point of view of an adult's elbow and, far from being helpless, standing his or her ground *without power,* with nothing to back him or her up, no authority, and nobody's aid? Children are in these situations all the time, no matter who loves them or what their environment.

Or the brilliant tactical retreats of children. I think of my friend Cora, who as a girl hid in her dark closet for hours and even days, to grow up (to become a therapist!) marvelously unafraid of the dark depths in herself or others. She didn't have a good time in that closet—she was in fear and pain, and she had reason to hide—but in that closet, letting her mind wander and telling herself stories, she learned how to think and to see in the dark. (Yet I wonder how she'd feel now if her four-year-old started hiding in the closet, whether she'd permit him the same training she gave herself.)

We have all seen children manipulate whole rooms of people. Isn't it possible to learn from the child how to have power without authority? And isn't this a crucial issue in our time? Children invented passive resistance and civil disobedience a long time before Thoreau, Gandhi, and King. I'm suggesting that a danger of the inner child ideology is that it simplifies children and childhood, exaggerates both their vulnerability and their powerlessness, and denigrates a lot of good survival skills as "symptoms." The child Picasso you wrote of, who had to be taken out of school because he refused to do anything but paint—today therapy would look to his home life to find out what was frightening him. He'd get pinned by some diagnosis (which would stick to him for the rest of his life) and would likely be tranquilized. And all this would be justified as "cure," not control.

More kid stories.

I remember at the age of five or six living in one of the then-new projects in Queens—this was 1950 or '51. We little kids ran in packs like dogs. We had not grown up with television (many families didn't yet have one). Most of us had never seen a movie or any extreme violence, nor had we known serious deprivation. Yet we were vicious and destructive. One day we went around kicking out all the cellar windows. I cut my ankle doing that, ran home, told my father I was playing and there was all this glass on the lawn and it cut me, my father sued the landlord, and that's how we got the money for our first TV. Some inner child, eh?

There was a boy in that neighborhood who couldn't have been older than seven but he was almost as big as an adult (though he wasn't retarded or misshapen in any way that I could see). We called him Giant, of course. He was always excluded from our pack. The pack had a Big Archie and a Little Archie. Big Archie was the nominal leader, but everyone feared Little Archie because he was so cruel. He was literally about half the Giant's size.

One day Little Archie led the pack up to the Giant. He hit the Giant in the stomach with all his might. You could see it hurt, but the Giant took the blow and said, "I can't hit you, you're smaller than I am." Imagine, Jim, how his parents must have dinned that litany into him. I remember clearly his serious and intelligent way of saying, "You're smaller than I am." Little Archie just kept hitting him. The Giant went down. Little Archie kicked him, then jumped on him with his knees while the Giant huddled in a fetal position with his arms up over his head to protect himself. Some of the others joined in with Archie to kick him.

The rest of us were silent and horrified. The Giant just kept repeating, in a broken way, "I can't hit you, you're smaller than I am." I remember so well how still I stood, overcome by fear and revulsion, ashamed that I hadn't the courage to help. Standing there, I had my first sense of thinking something important—important to me, I mean. It was simply: The Giant is very, very brave.

Where is all this when they speak of the inner child—where is Little Archie's viciousness, the Giant's heroism (I think that's a fair word), and my terrified recognition of his nobility? Where is *the life of children?* In this sense the concept of the inner child *represses our actual childhoods* and concentrates the fear, vulnerability, failure, and grief we feel as adults into an image that we can detach from our adult life—an image easily marketable and played upon. As you've said, we project the needs of the present onto the past, then try to fill those needs in that projected past via the therapist. (Thus, in one move, not only is our actual childhood repressed by the ideal of the inner child, but the present is both repressed and diminished by being treated as merely a symptom caused by the past.)

Memory is mutable, as we all know. Our perceptions of the past change as we change. But to introduce the ideology of the inner child into how we remember is in effect to substitute *a fictional character* for ourselves. That is what therapists who use this method do to their clients: they introduce a fictional character, the pure and wounded inner child, into the client's psyche; then this fictional character, like the protagonist of a novel, constellates one's memories around it, highlighting them to suit the theme of the character. A subtle, even insidious, transformation takes place. What happens to memories that don't fit this new character, events that are out of character, in which the ideal of the inner child could not have taken part? Those events lose importance, they fade, drained of *the ability to be remembered* because this creation through which we are now experiencing memory can't inhabit what happened. So parts of our life grow dimmer, dimmer, dimmer, until they disappear. This is what any ideology does—religious, political, psychological, feminist, mythological—when used as a lens for viewing one's life. The inner child is a fictional character produced by an ideology and introduced into one's memory, and, like a computer virus, its ultimate result is to repress, distort, and eventually even erase memory.

A similar thing happens when we accept or, as they say, internalize a diagnosis. A therapist convinced my friend Jean that her father suffers from narcissism, and since then she's interpreted every exchange with the man, past and present, as narcissistic. He's also my friend, and when, talking to her, I bring up aspects of him that are not clinically narcissistic, she either rejects them out of hand or gets grouchy. Another therapist has informed another friend that he's a borderline personality, and now he's interpreting everything through that lens and in the process forgetting, or at least discounting, what doesn't fit. Again, the diagnoses act like computer viruses, changing and erasing memories. You also see this in Twelve-Step groups; everything in one's life is interpreted around alcoholism or eating or abuse, a kind of psychological monotheism, and what doesn't suit the syndrome drops out of one's consideration like a fall from grace.

Now let's go back to your acorn, that thing within, which is our genius and daimon. One reason the concept is so valuable is precisely because it's hard to visualize, it's *not* a character, not a stand-in for ourselves, and still less a diagnosis. It's more like a spirit, "the guiding ghost," as you call it. The daimon announces its presence (and absence) in and through *events,* always forcing us back on ourselves and on the nature of the event rather than on an ideal of what should be or should have been (all diagnoses presume, unconsciously, an ideal of normality). The daimon makes us ask: What did this moment want of me? What did it do and undo for me, to me, with me? What did I want of myself? Is this my past speaking to my future, my future speaking to my past? I love your conception, Jim, because nothing is excluded or labeled and because *the life itself dictates the terms in which it can be thought of, imagined, and spoken of.* It can't be diagnosed, it must be contemplated.

The difference is enormous. It makes me think of what the poet Octavio Paz said was the difference between Mexicans and North Americans: "North Americans want to understand and we want to contemplate. They are activists and we are quietists; we enjoy our wounds and they enjoy their inventions. . . . North Americans consider the world to be something that can be perfected . . . we consider it something that can be redeemed." Isn't this the sort of thinking we are trying to introduce to psychotherapy, Jim? We don't want to cure little Manolete of clinging to his mother's apron, we don't want Cora to come out of the dark closet and stop talking to herself, we don't want Zanne to swallow her food, or Michael to behave so he won't have to copy out of encyclopedias. We don't even want the Giant to hit back, nor do we want Michael to become a hero and save him from Little Archie. And we don't want to reduce the present merely to a result of the past or reduce the past to a rehearsal for the future. (Linear, developmental thinking does both.) So what do we want? To silence the conceptual noise of psychological jargon and create, in the consulting room, an atmosphere in which moments speak to us on their own terms and we answer back in ours.

Therapy then becomes the discipline of searching out what those terms are *in each case*—jettisoning diagnostics in favor of inventing, therapist and client together, a shared language suited to this particular life. Then we are not trying to discover and treat a disease, we are trying to invent and speak a language. *That* is the treatment, to speak and listen to the life; and the goal isn't that the life heal, or become normal, or even cease its suffering, but that *the life become more itself,* have more integrity with itself, be more true to its daimon.

It's late. I'll pick up on this again tomorrow night and send it all in a pack (and resolve that my next letters won't be as long).

Michael

P.S. No, there are some loose ends buzzing around before I can sleep. The Jungians would say that a life having more integrity with itself is what they mean by individuating. I don't think so. The concept of individuating is based on a larger ideology that assumes original *wholeness*—an *a priori,* if you like, wholeness that we begin with, then it gets shattered, then we spend our lives reconstituting it. *Individuating*—the very word—locates that entire wholeness in the individual, apart from the world. But what if that's not so? What if, as you and I have been saying, we're not born whole, and what if the quality of wholeness is not located in the individual but in a community that includes the environment? How does all that, the-individual-as-part-of-community-as-part-of-environment, "individuate"? If, instead, we conceive of therapy as an attempt to invent and speak a language appropriate to a particular life, the world *must* be part of it because any life is a life *in the world.*

Another loose end: When I say "invent a language," I am not just talking about speech. I know therapists who use silence, song, dance, gesture, and ritual as part of the language they are trying to invent with their people.

Which brings me to the last and most important loose end: I know therapists who work in the way I've been describing *in the consulting room.* In practice, they've jettisoned diagnostics and the jargons of the various schools, and they've created a kind of underground therapy that's much as I've described—but they aren't allowed to say so. Insurance forms, professional societies, publications, hospitals, what-all, demand the jargons; this demand, in turn, enforces the jargons and intimidates the less individual and secure therapists (that is, the majority) into imposing on their patients thought systems they know are inappropriate. This corporatism of therapy doesn't care about lives lived with deeper integrity to themselves; it cares about a stable work force. But I know you've said this many times in your work and have never underestimated the push to equate "healing" with "normal."

More tomorrow night. (This damn letter's turning into a pamphlet.)

Well, Jim, you just skipped a line but I skipped a day. It's late, two nights later. There's some more stuff going on in my mind about the daimon, and be warned: I'm on the weird side of the street tonight, even by our standards.

I think our daimon tries to fight for us. I think there are events in childhood, mysterious and often violent, that are best understood as daring chances the daimon takes in order to send messages into the future—messages to the adult we will one day be and, even beyond us, to other generations.

More kid stories.

Judith (My god, I just realized she's a therapist, too! I promise you I'm not selecting systematically.)—anyway, Judith is a cold, rigid woman, whose major passion is to be conventional. That's not as contradictory as it sounds, for Judith goes about being conventional and imposing the conventional on those around her with a single-mindedness that can only be called passion. It's the only passion she displays freely. Yet this story is told in her family:

When Judith was very little, not two, her mother proudly had her eating out of a child-sized set of quality glass. Bowls, saucers, cups, that sort of thing—an expensive set. Little Judith took to some strange behavior: when she'd finish eating out of one of the bowls or drinking out of one of the cups, she'd throw the thing with all her might and break it. Her mother was furious and finally threatened that if it happened one more time Judith would never have her own set of nice things again. Later that day the little girl methodically broke every cup, bowl, and dish in the set.

I hear Judith's daimon saying, "They are too strong for me, the crushing-of-spirit in this family is too strong, I cannot stand up to it, I'm going to lose, but I'm going to lose *this* way, with a gesture that they won't forget. I myself would forget this loss over the years, that's how complete their victory would be if I didn't leave them this gesture that *they* will not forget. They'll keep telling it to me, it will be a 'family story.' If I get married they'll tell my husband, if I have children they'll tell my children. And perhaps one of them—or even me, maybe, when I'm old—will see that this, which is so 'unlike me,' was the last time I *was* me."

Wouldn't such an explanation fit many a family story that one hears, not necessarily in the consulting room but over dinner or when being shown an album of photographs?

Another daimon story:

Sam (age about four, who would become not a therapist, but a pediatrician) was on an outing with his mother in one of those little parks you see in New York City, parks which in those days (circa 1950) were still quite nice. This park, like many, had large outcroppings of gray rock, the kind you may have noticed in Central Park, sometimes rising as high as twenty or thirty feet. The rocks were such that it wasn't very hard for small children to climb up, but, once on top, it was difficult for them to get down. Most mothers didn't let their kids near them, of course. Sam doesn't remember how or why, he just remembers finding himself at the top of one of these rocks, at the edge, with no one around. He doesn't remember feeling anything in particular, and he doesn't remember falling.

He fell about twenty feet, landing on pavement on his head. He shouldn't have lived, but he did. It's told in his family as a kind of joke that little Sam had cried and bothered a lot before the fall, but after the fall it was rare to see him cry. I've heard several "falling children" and "children exposed to heights" stories that are startlingly similar.

I can hear Sam's daimon saying to all the selves that child housed: "Well, kid, here we are on the edge of this rock, and she's not looking, and she doesn't want to know. You keep needing things from her, and she just can't give them. That poor woman's deadness is going to kill us, too, unless I separate us from her *now.* It's going to take something very dramatic. We've got a hard head. I think we can make it. The shock of this event will separate her from us forever, her guilt and our anger will make a gulf that can't be crossed, we'll start focusing our needs in other directions, we can't learn to do without her unless we experience a real shock; if we keep needing her now we'll become as dead as she is. *That* life wouldn't be worth living, believe me. I hope we make it. I *think* we can. Over we go."

I've read that many child deaths reported as accidents may be suicides. How many of these—let's use the clinical word *events*—how many of these events can be seen as chances the daimon took but didn't have the luck?

I wonder how far this goes. When I was very little my mother withheld her sexuality from my father while pouring it over me like a sort of nauseatingly sweet syrup. It was the sticky medium of my childhood. Somewhere in my third year I contracted pneumonia. Get that verb, Jim? I *contracted* pneumonia, I made a kind of contract with pneumonia, it put me in the hospital and away from my mother and father for the first time. Antibiotics couldn't cure me, I refused to get well, I'd begin to improve, rejoin my parents, fall ill again, go back to the hospital. My daimon was working hard to keep me away from those people. The doctors went so far as to tell my mother that I wouldn't live to be five years old and she'd better have some more children so she could absorb the grief.

That illness did so much for my life. For years now I've felt it was my soul's (or what you would call my daimon's) move to get me out of the sexual sphere of my mother and the helplessness of my father, to keep me sick and save me. God knows what would have happened if she had had her ways with me much longer; I'd have become an ax murderer or something. And pneumonia taught me to survive alone, without my parents, in difficult surroundings—for the hospital was terrifying. My mother and father, bless their haunted hearts, hadn't the competence to hold a family together, and at thirteen I was in a foster home, while my younger siblings were in an orphanage. But by thirteen, surviving alone was old hat to my daimon, for my parents took the doctors' advice, had more children, and became far too preoccupied to supervise me.

I can hear my daimon saying to my body, "No, no, don't resist, let in the sickness, let in the virus, the closer we get to death now the farther we will be from madness later. I think I can make you well, but we *must* get away from these people for a time. Let the virus take you, let it in, cherish it a while."

We are back, as you said in our earlier conversation, to the realms of the Gods, where illnesses and events are about taboos and visitations. The "official" American worldview is largely an Anglo-Saxon, Euro-Yankee product, and psychotherapy is part of it. That view would say that all these stories are far too dramatic, life is not really like that. For the gargoyles and angels carved into the cathedrals have been forgotten and, worse, denied. The forest Gods of Europe have been forgotten too or ignored or reduced to anthropological oddities, while Europeans and Americans have actively hunted and defiled the Gods and holy places of tribal peoples everywhere. Even the great teaching tales recorded by the brothers Grimm are often banned these days as occult. We should be very, very suspicious when both academia and fundamentalism have equal hatred for the same modes of thought.

(But then, to borrow a metaphor from Isak Dinesen, academia and fundamentalism are two locked boxes, each of which holds the key to the other.)

It's late at night, I'm a little drunk, and the evocation of these daimons has left me in an odd place. Let it rest here. Let the daimons and Judith and Tom and the dark-eyed child close to death who stares at me from the photograph and all our obsessed mothers and haunted fathers—let them rest. "A flight of angels guide thee"—or rather, "speed thee." No, it's "*sing* thee"! "A flight of angels sing thee to thy rest," each and every one of thee. I hate every theory that reduces life, trying to make things less, always less, saying this or that is "only" something else, something quantifiable. On one of my mother's gentler psychotic journeys she smiled slyly—yes, and seductively—and said to me, "Once in a while I trip, trip, trip, but then I come back, back, back. And the world . . . is a much larger place than we thought."

Thank you for that, Mama.

Goodnight, Jim.

Michael

Psychiatry's Afraid

Dear Michael,

Did you see the piece in the *New York Times,* day after Christmas, headlined, "Environmental Illness May Be Mental"? Important. Look it up. The subhead asks, What comes first, a psychiatric state of depression or an ecologically attributed symptom? Do we feel down because we are sick, or are we sick because we feel down?

Psychiatry is retrenching. Fear in the practitioner's office. They want to believe that the new illnesses arising, allegedly, from the world—chemicals, electromagnetic fields, high-tension lines, noise pollution, food additives, radioactivity, rare metals, trace elements, and aluminum—are really projections onto pseudocauses by depressed people. First people get depressed, and then they delusionally think their symptoms are coming from the world. Psychiatry prefers to believe that the new diagnosis called "environmental illness" or "multiple chemical sensitivity" is a cop-out from the real problem: the patient is simply depressed. The headaches and nausea, the fatigue and lack of libido, the occasional dizziness and circulatory disorders start inside the patient. This is the old idea of self-caused (endogenic) depression. It's you, not the world, that is making you sick, so treatment begins with you, not the world.

Psychiatry doesn't want to lose its clientele to ecological activists or to a new kind of specialist called "chemical ecologist." All this ignoring the world, though we've known for years about miner's lung and the effects of factory routine work, food processing, quarrying and blasting, glassblowing, even throwing pots with cold clay in a dark room. The labor force in the old Swiss watchmaking industry was swallowing Valium. But for conservative psychiatry, the environment is still unanimated, dead matter. Sickness is the patient's fault, because he —mainly she—is depressed.

That the world can be the first cause is buttressed by other bits of news. One bit from Berkeley says that the principal causes of stress are not what we thought they were. We used to believe, and studies "showed," that stress came from inside the patient's psychic field of personal relations: death of a loved one, moving to another house, divorce or breakup, bankruptcy, failure, or being fired. These were said to be the shocks that the soul and body couldn't easily take and caused "stress" reactions.

But now new studies "show" stress arises largely from "the irritations of daily life," which I take to mean again the aesthetic disorders of the environment, such as racism, noise, crowding, traffic, air quality, crime fears, police cars, violence fears, legal threats, hypercommunication (too much info, keeping up), breakdowns and frustrations in the school systems, taxpaying, bureaucracy, hospitals, and making ends meet.

You see, Michael, at last therapy is going to have to go out the door with the client, maybe even make home visits, or at least walk down the street.

Jim

City

Dear Michael,

Take this as a P.S. It's a little letter from a woman after she read what we said in the *L.A. Weekly.*

> I suffered from a kind of low-grade depression for ten years that I lived in Los Angeles. During eight of those years I was working with a Jungian analyst. Three years ago my company moved to San Diego County. My analyst advised me against leaving Los Angeles because she thought I should continue to deal with it inwardly and not run away from it. I moved to San Diego anyway. And almost immediately, magically, the depression lifted. It returns, however, whenever I visit Los Angeles. I know now that a great deal of the depression I suffered in Los Angeles was due to the effect of the smog and other environmental factors which cannot be worked out inwardly. I also found that once I started freeing myself from the insidious bonds of Jungian thought, which can be just as dogmatic, narrow-minded, and damaging as fundamentalist Christianity, and the internalization of my emotions, I felt more alive, angrier, and yes, more politically motivated, which is where I was when I came in.

I'm publishing it with her permission (*not* to insult the Jungians—and that is not her intention either). She sent it to me and I send it to you as an example of "recovery" from the dogma of interiorization. But also it's recovery by U-Haul or Ryder; moving man as therapist.

Of course her testimony doesn't prove anything. As many if not more letters can and will come in testifying to being saved by therapy as this one testifies to being saved from therapy by simply moving to another city. I've already tried to explain that anecdotal evidence, like case histories, is not sufficient to establish the truth or falsity of an idea. Stories are illustrations. Witnesses and evidence move at a different level than ideas. I'm using this letter only to state in a vivid way that city strongly affects psyche.

Better said: city *is* psyche.

It took the last several decades for therapy to learn that body is psyche, that what the body does, how it moves, what it senses is psyche. More recently, therapy is learning that the psyche exists wholly in relational systems. It's not a free radical, a monad, self-determined. The next step is to realize that the city, where the body lives and moves, and where the relational network is woven, is also psyche.

The Greeks knew this. The *polis* was the other half of *mythos. Mythos* was lived in *polis.* The Gods take part in and are felt in civic life. We sense this often in nature; why are we so numb to recognize soul in the city? Blacks and Latinos do. What goes on in the city is not merely politics or economics or architecture. It's not even "environment"; it's psychology. Everything "out there" is you.

The collective unconscious, as Jung said, is the world, and—also as he said—the psyche is not in you, you are in the psyche. The collective unconscious extends beyond the great symbols of your dreams, beyond the repercussions of ancestral history. It includes the ground swells that ebb and flow through the city, the fashions, language, biases, choreographies that rule your waking soul as much the images ruling your soul. It's more than ozone levels and days of sunshine; a city is a soul. You, Michael, *are* Los Angeles. You may be Brooklyn and Austin too, but so long as you pull yourself out of the night world each morning in L.A. you are L.A.

What does this mean? It means each city ought to have its own school of therapy, like the Vienna School, the Zurich School, the schools of Nancy and of Paris. It also means you can't honestly do therapy apart from the city in which it takes place. It means therapy has reached its city limits.

Jim

What About the Watcher?

Dear Jim,

Words get in the way. (Sometimes I think that's their secret job.) Words like *mind, psyche,* and *soul* overlap and obscure each other. I started to write, "So much goes on in the psyche at any given time," but I realized that if I just said those words out loud, at a party, say, someone might think I mean the daydreams and shopping lists that move jerkily along the surface of consciousness. But, as you've written of so well, under that surface noise, and coexisting with all our concerns about getting through the day and through the century, are currents of grief, hope, fear, and love that seem (in my experience, anyway) almost independent of each other. Each current whispers a different history of our lives and seeks a different future. When we say the word *I* we speak only for some, never all, of those whispers.

Which is to say: psychology has to recognize community because the psyche *is* a community. No: *community* is too organized and peaceful a word. The psyche is a city like New York or Rome or Calcutta; you'd need a Dante or a Breughel to picture it. It's like having all the TV channels on at once and feeding into each other, late night film noir and afternoon cartoons speaking each other's lines, while epic events like revolutions have the feel of family feuds. It's an inner world that reminds me of something Henry Adams wrote after he had contemplated the gargoyles and saints of Europe's cathedrals for perhaps longer than was good for him, a sentence at the end of *Mont-Saint-Michel and Chartres:* "Truth, indeed, may not exist; science avers it to be only a relation; but what men took for truth stares one everywhere in the eye and begs for sympathy."

Isn't the psyche like that? Sit still long enough and so much comes up ("memories, dreams, and reflections," as Jung put it) begging for sympathy, for understanding, for a voice. And beneath that level . . . the depths go on and on. So, as I started to say, with all the psyche's innate tumult, with all its levels and voices, one feels so many presences at any given moment that there's no such thing as being alone. If you are the only one in the room, it's still a crowded room.

I'm thinking tonight of something many feel when alone in that crowded room. For don't you sometimes feel accompanied, especially when alone, in a way that you usually take for granted? I do. The people I compare notes with do also. I'm thinking of something I now call "the Watcher." "The Companion Eye," my friend George Howard calls it—that sense of a constant companion, who is you and yet more than you, and who seems always with you, watching from a slight distance. My feeling of it hasn't changed since I was small. It's always a bit older than I, usually silent, and its features are sort of indistinct, like when you see an old print of a black-and-white movie. It's not exactly passive but rarely active. Its action is to watch.

Robert Bly does a lovely job describing it in *Iron John:*

> When we do look into our own eyes [in the mirror] . . . we have the inescapable impression, so powerful and astonishing, that someone is looking back at us. . . . That experience of being looked back at sobers us up immediately. . . . Someone looks back questioning, serious, alert, and without intent to comfort; and we feel more depth in the eyes looking at us than we ordinarily sense in our own eyes as we stare out at the world. How strange! Who could it be that is looking at us? We conclude that it is another part of us, the half that we don't allow to pass out of our eyes when we glance at others—and that darker and more serious half looks back at us only at rare times.

But I think Robert's way off when he calls this presence "the interior soul," because our sense of it, as I said, is that it watches from a slight distance. Even in his example, it's outside of you, in the mirror, looking back.

A friend's therapist calls it "the objective ego," but the whole concept of ego implies a hierarchy in the psyche: Freud's id-ego-superego structure. Freud's idea, now nearly a century old, was a great breakthrough in thinking about the psyche, but as a description it's too simplistic, too rigid. And today the word *ego* carries too many associations to be specific or useful. Jungians might call this Watcher "the Self," exchanging Freud's linear, patriarchal-style hierarchy for a circular, matriarchal-style hierarchy, with the Self at the circle's center. I know *circular hierarchy* seems a contradiction in terms, but consider: what Jungians, feminists, and all sorts of antihierarchy people overlook is that *circles have structures too.* What's on the diameter is not at all the same, spatially or metaphorically, as what's on the circumference; and no circle can be a circle without a center from which the circle radiates. So the idea of the central Self is, in a horizontal way, as rigid as the vertical idea of the ego.

The Jungian model doesn't apply to the Watcher because, again, our experience of the Watcher is that it's not within, it's a little off to the side, just beyond the circle. (Or it's above: a friend of mine told me that as a child he pictured his Watcher as a television camera that followed him, off to the side, a foot or two from the ceiling.) In the same way, the Watcher isn't one of those inner selves I'm so fond of speaking of; my experience of them is that they're clearly, even defiantly, within, often clamoring to take charge. No, and the Watcher isn't your daimon, either, that impish genie that goads and tricks us toward our fates. Our daimon is, as you said, ghostly; it inhabits events and reveals its image, if at all, as a kind of haunting, or after long visual work. You can't see your daimon just by staring into a mirror.

Yet this Watcher—*is.* Anyone who's traveled alone for long distances knows their Watcher well, because we never travel all alone. There is the sense of being *in the company of oneself.* As I said, a you that is not quite you, a presence felt when you're alone, from which (from whom?) comes the mood of your solitude.

I think some people live in agony because they feel their Watcher doesn't like them. Alone with their Watcher, they feel not accompanied but judged, even threatened. Other people have endured horrors because their Watcher is, as my friend George puts it, a companion. Still, this is very different from "liking yourself." You may not like yourself at all, yet your Companion is calm and doesn't disapprove, and your solitude can be sweet at times because of this.

Things get multiple and murky in this realm. Which part of you isn't liking you when you don't like yourself? I don't know, but my experience is that I loathe myself often, actively, for long periods, and make a lot of trouble doing it. Yet my Companion, my Watcher, is patient—not condoning nor even reassuring, just patient. Though, as George says, "It's kind of comforting to realize that some part of you is actually seeing things as they are. It doesn't have to influence you at all, but it's not gonna give."

Another wrinkle: Marie-Louise von Franz says that Western civilization has put a little gnomish man on the shoulder of every woman and that this gnome does nothing but tell the woman that she's wrong, wrong, wrong. Thus a kind of artificial, oppressive Watcher has been installed. When I mention this image to women (especially writer women) they enthusiastically agree with von Franz: that's their experience, an almost literal voice buzzing in their ear saying, "No, no, your work's no good, it's worthless, you're wrong." In von Franz's construct (though she'd use different terms), women have to learn to ignore that gnome and recognize their real Watcher, whom civilization did not put there and whom civilization cannot take away.

I'm writing this because there is not, to my knowledge, a psychology of the Watcher. I've never heard of therapists saying, "What's your Watcher like?" Yet according to the people I compare notes with, the sense of a Watcher is so common it's taken for granted. My conviction is that during a bad time one's relationship with one's Watcher is crucial; it may be all one has. You'd think that would make it a therapeutic tool, but, as I say, you don't hear of a psychology of the Watcher.

When I think of fiction made from this experience I think of the 1950 Jimmy Stewart film *Harvey,* written by Mary Chase. Stewart plays Ellwood, a man who's considered mad because his best friend is a six-foot-tall invisible rabbit. His involvement with this "friend" is neither narcissistic nor cut off from the world. Ellwood cares very much for his sister and niece, with whom he lives; he's always saying hello to strangers, taking them seriously in a kindly way, inviting them to dinner, introducing them to the invisible Harvey. He takes nothing for granted. If a salesgirl asks, "Can I help you?" he replies, "What did you have in mind?" Ellwood doesn't care that everyone thinks he's crazy, because his Companion doesn't share their opinion. *Harvey* is a light and sentimental tale, but its great appeal is that we are watching a man's extraordinary relationship with his Companion, and we know something of such relationships because we feel a presence beside us as well. We feel relief at seeing this feeling addressed, for our culture is so limited in what it allows itself to address, and this limitation makes people feel so isolated.

(That's the real reason for censorship, whether it's the direct censorship of the state or academia's censorship-by-dismissal: the less you allow to be expressed, the more alone and cut off people feel. When certain feelings are unexpressed in the culture, people think those feelings are bad or crazy, and so they trust their feelings less; hence they're more vulnerable to pressure from above.)

Another fiction of the Watcher is Marc Behm's chilling 1980 novel, *The Eye of the Beholder.* (It's a literary crime that, while lightweights like John Updike are all over the shelves, Behm's novel is out of print.) Behm calls his narrator only "The Eye"—a private eye, or rather semiprivate: he works for a detective agency. The Eye trails a young female serial killer who marries then murders her men. The Eye falls in love with this killer from afar. He not only watches her for years as she kills, but, unknown to her, he keeps the police off her trail and commits every sort of crime to protect her. Slowly, over the years, she becomes vaguely aware of his presence, until an eerily beautiful moment when they face each other.

Behm is describing a psychological state: that the Watcher doesn't care about society or morality or the idea of good and evil. The Watcher cares about *you,* and, if it's on your side to begin with, it's all the way on your side. Thus you can be a psychopath and still have a healthy relationship with your Watcher (which is bad for society); or you can be a good, normal person and have an unhealthy relationship with your Watcher (which is bad for you), perhaps because you're not living the way it knows you should. (Maybe then you should try talking to it?)

So I bring this up to say that perhaps there is something in the city of the psyche that is absolutely apart from one's social community, something that, in and of itself, doesn't care if the whole world shrivels and burns, something focused utterly and only . . . on you. We began as a tribal race, we lived in packs and small settlements for millennia before there was such a thing as a city and, with it, the possibility of individuality, so perhaps this Watcher served as a kind of buffer or refuge from what was an inescapable community. (We must remember that even among tribal peoples, vision quests and walkabouts happen in solitude, or at least in human solitude, though nothing is quite solitary when you know that the animals and the moon and the rain are your brothers and sisters and uncles.)

(I don't pretend that all this could stand up as either knowledge or theory, by the way, Jim; it's just what you might call my fantasy of how things are.)

Interesting that both *Harvey* and *The Eye of the Beholder* are about psychosis. In a world like ours, where what's considered normal is a sickly compromise between how much boredom you can stomach and how much denial you can defend, new thoughts and explorations are often couched in terms of psychosis. (Modern psychology began with studies of psychosis.) I wouldn't let that put me off thinking about the Watcher, though. At least, I don't think I should.

Should I?

My Watcher, who is almost always silent, nods no.

Michael

Letter Writing

Dear Michael,

Last night on the phone you asked me what my letter about letter writing had to do with the theme of this book—therapy.

I take pleasure in expanding.

Therapy began with Freud's "talking cure," as he called it, letting a patient lie down and freely associate, speaking out loud whatever comes into the mind. Then, mainly owing to Jung, therapy developed into a dialogue. Two armchairs, face to face and knee to knee, as I recall the few occasions I sat with Jung. Whether in couples or groups, therapy continues the oral approach. Writing seems to be mostly confined to transcripts of the oral sessions and to case reports digesting the session. (Also, many patients keep journals and dream notebooks for themselves.) Now these transcripts and case reports are intolerable to read. They are universally the same and utterly boring. Not that the hours themselves were boring, but the written records certainly are. Why boring? Because the language consists of dead words, clichés, rhythmless repetitions, generalized conventional terms without the luster or the lilt of the soul's songs of itself. Yes, even depression—or, as it should be called, melancholy and despair—has a cadence and a pitch and a vocabulary.

How rare it is to *speak* well about ourselves. Write well, we can do. Poems, short stories of childhood, biographical excursions, even descriptions of intense emotions—these all are the very stuff of writing. But the soul seems reluctant to speak eloquently of itself. When I try to tell you directly what I feel and what's going on inside, personally, there comes a jumble of circumlocutions, coagulated phrases, interrupted qualifications, "Undisciplined squads of emotion!" as T. S. Eliot said. *Is this confused reluctance, perhaps, the very source of writing? As if the soul needs to find a way out of its own inarticulate morass by means of the hand's deft linear skill. Writing as the thread out of the labyrinth.*

Anyway, some years ago along came a man in Japan—was it Morita?—who let his patients retreat into solitude, writing their "confessions" and handing these written pages to the therapist without much talk between them. The therapist then commented (like an editor or a composition teacher) on the "problems" in the written material. Therapy took place largely by means of written documents.

You need to see here a BIG contrast with most usual Western therapeutic methods, which do not trust reflection as much as immediacy. Blurted truth is more true, we believe, than burnished truth. In fact, we believe, burnishing tends to cover up so that the raw is better than the cooked. This distrust of articulate form betrays the Romantic roots of therapy and its distance from the carefulness of classicism. Therapy might find its literary antecedents in Rousseau, Whitman, and garrulous Eugene O'Neill, whose characters go on and on as if they were at an AA meeting.

An exception to Western therapy's usual distrust of written reflection for personal expression is orthodox Jungian method. At least, Jungian method used to be a reflective exception in the days when I trained and practiced in Zurich. I refer to Jungian method since, after all, this is the therapy I know most about, having myself had—or been had by—a classical Jungian analysis and having practiced it for over thirty years as well. Jungians invite reflection by means of writing. Classical Jungians asked their patients, even required their patients, to write down their dreams and make drawings and paintings of their dream figures, feelings, scenes, and to write long interior dialogues called "active imaginations."

I myself have spent the larger part of my analytical hours paying my money for my analyst's dumb silence while he read through my written material. And, when I transferred to the other chair, having become an analyst myself, I sat still long times, while being paid of course, reading through a client's material.

Immediacy was not the issue. Content analysis. Quiet. Reflection. Constellation of unexpected emotions through tension and mulling. Thematics. Style of expression. Emotion compacted into words, images, colors, scenes, phrases, diction, voices. Attempts at precision, finer and finer. The personal relation between the two people, analyst and patient, was carried on in a good part via the material. The nebulous, ephemeral psyche and its fluid swirling moods and laconic resistant rocks caught on paper, materialized as traces of the *écrit,* the mind's marks on paper.

A lot of this, I suppose old-fashioned, style has gone out the window. Was it too European, too reflective, too educated, too literary for the American therapist who is into immediate feelings and on-the-spot transference reactions?

If we place our American style against schools of painting, our therapy is expressionist, while the therapist's response is minimalist conceptualism. Curious that therapy expects the patient to open up and pour out more and more vibrant color while the therapist responds with judicious reserve and the pregnant silence of a blank canvas. If we let studio art be a metaphor for what goes on in a session of therapy, then how in the world can the two styles work together? Sooner or later a war must break out, which is less a personal war than a war of schools, of styles.

The Jungians too have yielded to expressionist immediacy. They too have begun to distrust written material. Writing has become a "defense." Instantaneity is now privileged. Dreams are to be recounted on the spot rather than turned into texts to be read, and the therapeutic process has come more and more to mean what goes on between people rather than the spontaneous unfolding within the psyche as presented in written dialogues and painted images. Talk rather than writing.

Now, my point here is that something of soul is gained by instantaneity, but something else is lost. We know what's been gained: the capacity to react immediately. Bring your suspicions and perceptions and irritations right up front: confront. Tell it like it is, as they said in the sixties. Feel where you are and be it.

But what was shoved aside? The meditative scribe, the persuasion of rhetoric, the fictional sense of living in a plot rather than in the confines of a first-person narrative, the play of poetic formulation. Language has been reduced to the spoken word.

This spoken word in our white therapeutic culture tends to be limited in vocabulary, piss poor in the power of its adjectives and adverbs—sentences begin with *hopefully, personally, basically*—wandering in syntax (think of Reagan, Bush, Eisenhower, Ford), flowing with run-on sentences that would take the Army Corps of Engineers to channel toward an intention, misplaced modifiers, uncertain referents (the universal *it* standing in for everything), loaded with "I means" and "you knows," and a sparse scattering of images and metaphors amid a vast, exhausted field of therapeutically approved abstractions for feelings. Right here, Michael, I'm going to quote something I said at Eranos back in 1976:

> Go in fear of abstractions . . . " says Ezra Pound. "Use no adjective which does not reveal something . . . " F. S. Flint says, " . . . no word that does not contribute to presentation . . . " Our usual psychological language fails the precision of the image. What is revealed with such terms as "introvert" or "mother complex" [or adult child, addictive personality, avoidance behavior]? Moreover, these terms of typicality—unless imaged—bring further perceptions to a halt. Our language also fails the emotion. [T. E.] Hulme [*Speculations*] points out that emotions come in "stock types"—anger, sorrow, enthusiasm—words which convey only "that part of the emotion, which is common to all of us." Measurements of these emotions do not make the concepts or experiences more particular. Whereas art in images, defined by Hulme, as a "passionate desire for accuracy" presents each emotion precisely. Here image-speech takes precedence over emotion-speech. When we react to a dream image in terms of its emotions, or describe ourselves as "suicidal," "depressed," or "excited," we are again typifying, and moving away from the etching acid of the image.

Therapy's language makes all these mistakes. It talks in the general language of emotions and feeling, whereas written language tries to make precise the specifics. I'm claiming, Michael, that therapy's talking cure makes language sick and therefore the world worse.

Instead, I want to reach back a long way and recall what Confucius is said to have said: The reform of society begins in the reform of its language. I want to reach back to the Egyptians and their God Thoth, the primal baboon, God of written signs; and to the Ibis figure, the scribe; and to the sacred importance of the written, like the commandments of Moses cut into clay, like the cuneiform laws of Hammurabi.

One exception to this criticism of therapy's talk: I am focused on the white ghetto of psychological conceptual talk that passes for feeling, for insight, for communication. I am not taking into account the speech of the population outside the white psychological ghetto, the street talk that is often rich in rhythm, metaphor, image, phrasing, invention, and gesture. That talk might even cure our talk, maybe even help our writing.

I am insisting, however, on this: So long as therapy does not attend to language, which I contend it cannot do as long as it indulges in the spoken word at the expense of the written word, therapy cannot reform our society as it intends. In fact, therapy contributes to the decline of the civilization whose reform begins in the reform of language. So, if we are getting worse, we are getting worse partly because of therapy's linguistic callousness. Despite the emphasis upon the development of feeling, therapy actually invites the barbarians—a word that originally meant those who could not speak the language of culture, the Greek of the city. Feeling does not develop without the rhetorical and other arts, which give it differentiated expression.

As for reform, let's take that up when we have more time. This should get to the post office before the weekend. As for the post office, Michael, is there is a plot going on? Again they've raised the rates for letters. Is the government against writing letters? Why not make them real cheap and raise the taxes on long-distance phone calls? Just imagine the whole nation writing notes (not Hallmark cards), imagine millions and millions of carefully thoughtful feelings winging their way through mail-sorting machines, each letter in its privately sealed envelope, kissed closed with wet tongue and lips, each with its pretty little, frilled-edge, colored picture provided by the government glued to the upper right corner. Cheering isn't it? Cheers, Michael.

Jim

P.S. Maybe the fax will restore letter writing, but I'll still miss the envelopes and the stamps.

Telephone Versus Letters

Dear Michael,

We could be on the phone and instead we are writing letters. Why do we not simply talk long-distance coast-to-coast, Connecticut to California, taping the conversations as we did for the *L. A. Weekly* interview that started this whole book? What will happen when we write letters instead of talk?

You realize that by writing we are shifting the genre. No longer will the ideas come out hot owing to the double presence, back and forth, two chairs in a room together or pacing up and down or eating and drinking at a restaurant table or on a park bench. Now, alone, three thousand miles apart, each sits, pen in hand—or do you type right into the machine? This shift into writing is what the French thinkers today make so much of—the *écrit,* the paper trace.

Written words require a rhythm and a reflection so very different from the carefree spontaneity of the oral mode that jumps right out when we talk with each other. Therefore, these letters will be, supposedly, more cool and distant. And, anyway, wasn't that our point in including letters in this book—to give the book some cooling-off and reflective distance?

However—and mark my words, young man—I believe we may be actually closer and more truly communicating in letters than when talking. The vertical connection downwards and inwards, each on his solitary own, may be making a connection of souls through imagination, a connection that does not necessarily happen in live conversation or on the telephone.

I am saying, Mister Interviewer Ventura, that an interview does *not* have to take place "in person."

Now, if this be so, or enough "so" to be worth exploring, then the immense hypercommunication industry of portable phone and cellular phone, satellite dish and call waiting, of fax, beeper, modem, answering filters, and voice-activated recorders—all those oyster shell–colored, plastic-covered chip devices that turn the citizen into hacker, plugged into everyone everywhere—"I am because I am accessible"—does not, repeat, *not,* put an end to my aloneness but rather intensifies it.

If I must be networked in order to be, then on my own I am out of the loop, out of communication, null and void, nowhere. I can't be reached. If to be means to be reachable, then in order to be I must stay networked. Result: the contemporary syndrome, communication addiction.

One of the acute tensions of daily life strikes when the phone rings and you don't want to answer. Do you, Michael, let the phone ring and not pick it up? My daughter does. Do you put on your answering machine, call into your answering service, before going out the door so as not to miss—miss what, actually? What are we afraid of missing? The telephone ads recognize the right tie between loneliness and phoning. "Reach out and touch someone" reminds me how alone I am when not in touch. The more I feel alone, the more I phone; the more I phone, the more I am aware I am alone. A vicious feedback circle.

I hear you in my mind saying, "But Jim, it works." Phone sex, phone shopping, conference calls, family group calls; the red hot line that can start and stop a war. They say George Bush is on the phone a good part of each day. Can't be alone. And imagine this: Day in and day out an SAC plane flies around somewhere over the country, thirty thousand feet up, maintaining our national security communications center, a flying fortress phone booth keeping America safe. Even love works by phone talk. How many couples carry on their verbal intimacies long-distance! When I lived in Dallas, it was standard among families (maybe lovers too) to end their conversations with "I luv youuuu" breathed into the pastel, plastic, perforated mouthpiece provided by Southwestern Bell.

So, why write letters?

When I sit down to write, I've stepped out of the loop. I'm no longer in the addictive pattern. I'm simply here, on this frosty, moonless night, alone—but I am not lonely. It is silent, a little scratching of the pen point or the hum of the machine. I am not spread out through the network, not so much connected as collected. I'm not so much responding directly to you as I am pondering indirectly and generating, from my soul to soul, your image as recipient of this letter. I am not really writing to *you*. It's not the actual you whose voice I know on the phone, whose body I see when we talk. This "you" to whom I write is a visionary, imaginal Michael with whom my imagination is in touch, calling forth my imagination and freeing it from the confines of your actual voice and face. I enter an imaginal space, and that's what I mean by my phrase "generating from my soul to soul." We are connected by means of imagination. Imagination spins a web, *its* network, to ensnare your fantasies. This is less a communication than a cosmic enterprise that is really not bound by time or space. Isn't that precisely what the great letters of the past reveal and why they still appeal beyond space and time? Just think of the web of imaginative writing, written from ships after months away at sea, by explorers lost in wastelands, by those locked in prisons, written from trenches with sudden death imminent, written to lovers one has met but once or shortly—connections of imagination through imagination that are meetings of souls, in which there is no "relationship" going on at all.

Narcissism! Autoerotic! Fantasy! So might psychotherapy describe such outpourings. But wouldn't you rather get a letter of that sort than a phone call?

So, I believe I am actually closer to the soul of the person I am writing to than when engaged in conversation, and therefore, fundamentally—and here is the shocker—if this soul connection is going on in imagination, I am less alone when immersed in a letter, even if physically distant and not in touch. To keep in touch could now mean something altogether different: it could mean, "stay away—and write." The greatest of all letter writers, Mme. de Sévigné, said she was glad when her daughter took off so that the letters to her could begin again.

"Stay away and write" could be taken to imply that I don't like bodies, but that is not at all what I intend to say. I am merely contrasting the differences between talking and writing, because we need to make clear the difference between the parts of the book that begin in talk and the parts that begin in writing.

"Absence makes the heart grow fonder" reveals some truth about the heart's need to sink into its chambers to find its thoughts and put them into words that do not come to the lips in the presence of the other. How is it possible that works done in absence, in solitude, in remote distance, such as paintings and songs, poems and novels, works of imagination, communicate between the soul of the computer and the viewer, reader, listener? Again, Michael, we don't have to talk to communicate.

Let's keep clear the distinction between the vertical connection downwards, deeps touching deeps, and the horizontal connection outwards, beeps answering beeps. The tiny microchips, so light and fast, are the thin silicon wings of Hermes the divine messenger. (Get Ginette Paris's book *Pagan Grace* for the chapter on Hermes and communication technology. She shows the subtlety that makes Hermes both God of communication and patron of liars.) Our civilization has taken him over into its monotheism, a one-sided Hermes hypermania—and therefore concretized because one-sided—the hyperactivation of a single God. The subtlety is lost in the yes-or-no of information thinking. And we are moralized by this new Hermetic madness into slogans like: get plugged in; connect, only connect; never mind the message, it's the medium; keep networking. Info bytes; twenty-second bites; government reduced to "spin control." The Persian Gulf War shows that the incredibly difficult task of controlling Mars, the God of war, depends in our time on managing Hermes. As information is our new God, Hermes has replaced Yahweh, and, like him, Hermes too has become a God of war.

Hermes in antiquity was paired in the city with Hestia, she of the hearth, she who sat still, focused. (*Focus* is Latin for fireplace, hearth.) Letter writing requires a prolonged focus. It sits you down by the fire—the firelight of flickering reflections and the warmed imagination.

I used the word *recollection,* a Platonic word, implying that when we write letters the mind both focuses and also strays afield, seems partly under the influence of the muses.

A musing goes on that harks back to their mother, Mnemosyne, Memory. The phone just doesn't seem to allow all that to come in. Phone talk with the bill running by the second is especially foreshortened. Meandering costs money. Directness of phoning, the hand gripping the receiver, the ear hot under the pressure, leads to dreadful misunderstandings. How many devastations have happened in your life simply by wrong phoning?

So, to end this letter about letters, let's again remember the different feeling between love letters and love phoning. A love letter becomes a keepsake—or a time bomb in a divorce court! Love letters hold incredible potential. People used to lock them away, tie them in ribbons, burn them as they lay dying. They are documents of passionate imagination, frail sheaves of such pain. We write and rewrite them to find the right way, the right word. But with love phoning (even the term seems impossible), though the activity buzzes through the night all over America, we feel whatever went wrong can be rectified by another call. Hang up in fury and call back five minutes later to fix it. Addiction. And, too, a letter to a friend is different from a call to a friend. A letter takes a lot of effort. In the case of writers, letters to and from friends become publishable. But the way things are going now, with long-distance rates coming down and time under pressure, writers like you, Michael, will keep recording machines for your calls. Instead of publishing the collected letters, someday they will be selling tapes of the collected phone calls of Michael Ventura.

Don't hang up on me. Yours,

Jim

Talking

Dear Michael,

This is a P.S. I can't get off the subject of talking, writing, and phoning. It won't leave me. Maybe for a reason—to become clearer what's going on in this book. I think the book is beginning to take over my mind. Yours too? I hope so. Anyway, more needs to be said about the relation between our conversations and therapy, maybe even that our conversations may make the world less worse!

Psychologists are engaged in the business of consciousness. People come to see us about this or that problem, symptom, or trouble in order to become more conscious. We take things apart, that is, analyze problems, feelings, dreams so that they become more conscious.

Now what is this consciousness? What actually goes on in becoming more conscious? What goes on in conversation? If you listened to a tape of an analysis hour, an hour of becoming conscious in therapy, you would hear a conversation. That's all it is—conversation. You become more conversant with your dreams, about your relationships, your fears and needs.

Consciousness is really nothing more than maintaining conversation, and unconsciousness is really nothing more than letting things fall out of conversation, no longer talking about something—or what Freud called repression.

Conversation isn't easy. You know how hard it is in a family, what an art it is to keep a conversation going. You know the tortures of the family dinner table, how more and more is left unsaid. So, of course, Freud found repression mainly in the family. It's a place where conversation often has a hard time.

Or take a dinner party. Strike up a conversation and keep it flowing—not a monologue, not only opinions and sounding off, not only firing questions, but conversation as an exploration, a little risky adventure, a discovery, an interesting happening. Parties, doing lunch, and 7:30 A.M. breakfasts are terribly important in a city for keeping its conversation going, keeping the consciousness of the City at a certain intensity, moving its mind adventurously toward deeper discoveries.

What doesn't work, we also pretty well know: personalism—just talking out loud about what we feel. Complaints. Opinions. Information doesn't work—simply reporting what's new, where you've been, what you've heard. And lullabies don't help either—singing charming little stories to prevent anything from entering the heart or the mind. And boosterism isn't conversation either—broadcasting, self-advertising what we are doing, have done, going to do. You can't converse with a sales pitch of positive preaching. All these kinds of talk have to be cured in therapy; they interfere with conversation.

So, not just any talk is conversation, not any talk raises consciousness. A subject can be talked to death, a person talked to sleep. Good conversation has an edge: it opens your eyes to something, quickens your ears. And good conversation reverberates: it keeps on talking in your mind later in the day; the next day, you find yourself still conversing with what was said. That reverberation afterwards is the very raising of consciousness; your mind's been moved. You are at another level with your reflections. So, what helps conversation?

Here we need to look again at what conversation is. The word means turning around with, going back, like reversing, and it comes supposedly from walking back and forth with someone or something, turning and going over the same ground from the reverse direction. A conversation turns things around. And there is a verso to every conversation, a reverse, back side.

It is this verso, this exposition of the reverse version, that is, I think, the work of our talk. Whatever keeps us walking together with something and turns things around, upside down, converts what we already feel and think into something unexpected—this is the unconscious becoming conscious, which means doing therapy!

And to keep turning means that it's no use having fixed stands, definite positions. That stops conversation dead in its tracks. Our aim is not to take a stand on this or that issue, but to examine the stands themselves so they can be loosened and we can go on walking back and forth.

That is why the style of our conversation has to be somewhat upsetting, turning around the first expected direction of a thought or a feeling. And that is why we have to speak with irony, even ridicule and cutting sarcasm. Shocking even: because consciousness comes with a little shock of awareness, keeping us on edge, acute, awake, and a little awry. Instead of electroshock, psychotherapy uses *psycho*shock—that little twinge or flash that makes a situation suddenly seem altogether new.

This small book can hardly turn the City around, raise the level of its self-awareness, its reflection and insight into its unconscious repressions. Yet might these very conversations already be turning on the City Lights? For if we are working at curing our talk and less at talking of cures (for this or that problem) we would be engaged in true conversations, the very activity that does turn all things around.

Jim

What's a Client?

Dear Jim,

Just a note to wonder aloud when therapists stopped calling people patients and started calling them clients. You always have to be suspicious when there isn't a good word for something. It means people are uncomfortable with the subject. Therapists were obviously so uncomfortable with the medical term *patient* that they junked it. Was it because the tools they work with were conceptual rather than technical? Or because people feel more powerless when they think of themselves as patients? Or because a patient going to a healer expects to be healed, and, unlike in medicine, it's often hard to say when or how one is healed in psychoanalysis? Or was it just too heavy a word; did it make the sense of illness and injury (and the responsibility it puts on the healer) too vivid?

Still, it strikes me as a little odd that, in their search for another word, healers would beeline straight to the vocabulary of commerce. Looking up *client* in my Merriam-Webster, I think I've found the key. The second definition reads: "a person who engages the professional services of another; also: *patron, customer.*" But dig the first definition: "*dependent.*"

Lurking in the word they've chosen is the dependency that corrupts both sides in the consulting room. Psychotherapy's clients are customers who, instead of having the usual rights of customers ("the customer is always right"), are dependent on their therapists—therapists who in many cases even have the power to jail or hospitalize them—while the therapists, in turn, are emotionally and financially dependent on the clients who are also their patrons. The contradictory roles of this relationship, combined with its legal rules, are byzantine.

This subject is of course usually off-limits during the fifty-minute hour. If the client brings it up, it's evasion, denial, hostility, transference, and a waste of money (there are more pressing problems). And rare is the therapist who brings it up (though they do exist). So you have a relationship governed by a complex set of expectations and rules, the first rule being, "We're not here to talk about the rules of this relationship, we're here to talk about *your problems.*" It's almost as though both therapist and client have to deny that it *is* a relationship, and a strange one at that. And the terminology, expectations, and rules are also clearly a defense against the intense material that therapist and client are trying to deal with. But there's the same danger in this defense as in any: it can work too well, become a preoccupation in itself, and channel the healing process to fit the needs of the defense (instead of the other way around).

Now that I've raised all this I guess I'm supposed to have a new word handy. I don't. But I can fantasize about living in a culture that could say, "We don't have any words that fit what's going on here. Well, to hell with it! Let's not call it anything. Let's agree to leave a little silence in the sentence when we need the word we don't have, a little space on the page, to admit that when it comes to describing this particular thing we haven't the foggiest idea what we're talking about. This way at least we're not plugging in a phony or misleading word. Because if we plug in such a word we'll start to believe in it, even though we knew it was a compromise in the first place. This way, maybe we'll learn what we're talking about sooner or later and the good word will come."

Of course, a culture with that much sophistication probably wouldn't give much employment to psychotherapists and so wouldn't need to find a better word for *client.*

Michael

Empty Protest

Dear Michael,

Do you know the theological term *kenosis?* The idea from Greek means vain, hollow, fruitless, void, empty. In Christian theology *kenosis* refers to Christ's emptying himself of his divine power, of his unity with almighty God, in order to enter this world as a man. If it hadn't been for this *kenosis,* they couldn't have crucified him, and the expression of his emptiness is his cry on the cross to the almighty father, "Why has thou forsaken me?"

Kenosis seems now the only political way to be—emptied out of certainty. Otherwise, you become a fundamentalist united with an almighty ideology, protected from above by a cause. Therapy is just one more of the current ideologies keeping its believers from the panic of *kenosis,* the panic that comes when the whole structure of guarantees has collapsed. Therapy becomes a salvational ideology.

But I want to stay with politics for this letter. I could compare *kenosis* with the emptiness in Buddhist thought and the Zen exercises of emptying and the Oriental aesthetics of pottery and painting. But I'd rather connect *kenosis* with Gandhi and Martin Luther King, Jr. *Kenosis* is a form of action—not masochistic action, victimized, crucified, beaten with lathi sticks and billy clubs. Protest.

Politically, I am pretty empty. My state, Connecticut, has a huge deficit. What should we do? If we raise corporate taxes, we drive business out of the state and lose the tax base. If we cut the budget, we drop the level of our educational and social services that make this a quality state, attracting people and companies, which builds our tax base. If we encourage development to upgrade land values (and tax base) in small towns like mine, in the long term we are decreasing the value of residential property and thus decreasing the tax base. If we borrow with state-guaranteed bonds, then we run the risk of lowering our bond grades from AA to A and thus have to pay more interest on the borrowing. If we raise the sales tax, people go out of state to shop.

These dilemmas puzzle me. What a person usually does with political puzzles is make an either/or decision. Either I say it's beyond me and remain passive on the sidelines, or I follow the position of my political party coming down hard, say, against raising any taxes or against development or for social services and education.

I think now there's a third way. *Kenosis.* Empty protest. I don't know how to do the right thing. I don't even know what's right. I have no answer. But I sure smell something wrong with the government. And, within the federal government, for which I pay, something is wrong with airport safety, airline prices, gas prices, car efficiency, income tax loopholes, agricultural supports, PAC's, rail service, sabotage of the postal service, unions and union busting, aid to schools, military pensions, veterans' hospitals, drug testing, remedial education, busing. . . . Where does the wrongness end?

I used to get stopped cold in political arguments. I would be going on about something, and the other guy would say, "All right, if you're so smart, what would you do about it?" And I had no positive idea what to do, no program, nothing. It wasn't just that I was impractical; I was empty. My protests were suddenly emptied out because I had nothing positive to offer. They say that the '68 revolutions in Berkeley and in Europe among the students were so easily crushed or petered out because the revolutionaries had no positive programs.

Kenosis puts the emptiness in a new light. It values the emptiness. It says "empty protest" is a *via negativa,* a non-positivist way of entering the political arena. You take your outrage seriously, but you don't force yourself to have answers. Trust your nose. You know what stinks. Don't try to replace the helpless frustration you feel, the powerless victimization, by working out a rational answer. The answers will come, if they come, when they come, to you, to others, but don't fill in the emptiness of the protest with positive suggestions before their time. First, protest! I don't know what should be done about most of the major political dilemmas, but my gut (my soul, my heart, my skin, my eyes) sinks, creeps, crawls, weeps, cringes, shakes. It's wrong, simply wrong, what's going on here.

That we blasted thousands of Iraqis, mercilessly, for forty days and forty nights; that we kept this visual and verbal information from the citizens who pay for the war, who *are* the war, and who will carry the war in their souls into the future of our country; that America's president could say there are no more protesters, turning them into his political opposition, as if they were now wiped out like Iraqis (there are no more enemies); that our overkill—"to spare lives" (the Hiroshima argument)—resulting from the religious fanaticism called "unconditional surrender" (a tenet of Protestant rigidity and phobia of negotiating with the "enemy," going back to "Unconditional Surrender" Grant and the Civil War) is covered over by harping on

Arab fanaticism; that this enemy was created and armed by *us* just as Noriega was once our man (and where is *he* now?); that *national security* has become a shibboleth of a secret government much as *bottom line* is a shibboleth of ruthless business; that the deeply different mythologies of the Arabs and the West have only been driven further into self-justifying deafness; that we remain serfs to royal oil; that our victory comes from a totalitarian kind of plot between military, media, a cabal of administration, national security, and CIA together with a public that *wants* still to remain innocent of the full story—this signifies the death of the republic and the beginnings of the empire. That education henceforth will now mean technological electronics and not humanities, since the army's education program of the less literate and less advantaged proved effective (by measures of efficient spying on and destruction of the enemy); that the idea of enemy has now become reinforced and this reinforces the taproot puritanism of the American soul; that Vietnam is now rewritten, not as a tragedy of intention but as a handicap in execution (we shall not fight with one arm behind our backs, as in Vietnam, hindered by public opposition)—in short, Michael, America has suffered a devastating victory when we need rather a deeper humility and sense of our shadow in order to come off our high white horse. This victory is one more manic defense (like consuming, like fastness, like inflation) against the profound and permanent American depression that never ceases to call us both privately in our lonely souls and publicly in the despairing deterioration of the commonwealth. All this is wrong, terribly wrong, and this list could be compounded by your list and by lists of others who are far more perceptive than I am.

Yet, to the question "What would you have done with Saddam Hussein in August 1990, in October, in January and February, wise guy?" I have only my physical sense of something wrong. Only my empty protest. Therapy blocks this kind of protest. (I haven't forgotten our theme.) It does not let these "negative" emotions have their full say. It may value them, analyze them, but therapy insists they have to lead us into deeper meaning rather than immediate action. Therapy says, Think before you act, feel before you emote, judge, interpret, imagine, reflect. *Self*-knowledge is the point of the emotions and the protest, not public awareness. Know *thyself;* know what *you* are doing before you know the issue, and know the meaning of an action before you act. Otherwise you are projecting and acting out.

So, therapy would say, You can't protest in this empty way because you haven't made clear what the protest *really* wants and why and what for. It has to *mean* something.

An empty protest, however, hasn't got a defined meaning. It doesn't have an end goal—not even the end of blocking something it protests about. My protest about the Gulf War doesn't clearly say, "Stop the war!" Empty protest is protest for the sake of the emotions that fuel it and is rooted not in the conscious fullness of improvement, but in radical negativity. In theological language, empty protest is a ritual of negative theology. It's what the Hindus call *neti, neti, neti*—not this, not this, not this. No utopia, no farther shore toward which we march, only the march, the shout, the placard, the negative vote, the refusal.

What I'm suggesting here can't even become a new mode of conscientious objection because the C.O. must back up his position with a set of positive ideals (not taking life, all war is evil, peace, human community). It's not even anarchism, for the anarchist has as positive goal the literal ending of all governmental forms. Nor is it libertarianism, which again has a positive set of beliefs that can be put into programs of deregulating and dismantling.

What could be more unpopular than empty protest? Not only will you be seen as stupid because empty, but you will also be alone in right field and ninth in the batting order. I find it very hard to play the political game without falling into the usual American popularity contest, the public opinion poll. How does one enter the public fray and at the same time be unpopular? By this I mean I don't even have the honor of standing for the oppositional unpopular position like a Mencken, a Chomsky, a Jerry Brown, a Ventura. You, Michael, can be counted on to define an unpopular position but never truly an empty one. Your protests have beef. We read you to hear the "wrong" thing, whereas I want what I do to be applauded! Yet I am often roundly cursed (when understood) or, worse, approvingly smelted into someone else's arguments (because misunderstood).

Take this book, for instance. Because it attacks therapy it cannot help but be unpopular among people I most wish to reach—the psychological intelligentsia for whom therapy is now a sacred cow. When in front of a large audience my innocence is always surprised that the ideas I am deeply and passionately presenting are found to be intolerable. I haven't been able to separate being out there with being liked. So, empty protest for me is really a *kenosis*—giving up both the vanity of being admired and the surety of a sound position, and doing it in public.

You will probably refute all this by saying, "Jim, that's just negative politics. You're saying throw the bastards out. It's cynical disillusionment. Worse," you'll say, "you've removed your good mind from the engagement, letting others come in with their programs because you're not willing to do the hard work of thinking through to solutions."

Michael, you may be right. I have no answer. You've emptied out my whole argument. Still, I'm going on protesting, and protesting against therapy. Something's rotten in its kingdom, and I'll go on saying so, even if I have not been able to imagine what to do about it. Over to you.

Jim

The Edges of Behavior

Dear Jim,

Norman Mailer once wrote that psychology wouldn't come into its own until it could explain the psyche of the actor. I think he had something there. Don't worry, I'm not going to take on that job tonight, I'm just going to offer you some ruminations on acting and therapy. (An aside: Remember Stan Passy at the Pacifica Institute saying that his students, studying for their master's in shrinkery, often tell him that early on they wanted to be performers of some kind? And Stan going on and on about how therapy is practiced mostly by people who really wanted to be actors or singers?)

Maybe the difference between humans and animals is not that humans speak but that humans act. The words *action* and *activity* echo the word *actor*, as though to act (as in action) is also to *act* (as in acting). And then there's that psychological catchphrase that's become part of the common tongue: *acting out,* meaning, to follow through on emotions and thoughts that disrupt your life or someone else's. *Acting out* is an extraordinary phrase, really: it puts a negative spin on doing anything that involves the more molten parts of your psyche, while implying that such behavior isn't quite real. This implies, in turn, that to be authentic your behavior must be calm and considered. What a fear of disruption lurks in that phrase! What an anxiety about the way one is living! The more you think about it the worse that phrase gets; it denies whole realms of experience with one swat.

Where was I?

The phenomenon of acting as it relates to the phenomenon of psychology. Through varying degrees of effort and mistake we partly discover, partly invent not who but *how* we are—our roles. Then we play that part, some days poorly and some days well, for all it's worth and for as long as we can get away with it, until we're forced to change. "Getting your act together" is so central to our being that it's possible to dispense with psychological jargon and describe the crises of our lives purely in theatrical terms. The role doesn't work anymore, our timing's off, we can't say the old lines or even remember them, or they don't fit the scene anymore. We're too young or too old to play this part, too fat or too wasted. Our clothes, or costumes, don't seem to fit anymore; our space, or stage, has become too little or too much; the props are no longer right. A woman is sick of being typecast as a mother, a man can't act out his vulnerability. The girlfriend comes home with a new hairdo, the boyfriend takes to wearing a beard, and there's tension in the air: what does the need for a new look portend? Or someone walks into a party or restaurant wearing the wrong costume—too punk, too gay, too redneck, too casual, too formal—and everybody's sensitive that something is amiss. We expect from each other a certain level and consistency of acting. Rewrites and improvisations are not often welcome. Reject your lines totally: "catatonia." Put in wildly different dialogue: "schizophrenia." No one, least of all yourself, takes the part that you play lightly.

So if the art of acting in a culture changes drastically—if, that is, there's a fundamental change in the behavior we use to portray behavior—wouldn't that be an event of enormous psychological significance, with all sorts of ramifications for the practice of psychotherapy? That's what happened in America in the late 1940s, though deep thinkers in psychology and elsewhere didn't take much note at the time.

To comment on the changes at that time we have to make some distinctions among acting styles. Acting takes three basic forms, the most common of which is shtick. I suspect the ancient Greeks, who invented Western theater, had a word for shtick, for shtick has always been with us. We live now in a plague of shtick. Most TV and film, and all the commercials, display a kind of puppetry: no matter what the stimuli, schtick actors get by with two or three smiles, one expression of chagrin, one of sadness, and a grab bag of grimaces. It looks and feels like nothing, and it's supposed to. Such acting is meant to be absolutely nonthreatening: enter, charm, sell, exit. It doesn't matter whether the product is a douche or a movie like *Ghost.* Shtick acting is just a party mask. The fact that people choose to watch so much of it now is something for psychotherapy to ponder, but the style itself can't tell us much.

I'll call the second form of acting concrete or outer acting. This was the dominant form of acting in England and America for the first half of this century, and it remains so in England (as on "Masterpiece Theater"). It is the acting that made the old Hollywood star system great, and it is still done with mastery here by a few artists like Meryl Streep and Dustin Hoffman, as it once was by Laurence Olivier, Bette Davis, James Cagney, Cary Grant, Barbara Stanwyck, and on and on. These are people who mastered an enormous repertoire of behavior and could produce the most delicate shadings on cue. Their understanding of each gradation of laughter or anger is as precise as a great concert pianist's knowledge of the timbres that can be coaxed from each key. Even people acting in this style who, like John Wayne, didn't have a large range, still had total mastery of the gradations within their range, so that (like Wayne in *Rio Bravo* or *The Searchers*) they worked marvelous subtleties into their characters.

The third form I'll call abstract or inner acting. (As I said in another letter, this took hold in America when painting and jazz were moving in the same direction.) If the concrete actor is like the classical musician, the abstract actor is like the jazz player. The technical demands are just as great, but the technique is used differently. To see the difference starkly, rent yourself double features of Laurence Olivier and Montgomery Clift, Humphrey Bogart and Marlon Brando, Jean Harlow and Marilyn Monroe, Katharine Hepburn and Gena Rowlands. They perform equally well, but with different objectives. An Olivier or a Hepburn will project their roles at you as precisely as a laser, focusing on a moment's absolute center; Clift or Rowlands will play the same moment at its edge. Olivier or Hepburn will play the moment where it's most itself, where it is *that* moment and no other; Clift or Rowlands will play the moment at the border, where it's begun to change into something else.

Each style, the concrete and the abstract, embodies an entirely different experience of personality. The older, concrete style expresses fixity: no matter how much characters may change in a movie like *Gone with the Wind,* it's their behavior rather than their essential psychology that's at stake. Their relation to the story changes, but they don't, not really. While characters played in the abstract style—James Dean in *Rebel Without a Cause,* Montgomery Clift in *From Here to Eternity,* Gena Rowlands in *A Woman Under the Influence*—sometimes seem to be registering major changes every minute. At any given time in the story their characters seem able to go off in many directions; they seem to include several, often contradictory, motivations in the same line of dialogue. Such a performance gives ambiguity to even a very concrete story like *From Here to Eternity,* while Gena Rowlands's performance in, say, *Opening Night* has an almost unbearable sense of *possibility;* she trembles with it, is tortured by it, and is finally redeemed by it.

It's a style that tells nothing yet reveals all. It tells nothing, in that its interest is in the ambiguity and paradoxes of human behavior. Yet it reveals all, in that the character seems to leap from one area of the psyche to another in the same scene, often in the same line. I think of the moment in *Opening Night* when Rowlands, in a kind of hallucination, sees a young woman whom she believes to be, literally, her younger self: it's a moment utterly peaceful yet totally mad. She smiles with a kind of sly wonder, and her lips form but do not speak the word *hello,* and you don't know whether to be glad or afraid for her. Or in *Minnie and Moskowitz* when she watches Seymour Cassel cut off his moustache to prove his passion for her: is she in a state of love or horror? Both, and the very fact that love and horror can blend so perfectly on her face is terribly disturbing. Or in *Another Woman,* where she shows the most intense inner activity by an almost perfect stillness of expression, it's as though you could peel back her forehead and see the turmoil.

So our culture shifted, in its serious acting (the behavior we use to portray behavior), from the style of James Cagney and Katharine Hepburn to the style of Marlon Brando and Gena Rowlands; from fixity to flux; from clarity to paradox. Cagney could summarize his style brilliantly and simply, as he did: "You walk in, plant yourself, look the other fellow in the eye, and tell the truth." Compare that to what Ellen Barkin (who does a fine, earthy rendition of the inner style) said of Marlon Brando: "When he's up there he's telling a secret about himself that's not for sale." Cagney tells the truth, Brando tells a secret.

As psychotherapists would be the first to observe, there's all the difference in the world between truths and secrets. Something claiming to be a truth is taking a definite stance in relation to a shared reality; but a secret may not be "true" in any sense of the word, a secret may be a lie or wish or a dream. And the stance of a secret toward shared reality is clear: secrets don't trust it. As I said in an earlier letter, a stance of suspicion toward the outer world is taken for granted in the Actors Studio style. Where Bette Davis and Clark Gable walk into a room as though they're expecting to take it over, Paul Newman and Warren Beatty (even in roles that call for great authority) walk into a room as though they're expecting to have to leave, and very soon too.

Date the shift from Brando's 1947 performance in *A Streetcar Named Desire* on Broadway, under the direction of Elia Kazan (though the styles of Brando and Clift were already formed by then). The next year Kazan and Lee Strasberg founded the Actors Studio, where the new style flourished. Is it enough to say that this generation of actors was the first to grow up wholly in the technological world that followed the Great War, the world of movies, radio, telephones, airplanes, and cars? And that they hit their adolescence during the Depression and came of age during World War Two? Perhaps. But perhaps, too, the effect isn't so much causal (developmental) as simultaneous.

Consider, Jim: it usually goes unnoticed that technology is an *expression* before it's a cause. All these inventions began as human expressions, just as poems and songs and psychological theories are human expressions. The inventions of technology emerged from the human psyche before they affected the human psyche. So we don't really know if the fragmented experience of personality expressed by these actors was caused by a technological environment or if technology itself was one symptom of a change in the collective psyche that was experienced individually as fragmentation.

Take this a little further:

We can say with some certainty that the popularity of the Actors Studio style (*method* was always too rigid a word) should have taught therapists something. America began identifying enthusiastically, and in large numbers, with a sense of personality that had no center and with portrayals that could easily be diagnosed as neurotic, narcissistic, schizophrenic, and psychotic—in the late forties and early fifties! In other words, before there was a television in every home, before the dominance of Madison Avenue ads, before rock 'n' roll, before the civil rights movement, before permissive childrearing, before the sixties, before Vietnam, before feminism, before the collapse of American manufacturing, before everything that gets blamed for our ills. *What the art of acting tells us is that our sense of psychological fragmentation didn't follow these developments, it preceded them.*

I'm saying that your critique of developmental psychology may be applied to the collective as well as to individuals. We need another way to think about *events.* Period. Another dialectic regarding history, if you like. Because if individual histories aren't developmental, then can national and cultural histories be developmental? Not likely. I'm suggesting that one way to talk about the last century is to say that a fundamental change in the human psyche, for reasons not yet knowable, loosed a flood of inventions, ideas, and events; and that those creations, in turn, acted as a kind of feedback loop to further stimulate the collective psyche's change. And we live in the maelstrom of that change and will until that change completes or exhausts itself. And our political and cultural struggles, all these conflicts focused around all these issues, are *not* political or cultural or economic at all; rather, in the context of the collective psyche, they are more like dreams—complex constructs in which all the elements of the dilemma are given free reign. In that light, Stephen Daedalus's sentence strikes home: "History is a nightmare from which I am trying to awake."

Where does this leave protest, empty or otherwise? Where does this leave politics? Where does this leave belief or the life of the citizen? In a dream. A dream not like those of Freud or Jung, but like the dreams in the *Nightmare on Elm Street* cycle, that series of movies in which Freddy, the mad, surreal child murderer, follows children into their sleep and kills them through their nightmares. (These movies are rented *by the thousand* every day, all around the world, by children. They feel a truth here.)

And this takes us back (by quite a circuitous route, I know) to the consulting room, to the therapist facing a person who has come to that room to wake from the nightmare and get his *act* together. I am saying that the therapist has to deal with everything you speak of, freeways and fluorescents and furniture, *as expressions of the collective nightmare,* dangerous as Freddy and which, like Freddy, have to be dealt with in the real world *so that the action will register in the dream.*

This direction is double-edged. On the one hand, the consulting room becomes a cell of revolution, as you wish it to be; attention is focused upon the way we really live, today, now. On the other hand, it's recognized that in order to attend the psychology of one person you must include the fact that this individual is part of a collective psychological entity that is expressing itself *as his world.*

Which is the somewhat unwieldy point I've been headed toward or circling around, again: that this world is not something happening *to* us, as individuals, but is the expression of a change *in* us, as a collective psychological entity. When we act upon the world we act upon the dream; we *consciously* enter the nightmare of history, instead of living lives that are no more than a tossing about in collective sleep. To enter that nightmare consciously is to remember that, even when we act politically, we are in the realm, the realm upon realm, of the psyche.

It is like being an actor who is intensely aware not only of his role but of the entire play.

Fondly, your circuitous friend,

Michael

Welcome to the Dreamtime

Dear Jim,

Occasionally I've spoken to you about what I call, in conversation's shorthand, "the avalanche": simultaneous, massive changes on every level of life everywhere, that have built up unstoppable momentum as they speed us toward God knows where. I wrote the clearest statement of what I mean about three years ago. I'm going to retype it for you now, adding things about our good ol' theme, therapy, as I go along, because I think it belongs in this book, which we are not so much writing as improvising (and I mean that in the best sense, as they say).

And why do I have to retype the thing instead of just photocopy it and staple on additions? Because I don't write in my head; the thing has to pass through my hands for the thoughts to come. But if I go off now on the part of writing that everyone, especially literary critics, ignore—the *physicality* of writing—I'll really get derailed. Ventura, shut up and type.

So: An Inventory of Timelessness.

Human beings once woke with the sun and usually went to sleep not long after dark. Depending on which archaeologists you believe, this went on for anywhere from a quarter of a million to three million years. It has changed utterly and drastically in the last one hundred. One hundred years is such a tiny part of the human time line that as a collective we're in the first split second of this change; we've barely had time to blink twice. Say it slowly: we have dispensed with what the human nervous system knew as time, and, since we know that time and space are intimately related, to be lost in time is also to be lost in space.

Therapy takes the stance of trying to orient us, but, as Bertolt Brecht once said, "It is scarcely possible to conceive of the laws of motion if one looks at them from a tennis ball's point of view."

Item: Wells Fargo bank has introduced a twenty-four-hour-a-day, seven-day-a-week telephone service. You can now pick up the phone at any hour, from anywhere, and talk to a person, not just a machine, who can answer any conceivable question about your banking needs. This stretches the term *banking needs* beyond all previous definitions in the six hundred–year history of Western banking. Why do my bankers anticipate that I'll need them at three o'clock of a Sunday morning? Partly because there's no telling where I'll be—Tokyo, Barcelona, Moscow, desperate to know what my balance is before a market opens in Berlin or Hong Kong. Yet a hefty percentage of the calls are from Wells Fargo's home time zone and involve personal, not business, accounts. Which means that 'round about midnight, in these United States, a number of demographically ordinary people feel the pressing need to question their banker.

And it's not just that you're thinking about your bank in the wee hours. Your bank is thinking about you. It has decided that there should be less of a boundary between its needs and yours, and when you make such a call you are in effect agreeing with that decision. So the bank, a traditionally conservative institution, has redefined a fragment of time and space.

Psychotherapy talks a lot about boundaries. Especially in issues of relationships and of abuse, boundaries are considered crucial. I'm talking about boundaries, too, the boundaries between intimate time and business time; between home and work; between night and day; between individual and corporate; between private space and public space; between environment and psyche. Fuzzed boundaries. Areas once distinct that now bleed into each other. Dislocated time. Timeless space. We know that, within families, when boundaries this important are violated, people start to lose their sense of themselves. Historically, it's clear that this is also happening on a mass scale.

Twenty-four-hour bank call-ins and automatic tellers are in themselves insignificant details of contemporary life. But as part of a pattern, it speaks of a people increasingly coaxed to live without pattern. And increasingly *demanding* to live without pattern *in terms of services,* while they bemoan the loss of pattern in their morality, their love-life, their thought—and are unconscious of this contradiction.

If one individual demanded to do his or her banking at three in the morning, it would appear to be behavior that had gone over a risky edge. Some would begin to question other aspects of that individual's life. When a corporation provides the service, and meets the demands of thousands—then, in spite of what even the most conservative people might prefer morally or politically, their patternless consumerism disrupts the boundaries that made the old morality possible.

You spoke, Jim, of the importance of treating people's schedules therapeutically, but, see, the schedules of the collective culture have gone totally haywire, are out of control, *and this has been institutionalized in the form of services.*

Item: Life in Clarendon, a town of about fourteen hundred in the Texas Panhandle, revolves around its several fundamentalist churches. Like many towns in that part of the country, it's still "dry"; you can't buy alcohol within the city limits. But not too long ago an AM/PM convenience store opened. It never closes. And such stores exist now in even the tiniest towns, all over the country. Why do they need such a thing in such a town?

Until recently in the Texas Panhandle, you could tune in two, sometimes three television stations, depending on the weather. The stations signed off around midnight, often earlier. Now, with satellite and cable, there are many, many stations, dozens and dozens, and they never sign off. Some of those stations show porn in the wee hours. And MTV all the time. Constant news. And movies that no one in the Panhandle would ever have heard of otherwise. So a place that had depended for its way of life upon its isolation, upon its strict regulation of what it allowed into its boundaries, upon its rooted connection to what it imagined to be the morality of the nineteenth century, has been penetrated by what it views as a service. It is no longer separate in space; it no longer has a farmer's sense of time.

This is the technological equivalent of giving everybody in Clarendon LSD, not once but every day, in their morning coffee and in their evening tea.

Or take Utah, owned and run by the Mormon Church, a place with no separation of church and state. With satellite and cable, late night porn shows have become very, very popular in Utah, which means: Utah is no longer Utah at three in the morning. Night now turns Utah inside out. At that time, the space can no longer be depended upon to be the space it was intended to be.

Time and space, in such places, have become tentative, arbitrary. And this in the most concrete, personal sense. There are instruments in each home eating away at the time and space of people who have become addicted to those instruments. Consciously, these are people who see themselves as normal, righteous, and conservative, and they emphatically don't want this to happen to them. Yet something else is operating in them, some hunger that they follow without thought or plan, in which they indulge in activities that subtly but thoroughly undermine their most cherished assumptions. They want more and more boundaries, yet they live less and less within those boundaries. Isn't it fair, then, to assume that something else, something deeper within them, is doing this subversive wanting?

Poor psychotherapy, trying to treat Annie's anorexia or Jill's bulimia, Bobby's alcoholism or Jack's workaholism, when these people live in and are expressions of a voracious collective hunger that is, in effect, eating the boundaries of sanity on all sides.

Item: The electric light bulb. An invention barely a hundred years old, it has been in general use for roughly seventy years now. It marked the technological beginning of the end of linear time. Before the light bulb, darkness constricted human space. Outside the cities especially, night shrank a landscape into the space within arm's reach. (The moon figures so greatly in our iconography because it was all that allowed one to go far out into the night. But it was rarely bright enough and often obscured by weather.) But today there are few places in America or Europe truly dark at night. The glow of even a small town can be seen for many miles. Light gives us all the space we want, any time we want it. Psychoactive events of monstrous proportions can take place. Hitler's Nuremburg rallies, all those thousands with stiffly raised arms in the night, are impossible without spotlights. Light creates the necessary space, pushing back the boundaries of time. Dreamtime becomes a time for acting out the nightmare. What is nightlife, as it's called, but trying to find in the actual night the kind of things that once rarely appeared outside of dreams?

Item: The car is a private space that can go in any direction at any time. The motel room cinched that: *anywhere* you go, there will be a space for you—a fact unique to contemporary life and alien to every previous society. But the fact that there's a room for you anywhere makes the place where you *are* less substantial. Thus you are a transient, without having chosen to be. Human transience used to be defined almost solely by death. Now the fact of so much choice makes everyone a transient *all* the time. And, for most now, it makes any single choice almost unbearably tentative. Why be where you are, who you are, when you can just as easily be somewhere else, behaving perhaps differently? Again, this is a question that even most demographically average people ask themselves often in our society. How can it not make them more and more uncertain? Hence they crave certainty in all the wrong places: in politics, which has always been uncertain; in metaphysics, which by its nature is uncertain; in love and in sex, where nothing's ever certain. Many of these people blame the uncertainty, the tentative quality, of their lives on liberalism, humanism, relativism, and all the behaviors they attribute to those words —when what is really going on is that once they were prisoners of time and space, and they will never be prisoners of them again, and they miss those prison walls desperately.

How long will it take them to become accustomed to timelessness? This has become a crucial historical question. For until they acclimate themselves, they will continue to want reactionary solutions that can only increase the chaos. Psychotherapy is disgracefully behind in thinking about these things, for in this process psychotherapy could perform a crucial role, could help make millions of people conscious of these changes and their effects on a one-to-one basis. And that, in turn, might change the changes (in what direction I couldn't begin to predict). Some people have to start thinking about these issues within the terms of psychology, because it's obvious that without theoretical frameworks therapy can't begin to deal with this in the consulting room—at least not on any scale sufficient to be absorbed into the collective culture.

In order for that thinking to begin, it might help to look to the roots of our modern destruction of personal time and space.

And here we are back to Christianism, Jim, for this destruction began with Jesus.

Boris Pasternak, in *Doctor Zhivago,* saw this clearly:

> In the first [Western] miracle you have a popular leader, the patriarch Moses, dividing the waters by a magic gesture, allowing a whole nation—countless numbers, hundreds of thousands —to go through. . . . In the second miracle you have a girl—an everyday figure who would have gone unnoticed in the ancient world—quietly, secretly, bringing forth a child. . . . What an enormously significant change! How did it come about that an individual human event, insignificant by ancient standards, was regarded as equal in significance to the migration of a whole people? . . . Individual human life became the life story of God, and its contents filled the vast expanses of the universe.

We don't know how it came about, but we know the enormity of the result. In Judaism, God redeemed a race. In Christianism, God redeemed *you*—an absolute reversal of metaphysics as it was practiced everywhere else in the world. Everywhere else, with the exception of the most highly sophisticated Buddhism, worship was always tribal: a people propitiated existence for comparatively small favors. But now, in the West, the *individual* was entitled to the full and undivided attention of the universe—a staggering change in individual space and eternal time.

It was a far smaller, slower, rigidly stratified world—a world in which most owned nothing and could go nowhere—so it took the better part of fifteen hundred years for this change to truly take root. First came the creation of perspective in painting; individual sense of space leaped past previous boundaries into an infinitely receding background. Foreground had been all. Now, foreground was arbitrary, made small by background. But the great catalyst of change was

Columbus's voyage to the Americas in 1492. The dream inherent in artistic perspective was made reality. The alluring, and to all intents and purposes infinite, background was now being mapped. Europe, and the rest of the world, now had somewhere to go. *Nothing needed to be permanent anymore.* Some Europeans went by choice, some were driven. Africans were dragged off their ancestral lands by force; Amerindians were pushed off theirs. The social glue of every culture in human history, the relation of a people to a land, a particular space, disintegrated. With that sense of space destroyed, it was only a matter of momentum before time would be destroyed as well.

The Christianist sense of the individual being the center of the universe now had the space to become daily reality. Later, the technological invention of timelessness—of it not being important to human activity what segment of day it was—would, in the context of such space, create spacelessness as well. The individual, the center of the universe, no longer had a definite ground to stand on. Neil Armstrong on the moon is the new image of what it means to be human—infinite space on all ends, living by several times at once, desperately carrying one's own power pack, one's own air supply, saying trivial things, to comfort oneself, to others hundreds of thousands of miles away who may or may not be listening.

It is no wonder that the United States all but abandoned the exploration of other planets for the next two decades. Liberal intellectuals fastened on the image of the whole earth hanging above the moon man and said it was a wonderful thing, and the vision of one earth would bring peace. But on other levels the society was more inwardly shaken than outwardly exhilarated by the precariousness of that human being in a space-time that brought on the fear of falling and the fear of suffocation, fears imprinted in our genes. What's the proof? Until we saw that moon man, the collective impulse to explore space was huge; after we saw him, it virtually stopped dead. But since the moon landing we've traveled farther in time and space than the astronauts. Now, with electronic instantaneousness at our fingertips all night and day, tiny towns in Texas and Utah might as well be the moon for all the temporal stability one can find in them.

Be careful of what you want, because you just might get it. The West has gotten what it has prayed for since the birth of Christ: every individual is being addressed directly, at all times, by an infinite universe.

In biblical mythology, this state of being is followed by Apocalypse.

Welcome to the Dreamtime, baby.

For what is Apocalypse? In Revelation it is described as the coming of the beast:

> Then I saw a beast coming up from the sea with ten horns and seven heads, and upon his horns ten diadems, and upon his heads the names of blasphemy. The beast I saw was like a leopard, and his feet as those of a bear, and his mouth as the mouth of a lion. And the dragon gave him his power and his throne and his great authority. . . . Then the whole earth went in wonder after the beast. . . . Who is like the beast, and who can fight with him?

From antiquity to Freud and Jung, the sea is the great symbol of the human psyche. So the beast is the manifestation, in the waking world, of what's deepest in the psyche. It's a multilayered, many-headed image, an image of simultaneity, which in itself is seen as great power. "And upon his heads the names of blasphemy": the expectation is that when this psychic beast appeared it would challenge all the laws.

These fearful writers of early Christianity sensed what had been started: That the new Christianist focus on the individual would sooner or later bring forth the secrets of the psyche, but in ways that would contradict their conscious morality. They saw this as, literally, the end of the world.

But perhaps they were being a mite too concrete. It is the end of *a* world, certainly—the world in which waking and dream are rigidly separate. When the "beast" rises from the "sea," the surrealities of our dream life become the daily facts of waking life.

For we in the late twentieth century live in the time-space of the dream. The dream's instantaneous changes, its unpredictable metamorphoses, random violence, archetypal sex; its constant cascade of supercharged imagery; its threatening sense of multiple meaning. For a quarter of a million years this dreamscape surrounded us only in our sleep or in arts experienced by the very few or in very carefully orchestrated religious rituals. Now, in our electronic environment, the dreamworld greets us when we open our eyes. It is the "something deeper" within us that creates all this subversive wanting, wanting, wanting. The long-suppressed psyche, as outrageous in conservatives as in bohemians, in capitalists as in socialists, in evangelicals as in atheists, has finally been freed to feed on the outer world, and so to grow.

In every other century there was an obvious separation between what's called the subconscious and the conscious. Individual daily life was more or less ordered, however unjust or distasteful, and cacophonous cross-purposes were left to be slept through in dreams. But now we live in a technologically hallucinogenic culture that behaves with the sudden dynamics of the dream, *that duplicates the conditions of dreaming.* Technology projects the subconscious into countless *things.* What distinguishes the twentieth century is that each individual life is a daily progression through a concrete but fluctuating landscape of the psyche's projections. The surrealism, simultaneity, sexuality, and instantaneous change that occur in our dreams also occur all around us. So the condition of our subconscious is now also the condition of this physical environment we've built for ourselves. And, as Freud was the first to point out, "In the subconscious there is no time."

Without time, there can be no space. Without time and space, the traditional filters, channels, and boundaries of human consciousness dissolve.

We reel between dream and dream—between the dreams of our sleep that speak to us alone and the dreamscape of this waking world in which we make our way through millions of dream fragments that collide around us, each with its flitting moment of dominance.

It was easy, or so it seems now, to love the world of rigid time and space. The world *was* a world, it held still long enough to be a world and gave us time to learn to love it. But loving this utter state of flux, where time has been shattered and space has been both elongated and compressed beyond rational dimensions—we want to love it, we have love in us to give it, but we do not know how, nobody does. Yet daily life hinges on what we are and are not able to love. So these changes in our time and space have cut through the foundations of what made daily life livable and what we found lovable in one another.

And yet—we made this world. We gobble up its instantaneousness and breathlessly want more. Could it be that our collective purpose is to revivify the psyche by making it deal with its labyrinthine *physical* image at every turn? Have we created this multifarious, timeless, spaceless world in order finally to learn to *live within and use* our own immense and cacophonous psyches?

Is this the collective thrust of our history? A genetic demand? Individually, the contemporary environment seems to have been thrust upon us. But collectively, I say again, *we've* made this world. And, both individually and collectively, we've eagerly welcomed each separate manifestation that has created this collective change. Radio, television, telephones, light bulbs, cars, planes, records, computers—all the building blocks of contemporary life in all their manifestations have been seized upon everywhere in the world. It is not enough to blame this on capitalism or consumerism. The very eagerness of the world's embrace of this hallucinogenic technology by the most different sorts of peoples is evidence of the deepest of longings.

For the human psyche is one of the great forces of nature, and what is most frightening about this space-time technology is that *it exposes us to this force within us* as nothing else ever has. We are standing in the storm of our own being. We are standing in a world created not by God (except indirectly), but by our psyches. It is undeniably our fate, so we must face the fact that it may be our natural habitat. We have willy-nilly broken through all the old rigidities, all the limits we thought were nature itself, and we can never go back. This is a new nature. Dream has become reality. And through that fact echoes what may yet be the great line of our culture: "In dreams begin responsibility."

This, Jim, is what I see as the unknown terrain that psychotherapy must either explore or become meaningless. This is the white space on the map, Jim, where the ancient navigators wrote, "Here There Be Soul-Eaters."

Michael

Substance Abuse and Soul in Things

Dear Michael,

I want to lay out—practically!—the connection between soul and things. Then it will be clearer what it means to be a "psychological citizen."

It all begins with symptoms—the classical beginning in depth psychology. That's where Freud started with his hysterical Viennese patients and Jung started with his schizy inmates of the insane asylum. Trying to understand the strange manifestations of the psyche, they began to invent the depth psychology of introversion, what was going on inside the patient's feelings and memories.

Follow the symptoms. Pathology always leads into new unknowns. Our whole field of psychotherapy may simply be a reaction to symptoms. As they change from decade to decade—we don't see cases like Freud and Jung saw at the beginning of the century—therapy invents new ideas and new interpretations.

What are the symptoms now? Alar on your apples; asbestos around your heating pipes; lead in the paint on the schoolroom ceiling; mercury in your fish; preservatives in your hot dogs; cigarette smoke in the diner; rays from the microwave; sprays, mothballs, radon, feathers, disinfectants, perfumes, exhaust gases; the glue and synthetics in your couch; antibiotics and hormones in your beef.

We awaken daily in fear of the things we live with, eat, drink, and breathe. "I am slowly being poisoned." The closest environment has become hostile. To live, I must be alert, constantly suspicious, on guard at the cave's mouth. But it's not a saber-toothed tiger that'll get me and my clan, it's the friendly family fridge ruining the ozone.

If I were of a different culture, we would say: spells have been cast, bad magic; we have fallen out of favor with the spirits; my vitality is being sapped by invisibles. By attributing death-dealing effects to things—microwave oven, asbestos, cigarette smoke, hot dog—I am saying that they have enough moxie to knock us out and do us in. The object has become animated by the symptom. It is an alien power to be wary of, eradicate, or propitiate. "Don't stand too close to the microwave while it's on; keep the windows unsealed so that the air can circulate; only ingest foods and drinks after reading the labels and warnings; throw away in a special container and at a special location: batteries, sprays, household chemicals."

You see what I am driving at: my suspicions and my precautionary rituals announce that I am living in an animated world. Things are no longer just dead materials, objects, stuff.

Take this one step further: perhaps the bad magic comes not only from the material cause of things, but also from their formal cause. (Aristotle explains that all events have a material cause like the stone or wood of a sculpture and a formal cause like its idea, design, shape.) Suppose we are being harmed as much by the *form of things* as by their material, where form means their *aesthetic quality.* For instance: styrofoam cups, fluorescent lights, bad doorknobs, unpleasant chairs, K-Mart fabrics and their colors, the hollow loud clack of objects set down on fake wood tabletops. Enough. The soul, which has classically been defined as the *form* of living bodies, could be affected by the *form* of other bodies (design, shape, color, innate idea or "image") in the same way as the matter of our bodies is affected by the matter of other bodies (pesticides, additives, preservatives).

Plotinus makes this clear (*On Beauty* I.6.2): "The things in this world are beautiful by participating in form. . . . A thing is ugly when it is not mastered by some shape" (form, *morphe*). You and I are psychologically in bad shape because our physical world is bent out of shape. And, Plotinus says in the same passage, this is because "when the soul meets with the ugly it shrinks within itself, denies the thing, turns away from it, out of tune, resenting it." Plotinus here describes the clinical condition of the psyche turning itself in for therapy: out of tune, withdrawn, resentful. The ugly makes us neurotic.

If it is the form of things that disturbs the soul, then the task of therapy becomes noticing noxious forms. Every citizen is already concerned with the material nature of things, their ecological value (recycling, protecting, conserving), but the special role of the psychological citizen is the awakening and refining of aesthetic sensitivity.

Why the *psychological* citizen? Because psychoanalysis teaches "seeing through," an intuition into what is invisibly going on, which particular forms are within and behind events —the nose for sniffing, the ear for hearing, the third eye. This means that the job for therapy becomes one of supporting the citizens' formal perceptions, and these require civil courage, just like the personal courage required in personal relationships. Civil courage in an ecological age means not only demanding social justice, but also *aesthetic justice* and the will to make judgments of taste, to stand for beauty in the public arena and speak out about it.

Consciousness of form would make us feel how assaulted and insulted we are all day long by the thoughtless ideas in things: by pretentious buildings, noisy ventilation, oppressive meeting rooms, irritating lighting, vast undetailed parking spaces. The aesthetic eye would require things to be thoughtfully designed. And this attention turned from self to things would begin nursing back to health the soul of the world. Aesthetic hygiene. The therapy session would then be engaged as much in talking of the things and places that affect our moods and reactions as of the people. Deep ecology begins in our aesthetic responses, and the citizen's reentry into political participation starts in his or her declarations of taste.

We would begin to revision substance abuse, perhaps for the first time recognizing that material substances into which we have concretized "abuse"—alcohol, drugs, caffeine, sugar—are acute concentrations of the chronic abuse we unwittingly tolerate and that comes from the abusive substance or form of things. (Substance in older thought was often equated with the form or idea of something rather than with its matter.) You see, it's very possible that we become addicted to material substances by getting into that an-aesthesia, or hyper-aesthesia called an altered state so as not to sense the aesthetic insults we are suffering.

All of a sudden there seems hardly any difference between depth psychology and design. Imagine that! People have been trying to dissolve depth psychology back into religion, saying you go to your analyst like a priest or confessor, and they have been dissolving analysis into Asian wisdom philosophy (analyst as guru); into education (analyst as tutor, mentor, coach); even analyst as mythmaker who rewrites (reframes) the story of your life. I won't even mention other dissolutions into wet-nurse, mother, pseudolover, guide, midwife, and so forth. Here I am coming up with yet one more way of dissolving therapy into something else: interior decorator, architect, urban planner, product designer.

There's a difference, however. I think therapy and design part company at the point where design strives always for the good, that canon of pleasing unity and harmonious balance—"good" taste—whereas therapy as aesthetics would want mainly to sensitize imagination. Now, here's the rub: peeling away the skin and opening the imagination always invites the demonic, and that disrupts "good" design. It's not enough to be in a tastefully decorated room. White bread therapy has all along secured itself in well-appointed consulting rooms, with comfortable chairs and artistic ornamentation. "Good" design can lead to the mediocrity of normal adaptation rather than into the depths of soul.

Depth means death and demons and dirt and darkness and disorder and a lot of other industrial strength *d* words familiar to therapy, like dysfunctional, disease, defense, distortion, drives, drugs, and despair. So design that invites depth will indeed focus on form, but this focus will not exclude the pathological. The problem for the designer, like that for the therapist, is to coordinate the pathological within design, so that psyche's *d*'s are neither excluded like a Disneyland mall nor running around loose like an urban sprawl. Therapy has to be sublime. Terror has to be included in its beauty. So too in design. It seems only our war equipment so far shows this sense of the sublime in design.

By this I mean "good design" elaborates the syndromes so that the pathologized psyche can find a home in the world. To get our souls out of the consulting room and out of our private interior space, we need space in the world for the soul's pathology. Then we can relocate the syndromes. The world can then help carry our disorder, for like cures like. Our obsessive ruminations that go on and on also appear in the repetitious patterns of mosque tiles, friezes, and in Celtic manuscripts; in the hysterical theatrics of baroque altars; in the anorexic emptiness of high, glass-enclosed atriums; in the oppressive claustrophobia of low-ceilinged, overstuffed trailers; in gaudy escape from despair through the slot machine casino and provincial red-light district.

The movies tie landscape, architecture, furniture, light, human movement, and talk into a single shot of soul. The set presents the pathologies of the plot as much as do the dialogue and the action. And the citizens, just come from their therapy hours and now sitting in the audience, gain in the movie house deep psychological learning simply by participating in the aesthetic details displayed through the camera.

These are the models for thinking about therapy that I am looking for because they are rooted in the psyche of the world. As this century closes we have begun to think of the human mind less as a part of physical nature and historical culture, as in Freud's and Jung's day, and more as a participant in media images. Interiority is all in presentation. If design can form the faces of the world into receptacles for the soul's strange predilections, then therapy can notice the things and places where the plot of human lives—and the Greek word we translate as plot was *mythos*—takes actual shape and can begin to care for, even heal, the soul out there.

If we keep pushing this parallel, if we keep revisioning therapy as an aesthetic activity, some surprising consequences emerge. For instance, the clinical hierarchy of psychiatrist on top and art therapist as adjunct on the bottom gets turned upside down. Instead of the expressive arts people—dance, music, and arts staff—getting the least pay and respect, they would become more valued than the Ph.D.'s and M.D.'s. A true Saturnalia would reign in which the dispenser of chemicals (psychiatrist) would drop down to the minor role of strait-jacket man brought in as last resort.

Everything to do with forming—speech, theater, dress, athletics, movement, gesture—would become the indications of improvement rather than insight, understanding, emotional balance, and relating.

This little revolution that raises the aesthetic to top rung would help reimagine therapeutic work as a deanesthetizing, an awakening, lifting the "psychic numbing" that Robert Jay Lifton claims to be the disease of our times. Each thing we notice springs to life: reanimation, reenchantment. The persons hidden in things as their forms speak up, speak out. The clinic becomes truly a madhouse, everything alive, and our concern turns from ourselves to its life. Door, how do you feel that nobody can close you right and you have to be slammed shut? Little plastic cup, do you like being thrown away? Wouldn't you rather be a real hard china mug touched by eager lips many, many times, washed out, kept on a shelf? Big blank bank wall, three stories tall, don't you crave a face with character, aren't you asking for some fantastic graffiti? Parking lot, isn't there any way you could have some fun, have some special cartoons painted on the asphalt, or labyrinths or maps or slogans—some way to make yourself not so endlessly, boringly self-same?

Shifting us into an aesthetic loop will run us into a host of prejudices backed by academic arguments. Such as: aesthetic taste is a subjective personal affair in the eye and tongue of the beholder and cannot provide empirical, sound theory for therapy. Such as: aesthetics is always secondary to the major therapeutic issues like healing, moral improvement, and societal cohesion. Such as: concern with aesthetic form and design is luxury compared with the real problems of material toxicity and the real economic problems that are harming the patient. Beauty never solved anything.

Unlike ancient Egypt and Greece or modern Bali or the bird-feathered, body-painted, masked "primitives" of Papua New Guinea, our culture just can't accept aesthetics as essential to the daily round. The prejudices against beauty expose our culture's actual preference for ugliness disguised as the useful, the practical, the moral, the new, and the quick. The reason for this repression of beauty, in therapy too—for beauty doesn't come into therapy any more than it comes into the mall or the workplace—is nothing less than the taproot of all American culture: puritanism.

You see, taste, as the word itself says, awakens the senses and releases fantasies. Taste remembers beauty; it enjoys pleasure; it tends to refine itself toward more interesting joys. Puritanism would much rather focus on hard realities and moral choices that you have to suffer through and work for. But for me, the greatest moral choice we can make today, if we are truly concerned with the oppressed and stressed lives of our clients' souls, is to sharpen their sense of beauty.

In one stroke we've made peace between the moralistic superego and the pleasure-driven id, ended that chronic war between guilt and greed, denial and lust, shame and appetite. It was a battle created by therapeutic theory, not by the psyche; a theory that says therapy fosters moral improvement (called developmental maturity) rather than the refinement of pleasure. No need for that war if we imagine the superego to be an aesthetic rather than a moral principle. Then the id would not be condemned for its desires or dissuaded from its pleasures, but would be encouraged from above to find for them more fertile fantasies and superior forms.

Otherwise, therapy remains Victorian, stuck in its nineteenth-century moral individualistic origins and its inherent contempt for the world, which ever seduces the id into acting out its pleasures. Each time therapy suggests for a client to make a commitment or decision in order to promote "maturity" and "control," the heroic ego resurrects—that grim-jawed, determined puritan for whom the pleasure principle is a dragon to be slain. Remember this marvelous definition of beauty: "Beauty is pleasure objectified. Beauty is pleasure perceived as a quality of an object" (George Santayana). So the road to beauty follows the signposts of pleasure. And Mr. Clean stands in the way.

Puritanism is no joke. It's the structural fiber of America; it's in our wiring, our anatomy. And, if Freud's right that anatomy is destiny, then we *all* descend from the *Mayflower.* Then there is no hope for an aesthetic awakening. We can't overcome Lifton's "psychic numbing" because its ground is puritanism. We are *supposed* to be sensually numb. That is the fundamental nature of puritan goodness. We are numb because we are anaesthetized, without aesthetics, aesthetically unconscious, beauty repressed. Just look at our land—this continent's astonishing beauty—and then look at what we immigrants, Bibles in hand, priests and preachers in tow, have done to it. Not despoiling, not exploitation, not the profit motive; no, as a people we are void of beauty and devoted to ugliness.

Yet we each know that nothing so moves the soul as an aesthetic leap of the heart at the sight of a fox in the forest, of a lovely open face, the sound of a little melody. Sense, imagination, pleasure, beauty are what the soul longs for, knowing innately that these would be its cure.

Instead our motto is "just say no." And we pass laws to make everything "clean" and "safe"—childproof, tamperproof, fallproof, bugproof. Start each meal with preop prep—iced and chlorinated water to numb the tongue, lips, and palate. Laws to protect children in moving vehicles so they can be kept alive to be ignored, scolded, and homeless. Laws for order, once the inherent *cosmos* (the Greek word for aesthetic order) of the world is no longer sensed. This is the promised land, and the laws are still coming down from the hill. Prohibition is the ultimate law of the land. Watch school kids of eleven and twelve debate on TV whether or not to turn a friend in to his parents for smoking on the sly, because smoking is bad for the friend's health. Is this friendship or is this espionage for the sake of the law?

Maybe ranting is one of the last pleasures the mind *in extremis* can enjoy. So I shall not be stopped. Besides, aesthetics and a therapy of things is also eminently practical. Take our trade war with the Japanese. We believe we have lost out to them because they have better management techniques; because they plan farther ahead; they coordinate better among the bankers, researchers, industrialists, and government; because they work like slaves. These economic reasons don't cut it. There is also an aesthetic reason for their guaranteed quality, which our puritan mind simply cannot even imagine. The Japanese are trained aesthetically early on and live in a culture devoted as much to the chrysanthemum (beauty) as to the sword (efficiency)—to use their symbols.

Japanese people—ordinary people—have hobbies of calligraphy, flower arrangement, dance gesture, paper twisting and cutting. They live in a world of very small detail, which we call quality control. Their eye is trained to notice, their hand to tastefully touch. Watch the sushi chef. Even their language takes immense care. It's *aesthetic* training that gives them the economic edge, even if they get as drunk as we do and as tired.

Puritanism, not aesthetic pleasure, also runs our prisons, the major social disaster of today. At the Kinsey Library in Indiana, I saw piles of drawings, notebooks, and letters confiscated from men in prisons because the material was redolent with erotic fantasies. The material must be taken away from the prisoners because sex in the mind or in art forms is just as bad as sex in action: so says the puritan mind. So instead of imaginative sex, we have buggery, rape, punk system, sadomasochistic violence. Wouldn't it be wiser to bring in artists to direct men in elaborating great erotic murals on the walls of the penitentiary, and dancers brought in to form rituals of the body, if these aesthetic therapeutics reduced, by means of beauty, incidents of rape, jealous knifings, and sadistic pleasures in those same bodies behind those same walls?

Exhausted. The towel, the towel! If all this sounds punch-drunk and hardly an adequate replacement for one hundred years of psychotherapy, let it be. Let it stand. That's the point, isn't it—to break old bottles with new wine, strange as it may taste?

Jim

Recovery

Dear Michael,

It will be charged that what we are saying is wacky. Any more wacky than what now goes on in therapy?

Item: A man reports in a letter to a male journal (*Wingspan,* circulation 120,000) that he raped his girlfriend and that he is now a "recovering rapist," attending an Incest Survivors Twelve-Step program. The girlfriend (now an ex-) is in a "support group for women who have been raped, slowly healing from the betrayal of trust and respect. . . . " What actually happened? "She was passed out asleep on the couch after we'd been drinking. I woke up in the middle of the night horny, so I fucked her. She didn't wake up. . . . I told her about it in the morning. She was furious. 'You raped me!' she said. She called the rape crisis center. . . . "

That he felt "sleazy," as he writes, and learned from this event, and that it brought back the violence perpetrated on him as a little boy is not here at issue. Nor that she was badly used as a soulless object—or did he hope she would wake up? What I question is the infiltration of therapeutic morality into their affair, which had existed for eighteen months previous and was sexual. Is this wacky, or am I out of touch? That she was entered without verbal consent is utterly clear, but was there bodily consent? Had there been pain, it did not awaken her. The new morality and legality declares rape took place according to *his* testimony, even though, in my particular mind, rape means genital contact on command by force and terror.

He is now a "rapist" and identifies himself as such; she is now "slowly" healing from something she did not experience, was only told about. Their love together is over. She finds love in her support group, he in his. And they have new identities: "recoverers."

For more on this new field called date rape (on college campuses) see the piece by Phillip Weiss, *Harper's Magazine,* April 1991, where it becomes clear how puritanism, in order to protect women against male violence—a most worthy aim—has substituted the rule of law for the rule of eros. Where once passivity on the part of either partner was read as acceptance, now it is read as refusal. For there to be any sexual approach at all, there must first be a contract, a verbal agreement of consent. How does one dance the dance, flirt, seduce, parry and thrust, turn away, turn toward, turn on, and move into that awkward entrancing ambivalence that heightens arousal and is necessary for sexual acts, at least among many animals, as long as the rule of law obtains—a law that follows the slogan against drugs, but in reverse: "You must say yes"?

I am accusing therapy of this new puritanism, rather than blaming radical feminists, because the issue turns on *feelings* of injury rather than on acts, witnesses, testimony—and it is settled by recovery, separately, rather than between the parties, together. If a party feels "raped," even if unaware of it, as in the case above, and even if a three-minute pawing, perhaps mutual, is brought to public light three years later (see Weiss), this is rape. My personal feelings determine the definition, yet my personal feelings are subject to the ideational influence of the therapists in the rape crisis center and the college counseling office. They have theory, influence, authority. Frankly, I see little difference in the long run between this creeping therapeutic invasion of private relations and the statist propaganda that persuaded children to denounce their parents and lovers to denounce each other in Europe in the thirties. When my personal feelings, which are subject to collective TV morality, mass hysteria, and therapeutic intervention, determine the definition of an event to the neglect of the actions—their motivation, the circumstances, the past history, the tone of verbal exchanges, the moods of the persons—then we have a simplified legal formula: if I *feel* raped, then I was raped. We are no longer in the realm of real human life; we have entered the wacky world of therapy.

Of course the rape issue has been complicated by power struggles between genders. Always it is discussed as happening between strong males and weaker females. As Weiss says, "[If] all sexual relations took place within the context of potential violence against women . . . [then] it follows that the individual man is always responsible for the general problem. . . ." But recast the scene. Let it be played out by two lesbians or two gays; then it's not a gender issue at all, but one of who initiates, and all responsibility falls on the initiator. Result: don't initiate, make no sexual advances, for any move can be *felt* as rape, even if it is not actually felt. Puritanism wins again, achieving its aim of controlling the sexual impulse through internal fears.

Michael, when I say that therapeutic puritanism has substituted the rule of law for the rule of eros, I don't mean that all these ugly social miseries aren't real. Child molesting, incest, overeating, domestic violence, and all the true addictions to drink, drugs, and sex of course need attention. So too date rape. But the spirit informing these diagnoses, and therefore the treatment of these conditions, has the effect of repressing eros in favor of bureaucratic institutions like crisis centers and legalistic solutions. Logos represses eros, Apollo represses Dionysius, yet all these phenomena—domestic violence, child molestation, sexual harassment, incest, overindulgences, date rape—are strongly, passionately, if not basically erotic Dionysian disorders.

Where does eros go if repressed by logos solutions? I think it appears in the recovery programs, in that deep affection for and blind defense of the group for the good it's doing. That's why recovery works, it's erotic, as far as it goes.

Item: The *New Mexican,* 11 April 1991: Data listed under "Santa Fe Today: These groups will all be meeting: Debtors

Anonymous; Incest Survivors Anonymous; Adult Children of Alcoholics; Survivors of Suicide; Narcotics Anonymous; Co-Ed Incest Therapy Group; Manic-Depressive and Mood Disorder Support Group; Illness, Loss, Grief, Personal Growth Support Group; Arts Anonymous (artists recovering through the Twelve-Step Support Group); Support Group for Persons with Environmental Illness; Bereavement Support Group; La Nueva Vida (group therapy meetings for parents of adolescents who are using drugs/alcohol)." These are the listings. A few others, very few, having to do with civil affairs are also listed—a meeting on a proposed interstate highway project; Kiwanis Club; Disabled Veterans; Citizens Environmental Task Force—but clearly the main thrust is recovery and support. Citizen as patient.

Item: Letter to the *Dallas Observer*. "As a survivor of Delta 1141 plane crash, I entered therapy the day after the crash to help with my fear of flying. . . . I am still in therapy for one simple reason: it has changed my life—so much that I am starting a master's program to become a psychotherapist myself. Most of my friends are now in therapy, and I prefer to date men who have had at least some counseling or are willing to go. . . . I love mental health and hope that more people can discover that therapy is where inner peace begins."

Is this the language of insight or conversion, of psyche or spirit, of therapy or religion? Does "recovery" know a difference? Notice the moralism, the exclusivity in her dating preferences. Eros trapped in the new church. Let's move this in time warp back to Rome, the year 300 or 400: Most of my friends are in the new sect of Christians, and I prefer to be with men who are in the community or at least willing to attend our meetings. I am studying to be a minister of souls myself.

I am not unfair in this comparison with religion; besides, why shouldn't therapy release the soul's native religious concerns? It does and should, only it ought to bring insight into shadow as well, so as not to move simply from one style of unconsciousness to another, one that happens to feel better.

Item: More on the language of therapy. Descriptive phrases about courses for professionals held at the Cape Cod Summer Symposia (1991): "Personologic Assessment and Diagnosis; Therapeutic Stances—Circular Questions and Comments, Structural Assumptions and Interventions; The Construction of

Realities in Systematic Practice; Abnormal Grief Reactions/ Grief Goes Wrong; The Concept of the Selfobject and its Developmental Significance; Direct View of Multifoci Core Neurotic Structure; Has an Ambient Process Been Established?; Designing Effective Home Token Economies; Addressing Issues of Treatment Adherence, Nonadherence, Client Resistance."

This last (client resistance) is no minor matter. "At general psychiatric clinics, 20%–50% of the patients drop out after the first session" (*Newsletter,* Sterling Institute, Stamford, Connecticut, 1990). Michael, do you wonder why? Unfair again? The random selection of language from any specialized field, including a list of course descriptions I myself have given on Jungian thought—myths and dreams, for instance—would sound wacky too. Still, I always tried to keep in touch with soul using words of feelings, figures, and images rather than a specialist language that separates and alienates. Why can't therapist and patient speak the same tongue, not only in the consulting room, *but about it?*

This is, as you implied, more than a difference in rhetorical styles, the poetic versus the theoretical. It reflects the very reason why therapy can't make it over into the world. It talks to itself, a self-isolating, abstracting language much like minimalist nonfigurative painting. Shall we call it, to use that language, iatrogenic narcissism or grandiosity, a narcissism that begins not in the patient but in therapy's grandiosity, to which the patient must adhere and within which the patient shall conform? Patients are patients and not citizens, first because they are trapped in transference, then because they are trapped in doctrinal compliance that reduces them to childhood, and, not least, because they are trapped in therapeutic language. Their speaking about themselves has replaced their speaking from themselves. For further advice, see Woody Allen and read Thomas Szasz and Ronald Laing. Or, to put it another way: is there recovery from therapeutic language? Am I, Michael, by means of the tough talk, the street talk, the rhetorical style we've chosen for this book, beginning my own recovery program? Am I a recovering psychotherapist, you, my sponsor, my mentor back into the city?

Item: The *Boston Globe* (29 April 1990) reports that "each week, 200 types of 12–step recovery groups such as Alcoholics

Anonymous or Overeaters Anonymous draw 15 million Americans to 500,000 meetings across the nation." In Boston, there is a national self-help clearinghouse for finding the network to meet your therapeutic needs, your kind of recovery.

Meanwhile, where are the small political meetings, the ward heelers of yesteryear? Where are the Irish, the Italian, the Polish groups—the little ethnic and neighborhood groups—who met about city power (yes, graft and nepotism too), but who came together to push politics? There was a common cause as well as self-advancement and protection (support).

Before I go on, I must say why recovery groups have been, and still are, necessary. Someone, somewhere must pick up the pieces. The world is getting worse; ask the animals, ask the trees, ask the wind—but also ask the citizens declared mentally ill. "Not since the 1820s have so many mentally ill individuals lived untreated in public shelters, on the streets, and in jails" (1989 report of the Public Citizen Health Research Group and the National Alliance for the Mentally Ill, a report called "laudable" by the American Psychiatric Association, despite the report's hefty attack on psychiatric care in the United States). "There is near total breakdown in public psychiatric service in the United States," writes the psychiatrist who is lead author of the report.

Item: We are back to the 1820s because criminality and psychic breakdown are now confused: the poor, the misfits, the backward, the ill, the crazy, and the criminal are again held in the same compounds, like the hospices in the Middle Ages, even if these compounds are now the streets. For example, in Idaho the mentally ill are regularly brought to jail first and fingerprinted before seeing an "examiner." In Boston, the Pine Street Shelter houses half a thousand mentally ill people each night, making it the state's largest mental institution. The largest *de facto* mental hospital in the United States is the Los Angeles County jail, 3,600 of whose inmates are mentally ill. All this is intensified beyond your or my imaginational powers by racism. Michael, what would it be like today to be a seventeen-year-old, or even twenty-seven-year-old African American man, with a few quirks like us? If we were alive at all, we'd be in jail, criminal and crazy both.

Of course the trickle-down, rip-off, national security gang that has been running (spelled: *ruining*) the nation for the past decades would question the diagnosis "mentally ill," so that with one sweep the problem disappears and the people formerly so classified (and felt for) are no longer a concern of the citizen but a burden on the taxpayer, labeled as welfare cases or homeless, people who didn't make the dream, like we literate suburbanites who read about them in reports.

But it's not all bad. Recovery groups do lift men and women out of their sofas and away from the tube to meet regularly, faithfully, with deep emotions. In today's language, bonding is going on. And, nomadic as we are (20 percent of the populace moves each year; in five years every statistical citizen has changed address, all 250 million of us), recovery groups will take us to heart wherever we go in this land.

There's plenty for a recovery group to give their love to besides one another; there is the world.

During Franklin D. Roosevelt's presidency, recovery meant dealing with one-third of a nation, which he said were ill fed, ill clothed, and ill housed. He invented the NRA, the National Recovery Act. With a little spin and a little shove, all the 500,000 recovery meetings going on each week all across the U.S.A. could turn from individualism to the body politic, recovering some of the political concern for the plight of the nation that necessitated recovery groups in the first place. As I see it, we cannot recover alone or even in support groups. We need communal recovery, recovery of communal feeling, and each group provides the nucleus of that feeling.

"Communal feeling" (*Gemeinschaftsgefuhl*) is what Alfred Adler, one of the therapeutic pioneers besides Freud and Jung, regarded as the final goal of all therapy. Today, communal feeling is arising from the common sense of victimization. The groups gather because they feel individually disempowered, abused, victimized. Yes, we group according to our symptoms, but we group as well around shared compassion as victims of brutality, of compulsion, of disease like AIDS. We have come to feel ourselves as survivors, which means that behind the support group, at its root and soul, is death. In the group is a subliminal recognition of a dying civilization. We are each marginal, liminal, being carried along by what we do not comprehend, and a kind of group love is being born at the fringes, among the victims of an abusive system. We gather (huddle) in the boxcar, hoping for empowerment, taking one day at a time, because we smell the gas ovens if we think too far ahead. But where are the guards, who are they? Would we not do better to look outward at what is railroading us rather than at one another for comfort and courage if the train's destination, despite what we do and say, is death?

Only this apocalyptic vision gives justification for the ubiquitous use of the words *victim* and *survivor* in recovery groups. Otherwise, to use these terms is a travesty of the Holocaust and the victims and survivors of the political genocide destructions, the death camps, massacres, and species extinctions that have marked our century.

We huddle because we still believe we die alone and ask for protection from the group to keep this basic belief of our culture from coming too close. Our imagination of death is Jesus alone in the garden denied, on the cross forsaken. Fundamental to the doctrine of individualism is that you die alone. We believe that each of us makes his or her own death. Even if comfortable, clutching at the coverlet, loved ones present to ease the parting and to remember the last words, we still believe we meet death alone.

Ours is a religion of individual death. Maybe individualism begins in our idea of death, an ego's idea of death, which is also to say that the separated ego and the idea of an individual self are representatives of death and therefore destructive. Perhaps for this reason people in recovery so often attest to the group having saved their lives from death. *They have been saved by communal feeling from individuality.*

Death has become a substitute word in our philosophy (existentialists, Heidegger, Unamuno, Spinoza, Socrates) for aloneness. Yet, as I move more and more toward communal feeling, death occupies me less and less, and the meditation on self calls with ever-weakening voice. For the meditation of self on self is but another name for the meditation on death. I guess that's really why I once rudely called meditation "obscene."

That we die alone is an idea of the individualistic self, is part of its dread and part also of an individuality that believes its life is its own and so too must be its death. A person owns it all and death will take it all away. As Jesus said, you can't die rich and famous. But we do die rich if we shift the images to a

Mediterranean village funeral procession, the slow march, the trumpets, the casket through the streets, everyone somber and celebrating. Or a Protestant burgher's *Festmahl* (funeral feast) in a Baltic city, with food and drink and flowers, with anecdotes and memories. Or an Irish wake. These are the ultimate recovery groups flamboyantly demonstrating that we do not die alone, that the passed away are passing over and through the communal body.

We do not die alone. We join ancestors and all the little people, the multiple souls who inhabit our night world of dreams, the complexes we speak with, the invisible guests who pass through our lives, bringing us the gifts of urges and terrors, tender sighs, sudden ideas. They are with us all along, those angels, those demons. Evenings when I go to sleep, fourteen angels guard my keep. The freak companions—they are indestructible.

Once individualism dissolves its notion of self, and self relaxes into a communal feeling beyond bonding (tying, tightening, gluing, adhering, obligating), you can't possibly die alone, because there is no alone. We are simply a repository of *Gemeinschaftsgefuhl.* Not compassion, or altruism or empathy, and not the Other, for these are all constructs and commandments of the I, that first person singular. Rather and simply, *existence is multiple* and does not cease with your cessation. The chord, the flow, the herd, the hive dances on. By this I do not mean a New Age unity of all things. No, I mean that support is always there because the very ground is everywhere else. I am never only myself, always out of myself, out of control. And I can never recover.

Jim

On Being Practical

Michael,

"How?" you ask. How to analyze the world and discover soul in things? How to do therapy with ashtrays and toasters? How to turn analysis into a cell in which the revolution is prepared? How is the soul made in a practical context? You want some practical examples. What do I mean *practically?* I will try to answer, but there is something major to clear up first.

We have to address the idea of the practical before we can begin to be practical. What do we mean by *practical;* why do we separate thought and practicality; why are ideas merely ideas and not practical?

Critics of the American style of mind from de Tocqueville in the early nineteenth century on down have said this is not a land of ideas. We are superb at implementing, at making useful (practical?) inventions, but we are not philosophers. Europeans think and Americans apply. The major psychological ideas with which we practice come from Europe. This is the case whether in introspective psychology, laboratory psychology, child psychology, or, of course, depth psychology. Only Harry Stack Sullivan, B. F. Skinner, and Carl Rogers of the classics are truly natives, and certainly their strength is not in their ideas. Just look at the "furriners" in the ranks of therapy: Laing, Bateson, Erikson, Frankl, Minuchin, Alice Miller, Kübler-Ross, Watzlawick, Gendlin, Szasz, Lacan, Piaget, Bion, Kohut, Perls (to say nothing of the first generation: Freud, Jung, Reich, Reik, Rank, Rorschach, Stekel, Horney, Adolf Meyer). William James is probably the one great exception, yet he spent many years in Europe, as did, I believe, Henry Murray. (One of my own great difficulties is due to the many years I spent in Switzerland, so that I've never quite made a comfortable connection with the American way of psychology.) I have never offered a testable hypothesis, applied for a research grant, produced a program, found a gadget or a procedure that could be named after me, invented a "practical" test, elaborated an experimental model, or examined a particular population. I work mainly in a chair thinking, on my feet talking, in a library reading; it all goes on in my head while my body lives life. In this way, my work can be accused of being a head trip and not practical, because we believe, in America, that the head's activities—this head so full of blood and flushed with excitements of spirit—is not *practical.* But it's not the mind that's impractical or heady; it's the burned-out, ashen, conceptual language of academia and television that we have all been taught is the correct expression of thinking. It's this neutral, flatland language that is heady, not the impassioned head, popping ideas like grasshoppers.

My idea about ideas in America is that we burn them up too quickly. We get rid of them by immediately putting them into practice. We only know one thing to do with an idea: apply it; convert it into something usable. And it dies right there in the conversion. It loses its generative power. The Greeks spoke of a *logos spermatikos,* the generating word or seminal thought. As these are put into practice, concretized, they no longer generate further ideas in the realm of ideas. This sterilizing of ideas happens often when I give a talk. Someone in the audience asks, "How does that work?" "Can you give an example?" These are questions from what's classically called the Practical Intellect, whereas my talk was ideational, another aspect of reason altogether. In classic philosophy you don't mix kinds of thinking without destroying discourse altogether.

Besides, when a speaker puts out an idea and then answers a question about how it works, he or she is depriving the listener of the full impact of the idea and where it might carry the listener if pondered. My answer tends to channel the thought in only one direction, generally my direction. Recently I gave a long, complex paper on the colors white and black, of course intending implications for racism. But if I explain directly what my thought means for the race problem, I narrow the impact of the ideas into social politics only. *Explain* means to lay out flat.

Not only narrowed/flattened—my answering means I'm doing the thinking for the questioner, whose job it is to start thinking, not asking. That's why she or he came to the talk in the first place. Again, it's that latent child in the American head who believes himself, herself, unknowing (innocent), who asks questions and expects someone else to carry the work of thinking. That's why the interview in *L.A. Weekly* went so well. We were thinking along together, pushing out idea after idea, having fun with them, and feeling their implications along the way. Had you been questioning me, aiming at practicality, the flow would have stopped. Let me insert a passage here:

> Our society offers places where you can let your feelings out. You may go to group therapy or to sensitivity training, and no matter how silly or strange the feelings, they are received. There

are also places where you can improve your will: the gym or spa to work out, willing yourself to lift that contraption another twenty times, or to an EST meeting to develop your self-control and willful determination.

But where do you go to play with ideas? There is Church, where an idea may be presented to you in a sermon—more likely, though, it's a judgment, not an idea. There is TV; on "60 Minutes" there may be three ideas, presented as pros and cons, as if the point of an idea were to force you into a choice. Newspaper editorials urge ideas on you. But you aren't shown how to play with them. Where can we go to imagine an idea and move it further? In none of these places—Church, TV, Newspaper—do you let the idea swim way out and reel it back in again. You don't just relish the delight of the idea in itself.

One of the great difficulties in our American life is that we don't have places for entertaining ideas. And that is precisely what we're supposed to do with an idea: entertain it. This means having respect for ideas themselves: letting them come and go without demanding too much from them at first, like their origins (who said that first), their popularity (what if everybody thought that), their logic (but that doesn't fit with what you just said). Why can't they be a little crazy? We admit our feelings are crazy. We all have crazy feelings that might want to do this or say that. But maybe our ideas have arms and legs, too, and are crazy and want to get out and meet other ideas, air themselves, spend time with each other in public. The ideas themselves, not the people in whom they occur, just the ideas wanting to appear and be received, welcomed, entertained for a while.

What we usually do with an idea is put it into practice. Someone says "Oh, that's a good idea!" and he means: "Oh boy, I can save four bucks this way!" or "Smart. I can do something now that I couldn't have done before because I had a bright idea. I can hang the strap like this instead of like that."

That's what makes a "good idea" in our society. A good idea means useful, practical, immediately applicable. Isn't it a shame that we can value ideas only when we have them in a harness. I think it breaks their spirit. We don't let them run loose, to see where they might take us if we just fed them with a little attention and trusted their autonomy.

If you watch one of the more intelligent interviewers on TV, Dick Cavett, say, even he, when an idea breaks in, often says: "Well, it's just an idea I had." They move away from it. There is a little anxiety that the idea might get out of hand. "What will I do with that!" There is no skill in handling it, no way to dribble round the floor with it.

The media do not really favor ideas. They mix them with opinions. We have plenty of opinions on most everything—but opinions are personal. We get pugnacious. They involve belief. Ideas are much easier to live with; they don't ask to be believed in, and an idea doesn't belong to you even when you "have" one. You can become friends with an idea, and after a while it will show you more of itself, or you and it may get tired of each other and separate.

One thing is sure: ideas don't belong to academics. You don't have to have academic knowledge to have ideas. Knowledge might help work with the idea, enrich it, discriminate it more finely, or recognize its history—that it's not the first time that idea ever moved through someone's mind. So knowledge may save you the embarrassment of inflation and help you pick up some skills about polishing ideas. But knowledge is not necessary. You can distinguish things you have learned from ideas you have. Keeping these distinct—knowledge and ideas—ought to help you to feel that you can ideate without an academic degree. When an idea comes to mind, it asks first of all to be listened to and that you attempt to understand it. If knowledge helps do this, then fine. But first entertain your visitor.

That word "entertain" means to hold in between. What you *do* with an idea is hold it between—between your two hands. On the one hand, acting or applying it in the world and on the other hand, forgetting it, judging it, ignoring it, etc. So when these crazy things come in on you unannounced the best you can do for them is think them, holding them, turning them over, wondering awhile. Not rushing into practice. Not rushing into associations. This reminds of that: this is just like that. Off we go, away from the strange idea to things we already know. Not judging. Rather than judging them as good and bad, true or false, we might first spend a little time with them.

As I said, a "good idea" is a bad idea! I mean a good idea tends to imply a better mousetrap, ingenuity. "Genius"—which is your own guiding spirit, a daimon or angel, and who may be the transmitter of the ideas that come into your head—has now become "ingenuity," being clever, solving a problem. We lose the genius in ingenuity. Putting the idea in practice stops the play of ideas, the entertainment from going on. We put them into practice, however, in order to test them. In America we don't seem to know other ways of testing except by practice.

How else could we evaluate an idea? Is the idea fertile, fecund? Does it make you think? Is it surprising, shocking? Does it stop you up from habits and bring a spark of reflection? Is it delightful to think it? Does it seem deep? Important? Needing to be told? Does it wear out quickly? Especially: What does the idea itself want from you, why in the world did it decide to light in your mind?

This requires that you ponder it, which means weigh it, feel its weight, that it is substantial and has some gravity. Pondering is an action of its own and keeps you holding the idea, from letting it go into other kinds of action before it is fully appreciated. Meanwhile, you get a better feel of the idea.

The word idea supposedly originates in the Greek word *eidos,* which means both something seen like a form and a way of seeing like an eye, a perspective. So, ideas are not only things you can pick up and ponder. They also give you eyes, new ways of seeing things. Ideas are already operating in our perspectives, the way we look at things. We take our usual ideas for granted, and so, ideas have us rather than we have them.

Does this piece explain a little more why I am cautious about "being practical"? I worry lest I cage the birds and harness the horses to my own uses. Too soon, too soon. I want to *think* what comes into my mind asking that it be thought about. You know, to have an idea and thinking about the idea are two different things, and being practical often means skipping over the hard thinking part.

Each person has some talent. It's rare to have more than one. Mine is ideation, not practical, useful invention. I am a generator, elaborator, and scathing critic of ideas. I fall in love with them. I can't pretend otherwise, as if I knew what to do with the ideas. All I know is what not to do with them. Whether the ideas that have come to me and that I have fostered and pruned are viable or will bear fruit, I can't tell, but I refuse to pretend that their fruit is determined only by the one test of applicability to problem solving. (I even question the effort to solve problems, preferring to see them, sometimes, as permanent emblems under which the psyche struggles for more and more clarity. Let's call them "troubles." Can you imagine a blues singer going on about *problems?*)

For ideas to be therapeutic, that is, beneficial to the soul and body politic, they must gather in to themselves, garnering force, building strength, like great movers of the mind's furniture, so that the space we inhabit is rearranged. Your thoughts, feelings, perceptions, memories have to move around in new ways, because the furniture has been moved. A long-lasting idea, like a good poem or a strong character in a movie or a novel, continues to affect your practical life without ever having been put there. Ideas that live, live in us and through us into the world. Viable ideas have their own innate heat, their own vitality. They are living things too. But first they have to move your furniture, else it is the same old you, with your same old habits, trying to apply a new idea in the same old way. Then, nothing happens at all except the loss of the idea as "impractical" because of your haste to make it "practical."

Best to you,

Jim

Second, Third, and Fourth Sight

Dear Jim,

I'll give you a realm of experience that psychotherapy is terrified (and I mean terrified) of recognizing, writing of, theorizing about, or considering in any way—officially. At the same time, I know therapists who make a place for this realm in the consulting room, take it seriously, and even (truth be told) invoke it. Jung did too, but he had the rep to get away with it and was king of his own hill. The shrinks I'm speaking of are wary, even frightened, of letting these beliefs be known officially.

What am I talking about? I'll give you a few experiences.

I am making love, and I look down, and I don't see a face, I see an orb of light. This is not a metaphor. I *don't* see a face; I see, in the dark, an orb of fuzzy, barely glowing light, and through that light, just barely, a kind of face. The light glows stronger. I lift myself higher and I see not a body beneath me, but a vague bodylike outline of shimmering gray-white light. It looks like I could reach my hand through it. This dazes me, frightens me a little, because I know that for a moment we've slipped into the Other World.

It lasts only a few breaths. The strangeness of it jolts me back and I see and feel bodies again, and, safe now, I have the luxury of remembering how beautiful it was, what I saw. If I'd been able to relax with it, perhaps I'd have seen her spirit-body far longer, perhaps she would have seen mine, perhaps . . . but who knows?

The point here is that many people will say I didn't *see* anything, I imagined—though they are fairly sure that they see what *they* see. People are trained to blink away this sort of sight or to treat it comically or with an air that says, "Yeah, that was weird and maybe interesting but it doesn't mean anything."

It doesn't mean anything, for instance, that your phone rings and, before you answer, you know who it is. It doesn't mean anything that, especially while driving, you will without thought suddenly turn your head and find yourself looking into the eyes of another driver who's looking at you, or you'll be looking at someone and they'll suddenly turn and look directly into your eyes. I'd bet this happens at least once each day to everyone who drives a car. People are communicating nonphysically, telepathically, and utterly ignoring it.

Which is stranger, the communication or the decision to ignore it?

Of course, if you discount such very simple things, things that happen all the time, if you're so unconscious of them that they're experienced merely as reflex and they don't even cause a blip on your inner screen, then you won't be seeing shimmering, barely glowing orbs of light while you're making love, either. And you may scoff or even bristle at people who say they have, in order to protect your own state of unconsciousness, because small things in that realm are happening to you every week, if not every day, and to be conscious of them could mean changing your worldview. But which are you going to believe, your own senses or how you've been *taught* the world works?

I'm certainly not the first to point out that there is a great deal of pressure only to see what our culture permits us to see and not to see what is not permitted—or, if we see it, not to credit it and certainly not to speak of it. If we do speak of it, much less write of it, we are sure to be shunted off by a great many into a conceptual never-never land labeled mystic or spiritual or metaphysical or New Age—especially by Western intellectuals, even "radical" Western intellectuals, who are shilling for the old order because they are intimidated by any restructuring that can be labeled mystic or pagan.

Of course, we all know that the penalty for such seeing can be a lot more severe than disapproval. Many people, especially young people, are forced onto medication and/or into hospitals for seeing something like I saw, particularly when they see it more than once and have the naïveté or bad judgment to speak of it.

When a culture has gained a certain kind of power partly through *not* seeing, or ignoring various modes of seeing, then that culture will defend its not-seeing by any means necessary. Entire ("primitive") cultures expert at these types of seeing have been wiped out, then historically devalued, because the materialist Western worldview cannot bear to be questioned (a sure sign of how easily it is intimidated, that is, how unsure of itself it really is).

Again, an interesting phenomenon is how even the so-called radical elements of the dominant culture buy into its fundamental assumption that only a fairly narrow spectrum of the material world has validity. We see this in political "radicals" who rail against any sort of mysticism as insular or reactionary and insist, like their corporate counterparts, that everything be focused on material issues; we see it in psychology, where enormous funds are being spent to try and prove that all inner experience is chemically motivated; in academic literary circles, where "text" is all and "content" is considered practically accidental; and in the major, public cultural organs, where, for instance, writers of the Raymond Carver school, who focus microscopically on what I would not even call behavior but reflex, are considered "realistic."

Of course, a culture as manically and massively materialist as ours creates materialist behavior in its people, especially in those people who've been subjected to nothing but the destruction of imagination that this culture calls education, the destruction of autonomy it calls work, and the destruction of activity it calls entertainment. Such "education," "work," and "entertainment" (all focused solely on the material) in turn create behavior that is then cited as justifying the assumptions of the culture. It's a very vicious and efficient circle.

Is it any wonder that people hemmed into such behavior from birth are, at every level of society, turning to drugs by the tens of millions? And what are they using drugs for? To break out of the strictures of our corporately programmed environment of "education," "work," and "entertainment"—to satisfy, in other words, their craving for nonmaterial experience. Acid for visions, heroin and pot for differing sensations of otherworldliness, coke and crack for a hit of the energy that's siphoned off by their environment. The dominating culture *has to* make these drugs crimes, even though most drug-related criminal activity occurs *because* the drugs are illegal, occurs for the sake of procuring the drugs and not as a result of the drugs' effect on consciousness. Trying to break through to nonmaterial experience is the *real* number one crime in America today. The so-called drug war is a war against seeing reality in any but a strictly materialist, Puritan way.

But no culture has ever been as monolithic as its rulers and historians would prefer it to be. Nonmaterial experience is being lived and investigated on every level of society; the drug culture is only the most obvious case. Another is the growing body of so-called New Age (that is, nonmaterial) thought. Another is "deep ecology." Others occur within science itself —relativity physics first, and then systems theory, now chaos theory, and the various investigations of so-called psychic phenomena (more accurately, "seeing" phenomena).

A powerful example is this experiment done by Charles Tart, University of California at Davis, in the early sixties:

Person A is put into a sensory deprivation room and wired for brain waves, skin resistance, heart rate, muscular activity, and respiratory changes. Person B is put into another such room, also wired, and is electrically shocked at random intervals. Person A is then told to guess exactly when Person B is being shocked.

The results were as follows: Person A's *conscious* guesses "showed no relation to the actual events." But Person A's "polygraph reading indicated significant physiological changes at those instants when Person B was randomly shocked." The conclusion: "We may say the event did not register on the subject's 'conscious mind.' But obviously he *was* conscious of the event—on a fundamental biological level. The subject's *body* apparently knew of these happenings that his roof-brain did not know of." (The experiment is described in Tart's book *Altered States of Consciousness* and discussed by Joseph Chilton Pearce in *Exploring the Crack in the Cosmic Egg.*)

Our Western culture has put most of us out of touch with these faculties. But an Australian aboriginal tracker can precisely follow a random human trail *a year old*—a trail that has left no physical trace—and Australian desert tribes will suddenly get up and walk for days to a spot where there will be a brief rainfall. Muslims in religious ecstasy will cut their skin with no bleeding and no scars, and fire walkers in India walk the coals not only with no injury to their feet but also with no damage to their robes. These are only a few of hundreds of well-documented abilities by "primitive" peoples with the same bodies we have—abilities that include nonmaterial healing and lovemaking, and the perception of beauties undreamed of by all those Raymond Carver imitators.

"You can see beauty if you look quickly to the side" is how it was put by the Swedish poet Tomas Tranströmer.

So you are making love, and suddenly you see the spirit-body of your lover and feel your own spirit-body materialize. So out of the blue you think of someone you haven't thought of in years, and the next day you see them on the street or receive a letter from them. So you are in L.A. and speaking on the phone to a friend in Oakland about an old movie, and you learn later that this was the same moment that his wife, while out shopping, went into a video store and rented that very film (they had never discussed the film together, in fact her husband had never heard of it before). So you hear a voice, perhaps of one who has died, warning or guiding or even just kibitzing. Or you feel an energy in you that can, you rashly think, heal others, and you try it, and it does—sometimes. Or you simply walk in unexplained beauty for an unexpected day.

There is so much, Jim, so very, very much, that the West in general and psychotherapy in particular has shunted aside because it simply hasn't had the conceptual framework to deal with it. At each stage of development we've had to pretend that we know everything, when really we know so little. When Ginger and I were together, sometimes in the course of one of my dreams I'd hear something said in another room or hear a sentence shouted some distance away, and it would turn out to be (this became a joke with us) something that somebody had said in *her* dream. Or she would hear something in mine (actually, I'd usually hear and she'd usually see—interesting difference). And where does this leave all the theories of dreams, from the Freudian to the biochemical?

Theoretically,

Michael

Mediocrity

Dear Michael,

Let's keep working away at why the world is getting worse—getting worse not only in the usual sense, about Amazon forests and dead dolphins. That is the easy part to see, if not easy to correct. Our job is to show how *psychology* contributes to making the world worse.

Suppose we entertain the idea that psychology makes people mediocre; and suppose we entertain the idea that the world is *in extremis,* suffering an acute, perhaps fatal, disorder at the edge of extinction. Then I would claim that what the world needs most is radical and original extremes of feeling and thinking in order for its crisis to be met with equal intensity. The supportive and tolerant understanding of psychotherapy is hardly up to this task. Instead it produces counterphobic attitudes to chaos, marginality, extremes. Therapy as sedation: benumbing, an-aesthesia so that we calm down, relieve stress, relax, find acceptance, balance, support, empathy. The middle ground. Mediocrity.

You see, Michael, for me the job of psychotherapy is to open up and deal with—no, not deal with, *encourage,* maybe even inflame—the rich and crazy mind, that wonderful aviary (the image is from Plato) of wild flying thoughts, the sex-charged fantasies, the incredible longings, bloody wounds, and the museums of archaic shards that constitute the psyche.

Nothing about the psychic stuff that comes into therapy with the patient is mediocre, except, perhaps, the first level that is soon peeled away, that normal appointment-keeping, carefully reported early interview, and except, perhaps, the conceptual rationalisms of the therapist's language. Soon enough, the fears and desires and dreams are as mad as a tropical jungle and as salacious as Forty-second Street. I challenge psychotherapy's cool green consulting rooms, the soothing images and framed diplomas, because they are calming and cooling the *valuable* madness in our society so that psychology has become part of Henry Miller's *Air-Conditioned Nightmare,* his phrase for the U.S.A.

I know that the usual perception of America is that it is dangerously wild and crazy; that we should be grateful to therapy for what sedation and reason it can provide; that if anything we need more therapy to prevent crime and rape and violence, the acting out of hatred, jealousy, and greed. But this view of therapy associates it with security, the consulting room as a branch of your local police station. It's not suppression of American madness that we need but rather the *forming* of it. And form means art. Art as formed madness.

I feel so worked up about this theme that I am not saying it well. But give me a break. Don't read this letter to argue with it. Let me ride it out, and let's put it in the book, if only because it won't quite be appropriate, won't quite be mediocre.

You and I know this is a white bread country. The malls are made of white bread, the bread is made of white bread, and psychology is turning people into white bread. The genuine leaven that can ferment and erupt through the soggy, soggy dough is American psychopathology: sex, gambling, addictions, violence, insane religions, adolescent fads and attitudes —that world of which you write and to which your novel is a testament. (In case our readers don't know your novel, it's called *Night Time, Losing Time.*) Only the unconscious can save us: in your pathology is your salvation. Otherwise, the white bread ego rules and we will have Dan Quayle in the White House, the man without a quirk. I don't want psychotherapy working for Dan Quayle, normalizing and eliminating psychopathology, for I see our psychopathology as the "rough beast" in Yeats's poem, who is actually the Second

Coming, as the poem says in its very title. Psychotherapy has to take sides with the beast, walk with it, touching its shaggy fur, remembering it lives at the edge, along with Robert Bly's Wildman, demanding a place in the mall, like the Greek Furies were given a place in Athens. This is the "relationship" on which therapy must focus, the relationship with the beast; otherwise psychotherapy's clients become Barbie and Ken "working on their relationship," plastic dolls like Dan Quayle.

This sounds elitist, contemptuous, and anarchistic, as if I want all hell to break loose and the lions to roam in the streets. But is there no alternative to locking away the madness and the violence so that Disneyland may be kept safe for Pat Boone? We have one of the highest percentages of people in the penal system of all industrialized nations, of *all* nations. Three percent of the adult males in America are right now involved in the penal system: in jail, awaiting trial, appealing, booked, fined, subpoenaed, on parole, on probation, being pardoned, being executed. Repression does not work; it only makes the repressed invisible, but, as Freud says, the repressed returns, is not subject to time, and comes back in the same way—or worse. By advocating pathology I am not letting the lions loose in the streets, I am not promulgating permissiveness that breeds homelessness, poverty, and despair, a Republican permissiveness called free market economics. The choice is anyway not between punitive and permissive. The choice is between repression and art, and in this choice the valences are reversed. Art requires painful discipline; it is like a punition. Repression, by packaging its denial in the mediocrity of white bread and a smiling "have a nice day," becomes a universal permit for illusory happiness.

Mediocrity is no answer to violence. In fact, it probably invites violence. At least the mediocre and the violent appear together as in the old Western movies—the ruffian outlaw band shooting up main street and the little white church with the little white schoolteacher wringing her hands. To cool violence you need rhythm, humor, tempering; you need dance and rhetoric. Not therapeutic understanding.

Therapy has tried to stay in the middle, neither punitive nor permissive. It does genuinely seek to work with psychopathology so that it is no longer destructive to self and others.

Its balanced, middle-ground position wants both the individual and the system to survive, by accommodating the individual as best as possible to the system. The system as such, however, remains outside its purview.

Nevertheless, many psychopathologies seem to be focused on the system, as if symptoms are not merely personal disorders but social, even political, statements. Drunkenness, absenteeism, illiteracy and quitting school, fraud, defacing public property, noncompliance with regulations, cheating institutions—these are symptoms too, though not ones trumpeted about like child abuse and drug addiction. We need to read these symptoms as belonging to the body politic and not only the individual patient. Otherwise, we therapists continue down the middle of the road bringing people into line so that they can function within the system and cope. We continue to locate all symptoms universally within the patient rather than also in the soul of the world. Maybe the system has to be brought into line with the symptoms so that the system no longer functions as a repression of soul, forcing the soul to rebel in order to be noticed.

I can think of a middle ground, but not the one therapy tries to work, because that middle ground, I believe, is mediocrity, compromising symptom and system in such a way that in the end the symptom disappears and the "successful" case reenters society. The middle ground I would propose is the arts, in which the symptom becomes the marginal informing spirit or hounding dog that never lets go, driving the psyche to the edge.

I've been straining for decades to push psychology over into art, to recognize psychology as an art form rather than a science or a medicine or an education, because the soul is inherently imaginative. The primary function of the human being is to imagine, not to stand up straight, not to make tools and fire, not to build communities or hunt and till and tame, but to *imagine* all these other possibilities. And we go on imagining and imagining, irrepressibly. The repressed returns as symptoms, so our symptoms are actually the irrepressible imagination breaking through our adapted mediocrity. Hence, the pronouncement: "In your pathology is your salvation"—not salvation as adaptation, but salvation from adaptation. All our pathologies are imaginings, and so therapy's job is primarily to deal with the symptoms, just as Freud tried at the beginning, but now because the symptoms are the imaginings of the psyche seeking a better form.

When we were walking through the Los Angeles Museum, you reminded me of a passage in *Re-Visioning Psychology:* "I am working toward a psychology of the soul that is based on a psychology of image. Here I am suggesting both a poetic basis of mind and a psychology that starts neither in the physiology of the brain, the structure of language, the organization of society, nor the analysis of behavior, but in the processes of imagination."

If we begin in a poetic basis of mind, then psychologists have to be at home in the poetic, first of all, and that means not white bread. If our methods are to meet the madness in America, that eruptive violence, there must be madness in our methods. And, since our methods are our own personalities, which model the "cured psychological together okay person," then we therapists must admit the idiosyncratic craziness that is inherent to the poetic basis of mind, its fountain of strange imaginings. Our obligation to the soul calls for outrage and outrageousness, no warm support for compromising mediocrity.

Bob Stein—and I shall mention his book too, since it is a good one, *Incest and Human Love*—said that the profession of analyst, which he has practiced for close to forty years, has all but killed him because it has all but killed his craziness. Now, of course, there is crazy and crazy—a kind that you can and might want to live with and a kind that you cannot bear. I believe Bob is talking of both kinds, the bearable and the unbearable, which often flow into each other. His complaint, however, goes to the heart of professional mediocrity, for he claims that the therapeutic profession is so moralistic, so repressive, so competitive, so concerned with status, credentials, and respectability as well as distinguishing oneself and protecting oneself from the psyche of the patient, that he cannot age into his craziness, a major prerogative—if not necessity—of healthy old age. Psychotherapy oppresses those who practice it, and this atmosphere of obsessive pathological mediocrity is brilliantly sketched in Janet Malcolm's book *The Impossible Profession.*

There is a much deeper issue here than crazy versus sane, art versus therapy, or how to reimagine therapy as a practice deriving from a poetic basis of mind. This issue goes to the roots of the *political role of therapy.* If I am right that a major task of therapy is to work with the pathological ferment in the body politic, then compliance with normalization subverts its political task. (The antipsychiatry movement of Laing and Cooper said this in the sixties. But it seems already forgotten. And Ronnie Laing, M.D., is dead, protesting with his last breath as he lay stricken on a tennis court: "No bloody doctors.")

If therapy imagines its task to be that of helping people cope (and not protest), to adapt (and not rebel), to normalize their oddity, and to accept themselves "and work within your situation; make it work for you" (rather than refuse the unacceptable), then therapy is collaborating with what the state wants: docile plebes. Coping simply equals compliance. Community mental health, with its pamphlets giving advice on every "dysfunction" from thumb sucking to cock sucking, actually serves to keep the people pacified and satisfied with their white bread. Maybe I am an idealist, but I still believe therapy is engaged also in raising consciousness. I know this is not the intention of the behavior therapists. They seek simply to help people live their lives with less suffering and more freedom. Yet the actual styles of the therapists who model the cured, the straight and free person, show what is meant by less suffering and more freedom. These terms come to mean social adaptation, compliance with the rules of the system (such as licensing, insurance eligibility, and the continuing education racket), keeping a low profile and a low voice, out of trouble, less concrete, less spontaneously reactive, more reflective, less emotional, more conceptual. The therapist as person who has finally got his shit together. But, Michael, *what if the shit is not yours* to begin with, nor your parents', but George Bush's shit—and by that I mean a vast systematic denial of what truly matters to the heart and soul of us as citizens? Then adaptation may signify compromise so that dysfunction becomes a political statement. *Non serviam* rather than *Fiat mihi.* "I will not serve" rather than "let it be done to me."

I am talking about myself now, Michael, myself as a dysfunctional therapist. Imagine my predicament. I love therapy—

and have come to hate it. I was the truest believer who ever walked the streets of Zurich when I first began, and mostly ever since. I still love working on the conundrums of the soul. The psyche is incredibly fascinating, and it forces you to the edge in every hour. It's always turning things upside down, demanding the most radical thoughts you can come up with. It disturbs your usual patterns, your usual feelings. It wants the upside down so you have to think revolution.

But the psyche is not psychology, not psychotherapy. Let's keep that distinction very clear. In the good old days, psychotherapy was carried by revolutionary idealism and a crusading force in Freud and his confederates. This spirit was still alive in the early fifties when I got in. But gradually therapy, or is it me, has become more and more passive, boring, and repetitive, even trivial. My emotion was elsewhere: Salvador and Nicaragua and the bullshit of trickle-down economics and the bad buildings going up and corporate crookedness in government—that was where I was caught. Meanwhile, therapy was talking in pretentious scientistic language about childhood and gender and propounding French theories that carry no more weight than croissant crumbs and aren't even flaky. Training, ethics, lawsuits, licensing, dues, congresses, papers: institutional politics instead of real politics. It's a profession. Everybody's okay, even privileged, whereas, once it was secret, underground, shameful to be "in analysis." And that's what I love—that it doesn't permit unconsciousness, another word for comfortable mediocrity. And *I* was becoming mediocre, a gray man in a gray chair.

So, though I love you, depth psychology, I can't stay in the same house with you. We've both changed too much. Once you were like an artist, and now you're a homemaker. You never go out in the street; you've become content with yourself; what you say doesn't seem at all relevant. I can't bear the way you think and use language. You take pills. No one really crazy ever comes to call. I want to be loyal to our vow, but there is more death in staying than in parting.

When you walk out on a long marriage you feel dysfunctional. A container breaks, and you become a little crazy like I am in this book—and I can't thank you enough for instigating this chance to rant and rave. Not only crazy; you also feel morally bad. You think: "Something must be wrong with me. I ought to go back into analysis to see why I feel therapy is so wrong." And that's even more crazy! It's like leaving the Communist party and then turning to the KGB to find out what's wrong with your thinking.

I'm not burnt out. That's not the case. No ashes, no disgust, no frustration. Simply, my emotion and my humor have left the consulting room. I wasn't incompetent. I hadn't failed. I can still do a pretty decent hour. I have an ear and a skill. (But the practice of something is not justification enough for its practice. Else you can be a hitman or a torturer, justifying your work by saying you like doing it, you do it well enough, and people keep asking you to do it.) Maybe the only way to be morally honest is to become dysfunctional. And that's a messy place to be, Michael. But when it gets to that messy crazy place, at least you know you haven't succumbed to mediocrity. You can only let your emotions take the lead and follow your heart. My heart left therapy and it would be malpractice to do soul work without heart.

Let us go the other way with therapy, toward art. Then we may consider some of the pathology we have mentioned as political protests, as refusals to comply, and the consulting room as a safe house for revolutionaries. The symptom becomes a demonstration of a life force within the Winstons of our society (Orwell's hero in *1984*) that will not bend to big brother. Even when we try, even when we want to, the symptoms insist on depressing me so I can't get to work, sexualizing me so I harass and buy porn, enraging me so I shout in public, putting my money on horses instead of what the ads tell me to buy. I haven't kept faith with the economy (as they say a consumer must do). I haven't served Jesus by Christmas shopping. I have stopped consuming, stopped watching TV, stopped voting. My symptoms want something else, something more. In my symptoms is the soul's deepest desire.

This desire, which may mask itself as the depressive denial of desire, an apathetic exhaustion, cannot be encompassed by the marketplace. My cry is not a cry for help but a cry for more. Or, say, my cry to the therapist is: "Help me find more, be more, live more." I gamble because I want more; I fantasize orgies in Bangkok because I want more; I eat and I eat because my appetites cannot be stilled by the daily junk of white bread. As Eric Hoffer said, "You can never get enough of what you don't really want."

The catch in this statement lies not in the second phrase but in the first: "You can never get enough. . . ." That's the mystery. Why do all societies have some form of drunkenness? From the viewpoint of cultural anthropology, to take intoxicants, to drink alcohol, is normal. To "just say no" would be sick. Why is "never enough" so necessary to human life?

Michael, am I being clear? Are we getting to the invisible factors under the skin of psychology that are making the world worse? As long as therapy is engaged in adaptation, it is denying the raging lust and animal appetites that claim life is worth living. And my violent rage and sullen refusals are saying again and again: "What the system offers is what I don't really want." And my addictions show this hungry suicidal demand for more, higher, faster, fuller, spacier, looser, wilder, stranger life. Of course the addictions cannot provide this, but they offer it. And so the system is hell-bent on stamping out everything extreme, especially the extremes of pleasure, which come closest to fulfilling desire. But the psyche is extreme and the world today is *in extremis.* Both the psyche and the world show desires far beyond the normalizing capacity of therapy. In a nutshell: is the world *in extremis* because we won't go to extremes?

I have suggested an artistic paradigm for therapy, though I don't mean literal artists and art. For the arts and artists can be just as blithely self-centered and apolitical as the Berlin Philharmonic playing for a *Wehrmacht* audience. I have suggested the artistic paradigm because it satisfies the three requirements discussed in this letter. First, art *forms* madness rather than represses it. Second, the arts often act as the sensitive antennae of social justice and moral outrage, keeping the soul awake to hypocrisy, cant, suppression, and jingoism. And third, the fundamental enemy of all art is mediocrity.

Jim

Part III

The Second Dialogue: "Pick Up If You're There"

Ventura is staying at a friend's apartment high over Sheridan Square in New York City. The view faces north—real north this time, not a California "north." It's early of a Saturday evening in late February, but the cold and wind just seem to instigate more speed amidst all the taxicabs on the wide street below. The weather doesn't seem to have kept anyone inside. There are many walkers out tonight, leaning into the cold with their heads down and an intent, preoccupied air. Headlights, neon, windows lit as far as you can see, and people holding onto their hats while their scarves are blown straight out behind them—these, and the almost constant sounds of sirens and wind, sharpen the edge of the night as Hillman and Ventura try their second book-talk.

In contrast to the freezing, fuming mood out in the street, the apartment of Ventura's friend has a quiet mood. Her rug, her furniture, her wall hangings, her knick-knacks are smartly chosen and show a gentle, playful taste. Her plants look very much alive. Hillman and Ventura sit at a table by the window, and there's the odd sensation of the radiator near the table giving off heat while the window seems to radiate cold.

They have been talking about the women in their lives for an hour or so, and without realizing it they have segued into talking their book.

HILLMAN: Then she realized that what love is all about is heartbreak. And when you realize that what love is all about is heartbreak, you're all right. But if you think it's about fulfillment, happiness, satisfaction, union, all of that stuff, you're in for even more heartbreak.

VENTURA: Well, love is a very funny place to go for safety.

HILLMAN: A *very* funny place to go for safety.

VENTURA: You get totally vulnerable and infantile with somebody you're in love with, you're vulnerable to their moods, their needs. And you become more vulnerable to *yourself,* your *own* needs. Things you didn't guess were inside you will come out with a loved one, including the fact that you have needs that no one can possibly satisfy.

HILLMAN: The thing is that two people *do* go to love for safety, safety *for* their vulnerability. Both people want to be vulnerable, but as long as you're open and vulnerable nothing is safe. They want safety for their vulnerability, but because of their vulnerability they can't be safe.

VENTURA: My friend George Howard said a very disturbing thing to me in Austin. He said, "The Self is hostile to love. It will not long tolerate that preoccupation."

HILLMAN: It's got a lot of other things to do, that's the point.

VENTURA: Anyway, the reason you're with this certain person, this certain lover, is not about love, or at least it's not about "having a good relationship." You're with this person because your soul is hungry for them, your soul is seeking something with or through them, and it will insist on what it wants. It doesn't care what price YOU pay for that; the ego-driven, agenda-ridden *you* is not your soul's priority. The nice thing about getting older is that you learn to pay some prices more gracefully, but the soul doesn't care. The soul is absolutely merciless—toward you, and toward anybody around you. The soul doesn't give a damn about human values.

HILLMAN: The Gods do not care. That's the basic old Greek idea, that the Gods do not care about that kind of human concern. Our happiness, our security doesn't interest the Gods.

VENTURA: God has all of eternity to play with, and all thc worlds, so . . . God doesn't care about the price.

We are creatures of limited means, so I suppose we can't be blamed for worrying about the price.

HILLMAN: What *is* the price of love? T. S. Eliot says, "Costing not less than everything." So one of the things you begin to see is, what gets sacrificed in love is *love.*

VENTURA: Ohhhhhhhhhhh.

HILLMAN: Ohhhhhhhh.

You think you're bringing a lot of sacrifices to it, but the sacrifice demanded, the ultimate sacrifice, is the sacrifice of love itself. All your notions of love—*that's* what's given up. Your *idea* of love, what you've thought of love, what you expect from love, what you cling to as love—this is what you give up.

In that sense the real lovers, to my mind, are the burned-out lovers.

VENTURA: The burned-out lovers, eh? I've been thinking lately that you're never really married until you're divorced. Because at the moment of divorce, what's been done with the marriage has been *done.* Then it lives like a novel or movie in your mind, a memory you go back to and back to and back to, but you can't change what happened. And at that point you are *really* in the marriage, because there's no escaping it. You can leave a wife, but you can't leave an exwife.

HILLMAN: The philosopher Ortega y Gassett asked himself, "Why do I love this woman?" What does the psychoanalyst do with that question? Go into it: She's like your mother, she's not like your mother, she's your anima projection, she reminds you of your first love when you were seventeen or seven, "she's got these incredible qualities that I don't have" or "she's so different from me that it's extraordinary" or "she's just like me, we get along like brother and sister, it's remarkable." We dig and dig and dig to find the reasons why.

What does Ortega say? He says: "You love this woman because—because it is *this woman.*"

VENTURA *(trying the phrase out)*: "Because it is *this woman.*"

HILLMAN: And that makes her the unique woman. That's the important thing, the uniqueness. Because it is *this* woman, it's not another woman. It has nothing to do with any of the rational qualities. It's not, as Stendhal would say, because she's a little ugly and therefore you can see the beauty in her. It's not because she's beautiful.

VENTURA: It's not because she's your anima. It's not because she's your muse.

HILLMAN: It's not because anything. *There is no because.* The because is: it is this woman. And that gives love back to the Gods. You see, the Gods hit you with her arrow, or they hit her with your arrow, or you both got hit—and that arrow is the reason.

VENTURA: The Gods of the Hindus, the Greeks, the Romans, the Gods of Voodoo and Santeria—all of them have a figure, a God or Goddess, who can strike anyone, even the most powerful of the immortals, with uncontrollable passion.

HILLMAN: That has a lot to do with falling in love, but it also has to do with long-term love. It's the quality that makes people unable to let go. We call that in therapy an obsession or a sex addiction: you can't let go till *it* lets go.

VENTURA: Love is a madness, then. Think about that a second. "Love your neighbor," "Love one another," "God is love"—given everyone's *experience* of love, these become pretty disturbing statements.

HILLMAN: Love is a madness, *but what is the madness itself looking for?* Is it to make us more mad? Is it to grow wings, as Plato says? The question is not, why is it this woman or this man, but, what is the madness looking for? *What does the madness want?* Because in the madness we grow way beyond ourselves. Way beyond. It prompts us to write love letters, it prompts us to phone, to drive all night, it prompts us to do incredible things, I mean we're incredible when we're in the madness. You're a fourteen-year-old kid on his bicycle fourteen times a day going past her house, you're tattooing yourself, you're completely mad.

VENTURA: You're willing to change your entire life, hurt people, break promises, turn everything upside down so you can have *this* woman. The madness wants something not from but through this person.

HILLMAN: What does the madness want? That's the big question. If therapy could understand what the madness wants, then it would treat love very differently, instead of reducing it to terms of the relationship, and the reasons for the relationship.

I don't accept a single one of the usual sentences, like, "This was only a sexual affair," or, "We really understood each other, she had just to open her mouth and my mind already knew what she was going to say," or any of the others. None of them. There's a madness, there's an obsessive madness going on. What does it want?

And why do we think that if we marry it the madness will go away? Paul says, "It's better to marry than to burn." This burning is not just a sexual burning, it's the madness. And the Christians were right about that—marriage usually subdues the madness.

VENTURA: And we get very disappointed when it does. Marriage subdues the madness and we go, "Uh oh, the madness is gone."

HILLMAN: "Where did it all go?"

VENTURA: "Do you remember how it used to be?"

HILLMAN: "Do you remember what we used to do?"

VENTURA: "I don't wanna be married anymore, it's so boring without the madness."

HILLMAN: So we're chasing the madness, and then—we don't know what to do with it.

VENTURA: So we marry to get rid of it! That's not what we *think* we're doing, but since that's what so often happens it has to be part of a secret intent—secret from ourselves and each other.

HILLMAN: And the madness is not reducible to hormones.

VENTURA: Reducing it to hormones is just another way of saying "God" anyway. DNA is just another word for destiny.

We're a materialist, concrete culture. We have to say, "Okay, it's in this gene, your destiny." What the hell is the difference, destiny or the genes? Destiny being lodged in a gene doesn't mean it's not coming from Heaven, Hell, or wherever it comes from—the Other World.

HILLMAN: Whether it's DNA or a hormone, it's the angel, the ancient angel, the tiny little invisible thing that can dance on the head of a pin.

VENTURA: Yeah, yeah, DNA or angels, there ain't no difference. Or maybe the difference is, they think they can fuck around with the DNA. They'll splice this, combine that, they'll think they're controlling it. But all they'll do is take some angels off the pin—and expect them to behave and do as they're told. But angels don't do as they're told. They'll be as unpredictable as ever, it'll just be a new unpredictability.

On the one hand, I feel this paranoia of, "Oh my god, they're messing with the DNA, they're gonna ruin everything." And on the other hand I feel, "Okay, fellas, you wanna break the windows of Heaven, you wanna open the doors of night, you wanna invite the Gods in—let's party. You're not gonna change the basic situation: that life is unfathomable, unpredictable, uncontrollable. You're gonna get messed around, fucked around. It's gonna be with the DNA and gene splicing the way it was with electricity or plutonium. There is no escaping the fundamental wildness of the universe."

See what a state I get into when I talk about love? What were we talking about anyway? What *does* the madness want?

I mean, listen to all those sirens out there. Constant sirens. I don't think there's been a moment since we sat down without at least one siren wailing down there. Talk about, "What does the madness want"!

HILLMAN: The madness wants to be let in the room that it has been excluded from. It wants to come in.

VENTURA: No matter what that madness is—we're not only talking about love now—it wants to come in.

HILLMAN: Partly because—

VENTURA: —it's been excluded.

HILLMAN: That's Freud: it's repressed.

VENTURA: I think it's more than "repressed"; I don't buy that.

HILLMAN: Because that would suggest it would go away once it comes in?

VENTURA: Right.

HILLMAN: You don't believe that.

VENTURA: I think the madness is much stronger than that. It does not go away once it comes in. Freud may be right that we constructed civilization to keep the madness out, as a collective; and, with our nice little homes and lives, we try to do the same thing privately, keep it out; but it does not go away. It's right there, always, waiting, trying to get in. And once it comes in, it isn't easily appeased.

HILLMAN: In other words, you can't just give it a nice chair and a cup of tea and it sits down.

VENTURA: You can't say, "I acknowledge you, I own you."

HILLMAN: "I respect you."

VENTURA: "I respect you, I love that part of myself that is you . . . as long as you don't make any fucking trouble."

HILLMAN: "Or even if you make a little bit of trouble, I acknowledge you because really you're part of my creativity."

Hillman and Ventura laugh nastily. On the tape it blends in nicely with the constant background of honking horns from Seventh Avenue.

VENTURA: But the madness—at least my madness—doesn't care about being part of my creativity! Because in fact creativity is this fundamentally sane act, and the madness wants disruption.

HILLMAN: Ohhhhhhhhh.

VENTURA: Ohhhhhh.

HILLMAN: Well that suggests—you say the madness wants disruption, it wants disruption of the room that it's been kept out of. But that disruption is only from the point of view of that room. If you enter into the madness, does *it* want disruption? I don't think so.

From *its* point of view, it's walking in the door with a message, but you sit in the room and it knocks the door down and you think, "Shit, this is only bringing me disruption," but what does it carry in its hand? I think what it's walking in the door with are the Gods. I think the madness is the messenger of the Gods. And that's Plato, not Freud. Different forms of what Plato called *mania,* each of them associated with a different God. So the madness is calling us to the Gods, in one way or another either as a frenzy or as a love or as a ritual initiation into a new kind of life. Something more important than usual life is going on. It is drawing us out of one thing and toward something else.

VENTURA: Michael Meade says, "The difference between blessed madness and insanity is: insanity is following the wrong God."

HILLMAN: So madness differs from insanity. Madness would be the mania that Plato talks about, which is the way the Gods reach us, as all the Greek tragedies show. Or, as Jung said, the Gods are in the diseases. Insanity would be what the human being does in relation to that mania. That is, it follows the wrong God, or it serves its God the wrong way. It doesn't understand the ritual, or it literalizes the ritual. It gets inflated, it takes the mania to itself, takes credit for it, "The thoughts that come through me are mine, not the Gods'"; or it says, "I am an instrument of the Gods, I'm their favorite son or chosen person." Of all definitions of madness, I like the one in a poem by Theodore Roethke: "What's madness but nobility of soul / At odds with circumstance?"

You know that what we're saying ignores all the present systems of defining insanity—systems that say it's a biochemical disorder or a sociological disorder or a genetic disorder or an early childhood dysfunction. I haven't mentioned any of those as the roots of insanity, so I have omitted a whole set of contributing factors.

VENTURA: When you say something like "contributing factors"—it seems the starting place for any analysis of this culture seems to be the concept of a safe white slate. Anything that is not on this safe white slate is a "contributing factor" to evil and madness. Anything that disrupts a normal safe day—where this normal safe day ever was in history, I don't know—but anything that disrupts it is one of these contributing factors to madness. There's something very wrong with that kind of thinking.

HILLMAN: Many are now saying that the "normal safe day" was the matriarchy.

VENTURA: Scholarship should be classified as a form of fiction. You can prove or disprove anything. The arguments for the matriarchy, or any ancient life, are based on statues, buildings, and tools, and *that's* a woefully incomplete record, but let's say you had all the statues, buildings, and tools, say, of that city out there. What would you know about all its different ways of making music, what would you know about all the stories that its people tell or its poetry? How could you tell, from America's buildings and statues and tools, that we had feminism and the men's movement and the New Age movement and ecologists and Satanists and surfers and homeless and gay culture and Black culture? You couldn't. And what if the Neolithic stuff gives just as incomplete a picture? Such scholarship is a polemical tool, and that's all it is—and not a very honest polemical tool, either.

I've done it again, I've gone off—where the devil were we? You were going somewhere with madness.

HILLMAN: I think in order to protect yourself against insanity, you must every day propitiate madness. You must take your steps toward madness, you must open the door toward the mania, let it in. That would account in my mind for a great many forms of what we call addiction. These are ways of trying to open the door and to let the madness in. Whether it's getting drunk on a Saturday night or sitting for hours drinking alone in a melancholy to let Saturn in, whatever—these are modes of letting the madness in. And in a sense they keep us from going insane, and we don't know that distinction.

VENTURA *(singing)*: "I've always been crazy but it's kept me from going insane." That's a Waylon Jennings song.

HILLMAN: Crazy means "cracked," the cracks that let things in. It's not smooth, it's not safe. So what do you do, then, to let the madness in? What do *you* do to keep from going insane?

VENTURA: What do I do?

HILLMAN: Yeah, what do *you* do?

VENTURA: You mean other than hard whiskey, fast women, and loud music? Or is it fast cars and loud women? Hard women and straight whiskey? Could you repeat the question?

HILLMAN: I think you do one more thing, and I think I do too, and I think that's part of what this book is about—that we try to go out on a limb.

VENTURA: Oh yes.

HILLMAN: We try to go to unsafe places. We risk. With our minds, we risk.

VENTURA: With our work. In our work. Whether that work ultimately stinks or not is for others to judge, but it's risky, that's a fact.

HILLMAN: So we go *toward* madness; it doesn't have to just break in.

VENTURA: True. I am not happy unless I'm risking on that level.

HILLMAN: It makes me most happy when I can go the farthest out. Or as one writer said to me, it is not enough to go out on a limb, you've got to be willing to saw it off.

Now, could you connect how you let the madness in with keeping from going insane, in your life?

VENTURA: Every day I fear going insane. I've never had a day in my life when I haven't felt that.

HILLMAN: So letting the madness in becomes for you how you ban the Gods by giving to them. You keep them from possessing you by giving something to them.

VENTURA: Yes, but it's a dangerous game.

HILLMAN: Isn't it a dangerous game to close the door and sit on the sofa and depend on the locks to keep the madness out?

VENTURA: Much more dangerous. Because the madness is a lot stronger than the locks.

HILLMAN: I think the way of letting it in to most of our lives is pathology. The symptoms come—the marriage fights, the crazy child, the overspending, the drinking, the piling up of debt.

VENTURA: The dependence on TV, the compulsive schedules that eat your life, the endlessly repetitive family feuds.

HILLMAN: What goes on in the house is the pathology. Now, when therapy tries to cure the pathology, instead of seeing that the pathology is part of the crack or the broken window, and that something is trying to get in, then it seems to me it's creating more pathology and keeping the Gods even further away. And then they break in through the whole fucking society.

VENTURA: If we don't let the madness in, then collectively the society goes mad for us, and that's called "history." So in the long run there are enormous collective consequences for all these private evasions.

Speaking of the whole fucking society, when we saw the Kevin Costner film *Dances with Wolves,* I remember how struck you were at that scene—you know, the white soldier and the white girl who's been raised as a Sioux, they're getting it on, and the Sioux shaman is concerned about it so he asks his wife, "What are the people saying?"

HILLMAN: That's terribly important, "What are the people saying?"

VENTURA: Which is something you ask yourself when you get into a relationship, but you feel ashamed for asking. "What are the people saying? Do my friends like her, can they talk to her? Does she like them? Does my family like her—or, if I'm trying to break with my family, do they *not* like her? If we're thinking of children, do I really want something of her father in my son? How do I feel when I walk down a street with her? What are the people saying?"

HILLMAN: There's a communal aspect to love. Love does not simply exist as a private tryst or trust between two people in a personal relationship; it's a communal event.

VENTURA: When you bust up a marriage you find that out, because almost all your friends are pissed. Even the most understanding have the air of being a little disappointed in you. And some never get over it, some friendships are never the same afterward. Not just that you tend to lose the friends who came to you from the other side of the marriage; it's that, at least for a time, people don't talk to you the same.

HILLMAN: Why is "What are the people saying?" so important? After all, if this woman is your woman simply because she is this particular woman and no other, as Ortega says, what difference does it make what the people are saying?

VENTURA: The difference is, it's the context of the love. Your love is going to be lived, at least in part, in the medium, the environment, of "What are the people saying?"

HILLMAN: Is one of the people the therapist?

VENTURA: Oh yes. The therapist is part of that community. The therapists of everyone in that circle or community are part of that community, though they usually won't admit it.

HILLMAN: So she goes to her therapist and you go to your therapist.

VENTURA: And your therapist thinks you have a good marriage and need to save it, and her therapist thinks the marriage is worth saving. If *you* don't think so, then you're not up against one person, you're up against three. And by "up against" I mean you're standing up for your feelings against three other very important people, and that's not easy.

HILLMAN: So the question "What are the people saying?" locates the relationship in a context. The world is the context of the love. The sentence also is saying that love doesn't belong to the two people alone. What two people do with each other is very important for other people. And if you think that love is romantic and can lead "out of this world"—that's not it.

VENTURA: Or that's not *all* of it.

HILLMAN: I think the people are saying, "Is this good for us all?" And this is different from "Is it good for you?" They ask, "Is this good for us? Is this going to bring fruit and benefit to us? Or is this going to bring new disturbances to us?"

VENTURA: Yes. That's very strong. And we usually label that, or feel it, negatively, at least in this culture. We think, "Shit on them, what right have they got to an opinion about who I love?" And yet they do have some rights; they're going to be affected.

At the same time, if the madness wants you to say, "Damn you all to hell, we love each other and we're going to be together no matter what!"—if the madness wants that, you'll do it, and if you don't do it you'll never forgive yourself. From the ancient myths to *Romeo and Juliet* to *West Side Story* or Lorca's gypsy ballads, people never tire of telling such tales, which says to me that the collective in a funny way respects being violated by love, the way it respects other kinds of outlaws.

HILLMAN: "What are the people saying?" also says you've got a lot of inner voices, psychological voices, and *within you* you're being told, "Look, she's not good enough for you, she's lower class, uneducated. Look, she's had two broken marriages already, what are you doing getting involved in her patterns. Look, she's an exsomething—she used to drink, so did her father, it runs in the family."

VENTURA: "You're famous, and that's what she wants. She's gonna work out her father stuff on you, *that's* what she wants." While *she's* thinking, "Do I remind him of his mother, is that why he loves me?"

HILLMAN: And you've got to know all these things. There are a lot of voices going on, there are a lot of people in you saying a lot of things. Are these "the people" that we're talking about?

VENTURA: Inner voices, outer voices, both are "the people."

HILLMAN: What are your ancestors saying? What is your dead mentor saying? You're a woman and the only one who understood you as a child was your mother's sister, who's dead—what is *she* saying? What are the Gods saying?

VENTURA: You get along incredibly well, but her apartment is furnished and decorated so utterly different from yours, the furniture and wall hangings aren't compatible at all! What are your apartments saying? What are the walls saying?

You like to take walks on crowded streets, she likes to walk by the sea. What is the sea saying?

HILLMAN: Will our love be beneficial for the group, for the society, for the world?

VENTURA: Hold on, that's a lot to saddle two trembling people with.

HILLMAN: But in the Wim Wenders film *Wings of Desire* that was the whole point: they will dance and sing in the square because a man and a woman are in love with each other. And that was an old idea, that everybody comes to the wedding and everybody dances and sings at the wedding. Why is that? They are certainly not celebrating the "relationship" or a successful therapeutic outcome of couple's counseling! It's the joining of family, it's the joining of ancestors, it's the possibility of descendants, it's a whole lot of things being joined, including Heaven and Earth—more, even, than the world. It's not just you and me in a deep psychological relationship.

So "What are the people saying?" says, "This marriage, this union, this love affair, belongs to *us,* the people, that wide context called the world. It belongs to that street down there, it's going into the world of the sirens. And we, the people, are not concerned with whether it's good for you, Michael; we want to know if it's good for *us.*"

VENTURA: "And we have a right to know. We have a right to want it to be good for us. You are even being irresponsible if it's not good for us." Though, I must add, I personally reserve the right to tell all of you to go to hell.

HILLMAN: I don't know whether therapy realizes this point, because therapy's exclusively concerned with whether it's good for *you,* the private patient. Whether it will work for *you*. But does therapy ever consider the family, the neighbors, the colleagues, and, even more, the furniture, the sea, the effect on the world? See, the therapist isn't supposed to be involved in all that in any way. The basic frame of therapy is to withdraw from all of that, not to have "dual relationships." That is, the involving feelings of friendship shouldn't come in, so the therapist's concern is solely with whether it's good for *you,* not even with whether it's good for her.

That means therapy is not even talking about love any longer! If you can have a conversation with somebody about whether this, my love, is good for *ME,* beneficial, making me more conscious, making me more happy, making me more satisfied, making me more creative, all these words, without considering whether it's going to be good for *her,* that's not love. So that's not a real conversation about a relationship.

VENTURA: First Western culture invented the "romantic relationship," which cuts you off from community; now therapy deals with that relationship in such a way as to help cut you off from each other!

HILLMAN: Somehow we've got to see that "personal relationship" is a symptom of our culture. Read what the Muslims feel, what tribal societies feel, what we know of antique cultures, of Chinese culture today: they weren't hung up on romantic love, as we are, expecting all our sexual fantasies, and other fantasies, to be fulfilled by the person we sleep with. Why are we in our Western American culture of the nineties, in the therapeutic culture of the white bread world, so hung up on the significant other for fulfillment?

VENTURA: You tell me, Doc. 'Cause we're just like everybody else, you and I, full of longing to have our fantasies fulfilled—or at least serviced.

HILLMAN: All right, I *will* tell you! My obsessive sexual fantasies, and yours, come straight from Descartes. Because Descartes, the good Jesuit-trained Christian that he was, declared to Western civilization that only human persons have souls. No soul anywhere else. And, since love always seeks soul, you've got to have a "significant other," as psychology calls it. That's why we have all those images on billboards, in the movies, on the tube, of hungry mouths kissing, the divinely perfect man and divinely perfect woman with lost soft eyes and luscious washed hair, flying into each other's arms, getting it on. Notice these couples are always isolated. On an empty beach, a sailboat, a private bathtub. No other voices. Just us. They never ask or hear, "What are the people saying?"

VENTURA: They might as well be in a cemetery or in outer space. They *are* in outer space, encapsulated.

HILLMAN: That's Descartes. The world of trees and furniture and alley cats is soulless, only dead matter. There's nowhere for love to go but to another person. So the magnetic pull that therapy calls "sex addiction" or "loving too much" is nothing other than the end-station of our isolated individualism. The sexual fascination is the soul trying to get out and get into something other than itself.

Our genitals are right. Our hungry mouths aching to kiss are right. If we don't fall obsessively in love, we are all alone in a cemetery of Cartesian litter. What goes on between the legs in the muladhara cakra—

VENTURA: Mula-what?

HILLMAN: That's the psychic center at the base of the spine, in the perineum, at the bottom of where your cock rises. *Muladhara* means supporting the ground of community, family, the earth of one's place in this world. You see what I'm saying: the sexual desire that never lets go—

VENTURA: Ikkyu, that great Zen poet, says it *never* lets go. Even in late old age he wrote things like:

> "sick all I can think of is love and fucking the love song / hums in my groin listen my hair's white wild grasses uncut on / my meadow"

And I might as well add his:

"don't hesitate get laid that's wisdom
sitting around chanting what crap"

HILLMAN: That's the kind of Zen I like. Enough macrobiotics, sitting, and sword shit.

What I'm saying is that this desire that never lets go is the drive in the human, not only for union with a significant other, which makes it too personal and Christian, but for communion with something wider. With the community itself, the soul. We've identified communion with private intimacy. Our word for the muladhara region is *privates.*

VENTURA: Our love life is private, secret. It lets us out of the world, which can be wonderful, but the shadow of that wonder is that it reinforces our isolation.

HILLMAN: But let's get this straight. We are *not* isolated selves. It's individualism that makes us feel we're all alone.

VENTURA: And we're set up to feel that way by a long history of thinking. So when somebody says, "I trust my feelings," they don't know that what they're trusting isn't really all theirs, isn't their own invention or possession, but is instead part of a collective history, part of how they've been conditioned to respond by forces way out of their control that go a long way back.

HILLMAN: You bet, and that's why trusting your feelings without thinking about them can never work. They have a background. In fact, just trusting your feelings leads further into the trap of individual aloneness. *My* feelings, inside myself, about me, me, me, deep down. But those feelings come out of a whole nexus of ideas and influences. They're conditioned by history.

VENTURA: Therapy stops that history with the parents. It doesn't go back far enough.

HILLMAN: It still pushes the religious idea of private salvation, and we feel this when we are in the grip of passionate love. We feel love offers salvation of the privates from their cut-off isolation "down there," redemption of the repressed, fusion, ecstatic union, "coming" home.

VENTURA: So falling in love won't save me?

HILLMAN: You know why? Because as soon as two people pair off, they leave the party. They go elsewhere, his place, her place, for private salvation. Everyone else is left out. They don't ask, "What are the people saying?" Intimacy means anticommunity. And if the self means, as I defined it, the interiorization of community, then finding the one and only, the significant other, only reinforces individualism. And all those passionate images on the billboards and the tube are just more propaganda for private salvation. They are saying stay indoors, off the streets, out of the party. They are false because they are reinforcing the false self of individualism. They are pushing private enterprise. They keep our sexual desire, our Eros, harnessed to private salvation. Just fall in love and you'll be saved.

VENTURA: Getting it on doesn't even mean passion anymore, it means not being alone. "Let's just snuggle," she says, "we don't have to have sex." Statistics say that's what women want most. "I don't want joy, I just don't want to feel alone." We are deluded to feel that the only way out of individualism is private salvation, which is both bad sex and bad community.

HILLMAN: That's probably why the Church always said, "Outside the Church, our community, no salvation." So the Church and the old Bolshevists, and the Chinese Communists today too try so hard to regulate love. They see that falling in love is another kind of individualism. They don't want lovers to "leave the party" for private salvation.

VENTURA: You don't really want to come out agreeing with the Church, the Leninists who sold out the Russian Revolution, and the old men who ordered the Tiananmen Square massacre, do you, Hillman?

HILLMAN: Is that what I'm doing?

VENTURA: You just came awfully close. We don't want to confuse intensely private states of being with what passes for individualism in America.

HILLMAN: No, and we don't want to forget that in a true community there would necessarily be (as there is in the old tales, or in *Wings of Desire* and *Dances with Wolves*) a dialectic between intense states of privacy and the larger community. They pull to and fro in a dance of their own. "What are the people saying?" is part of that dance.

VENTURA: And when there is that to-and-fro between the lovers and the community, each questions the other, helps keep the other honest; the lovers and the community each give to the other what can't be gotten otherwise.

HILLMAN: But *that* only happens if we realize we're not isolated selves.

VENTURA: Exactly. Without that realization, the wonder that two people find together increases an isolation that in the end can only make them more desperate, and that desperation will eat and kill their love in the long run.

HILLMAN: A vicious circle. As long as the world around us is just dead matter, Eros is trapped in personal relationships. And transference, by the way, just confirms that, hour after therapeutic hour. It reenacts the problem not of my childhood and my love for Mommy, but the culture's hangup on an ideal significant other and salvation through tortuous love. *I want you*—that's our deepest cultural cry. And *you* have to be divine, since all the divinities, the ancestors, the souls of things, are dead.

VENTURA: I'm thinking of the one thing I love, have true passion for, I mean the one thing that isn't human, which is—

HILLMAN: —your car.

VENTURA: Of course. And, as you and my other friends know, I *really* love my car. And it loves me; I feel that.

HILLMAN: Right! And that saves you, Michael. I never saw that before, but your love for that car keeps you sane.

VENTURA: Hey, it's not just "that car"; it's a silky green '69 Chevy Malibu, and it's the only car I've ever owned and it's never let me down, and I've never let it down.

HILLMAN: To everyone else it seems insane that you take better care of that car than of any woman or child or yourself and stay loyal to it, but you are right, because your love of your car is the answer to personalized humanism.

No, don't stop me, I've got more to say.

A woman I know in Paris came back from Bahia in Brazil where everyone touches everyone all the time, either caressing and friendly or thieving, of course, but she saw a man make love to a banana tree. For us, that's perverse. The Church would say you can only put it in a person, and only in one place in that person, and only for one reason, procreation, and only if the Church marries you. But she saw a man making love to a banana tree.

VENTURA: And since it's a perversion, it's prohibited, and so we have to keep our erotic attractions to all the things around, like my car, hidden—I mean hidden from ourselves, from ever coming into consciousness.

HILLMAN: We cut the world out of our erotic feelings. But a "pervert" gets a hard-on from a nylon shower curtain or a piece of rubber. See, the perversion is already saying, "Look, you can make love to material things, dead things"—dead, that is, according to Descartes.

VENTURA: The pervert is then our leader out of the Cartesian dead, or rather deadened, world.

HILLMAN: Right, all those case studies in Krafft-Ebing's work—the fetishist, the sodomist, the coprophiliac who likes the smell and taste of shit—these are saying, "Look, the world has immense possibilities for desire. Go for it, even if Descartes says it is dead." See, Descartes makes our love for the world into a perversion: it's necrophilia because the world is just a dead body.

VENTURA: To love the world, the planet, is necrophilia—because to the Cartesian and scientific way of thinking anything not human is dead. This helps explain the real disgust some people on the far right have for ecologists and ecological issues—they're disgusted by our love of the planet because unconsciously they feel it's necrophilia!

HILLMAN: And what about this? Romantic love keeps the world dead. It insists, "Only you, only you, only you—you are my heart's desire. Forsaking all others." And here the "others" doesn't mean just other people, it means *all* others. No significant others can be had anywhere. Your car is out.

VENTURA: If romantic love keeps the world dead, then romantic love is an ecology problem?

HILLMAN: Right. It never asks, "What are the people saying?"—and by "the people" I don't mean just the tribe, I mean the banana tree and your Chevy and the sea. They will get jealous, and you know you can die from jealousy. Jealousy plots revenge. The world is taking revenge. Or maybe the world is dying from jealousy, jealous that humans with their huge heart capacity for love and their genital juices only give this to each other. How insanely selfish.

VENTURA: And what about this? Technological man treats the earth kind of like a wife beater or rapist treats women: his Eros is so twisted that the only physical relationship he can have with the planet is violence. That would go a long way toward explaining his insistence on violating the planet.

But you were about to say—

HILLMAN: If romantic love is an ecology problem, it's also a political problem. It's antisocial. It doesn't let my love into the community.

VENTURA: Are we now promoting free love, like the communes of the sixties or the old free sects and religions?

HILLMAN: No, I'm not setting out rules for a new practice. I'm not saying, "Let's construct a new society based on loving old cars and banana trees. Follow your fetish!"

VENTURA: I don't know—in the context of all this, "Follow your fetish" might not be the worst thing in the world to say.

HILLMAN: I'm still being a psychologist, I'm still saying, "Look at your personal love feelings, your romantic hang-up, your obsessive desire, not as something particularly wrong with *you*—or as something right with you either that shows what a powerful child of Eros you are—but look at it as a function of a Cartesian society. There will never be a solution to your pangs by just setting up a commune or preaching free love. The only solution can come when the world is reanimated, when we recognize how alive everything is, and how desirable."

Maybe that's what consumerism and advertising are really all about, unconsciously, compulsively: a way to rekindle our desire for the world.

VENTURA: "Rekindle our desire for the world." I like those words very much.

HILLMAN: Yes, rekindle our desire for the world.

VENTURA: Though the spiritual guru teachers would say that this world we're talking about is the thing that chains you to the flesh and to misery and to the cycle of unhappy rebirths.

HILLMAN: Maybe they're unhappy in the flesh, but I'm not. Do you think the man able to make love to a banana tree is unhappy? I think he's a Zen master, a fucking saint.

The phone rings.

VENTURA: I'm gonna let it ring, the machine'll take it. But the trouble with this machine is that you hear your own message with every call.

THE MACHINE *(Ventura's voice)*: This is temporarily the phone number of Michael Ventura. If you leave a message I'll probably call you back, but let's understand right now that that's not a promise.

The machine beeps.

THE MACHINE *(a man's voice)*: Come on, guys, don't hide. I know you're there.

VENTURA: That's Stan.

Ventura picks up the phone.

VENTURA: Hold on, Stan, I'm putting you on the speaker phone—condemning you to the echo chamber.

Ventura presses a button, puts back the receiver.

You still there?

STAN PASSY: I'm here.

HILLMAN: Hello, Stan. We're talking a book.

VENTURA: Bringing the ancient form of writing back to its origins—writing as dialogue.

HILLMAN: Thinking as dialogue.

VENTURA: Like a couple of goddamn Greeks.

HILLMAN: What's on your mind, Stan?

PASSY: There's something I want you to think about for your book.

VENTURA: That's the trouble with writing-as-dialogue, you get kibitzers.

HILLMAN: Shoot, Stan.

PASSY: When you told me the title of your book—

HILLMAN: Wow, that's interesting, writing-as-dialogue, thinking-as-dialogue, *does* let in, or at least imply? invite? the community—I'm not sure of the word, exactly. But because it's two people talking—

VENTURA: Though we'll spruce up the transcripts some and edit some—

HILLMAN: But we can't spruce up *too* much. It basically has to be speech. I know I'm interrupting you, Stan, but that's the whole point. Two people talking is, at least conceptually, open to the community. Open to interruption.

PASSY: Are you saying that's a function of community?

HILLMAN: We see it as interruption, as annoying, but the interruption takes you out of yourself, out of what you're doing, breaks the rhythm, breaks the isolation. So interruption has a value, is important, because getting taken out of yourself is important; it lets air into a stuffy room. That's part of the value of writing-as-dialogue, the important interruptions each makes into the other's thought, the sudden turns. So the page is more alive in that it's more like life, it moves like life.

VENTURA: Books are by their nature private *and* public —a book is a public thing, but it's read privately—but writing-as-dialogue is open to the community in another way: not everyone can write but everyone talks. So this is an open form, in that if people talk about the book in a way they're *doing* the book, extending and rewriting the book.

PASSY: So let me interrupt you, already.

VENTURA: Sorry, Stan. Like the man said, shoot. Where are you, by the way?

PASSY: Santa Barbara.

VENTURA: We're staring down on Sheridan Square, which from up here looks like an open-air madhouse.

PASSY: In Santa Barbara we go crazy quietly, behind closed doors.

HILLMAN: So go crazy quietly on us.

PASSY: The title of your book has been running through my mind. I was thinking, when did it go wrong, what happened, how did something that seemed so potentially great—I mean, therapy—get into the state it's in, pervaded by so many assumptions that undermine its original purpose?

VENTURA: Which was?

PASSY: The original notion had to do with philosophy. That is, the idea of psychotherapy grounded in philosophy is different from the idea of psychotherapy grounded in healing, medicine, shamanism.

HILLMAN: Should we be into "healing" and "help me," or into "who am I?" and "know thyself"?

PASSY: "Who am I?" has become a *healing* question; it's not "who am I?" as a philosophical question. That's so different. We don't understand the difference anymore.

HILLMAN: That's because "who am I?" has been reduced to "how did I get this way?," my childhood, and the answer is "who I *really* am is the inner child." That's how healing and "who am I?" have got confused. "Besides, I don't like this inner child, I hate it—"

VENTURA: "It's too frightened, too vulnerable, too needy—"

HILLMAN: "I want to get rid of it, which means I hate who I am. So I go to therapy to heal the inner child and be who I am." That's become the whole rationale: to make life safe for the inner child.

VENTURA: The goal of psychology, then, has become safety.

PASSY: Healing, help.

VENTURA: But healing as in "How can I be safe? How can I be well?"

HILLMAN: Well-fare.

VENTURA: Then we forget what Jung said, which is that the most terrifying thing in the world is to know yourself. That's very different from healing the inner child. And when you forget that difference you get the obsession with incest and abuse.

And don't tell me *obsession* isn't a fair word. A woman "working in child abuse," as she put it, told me not only seriously but earnestly that for a parent to favor one child over another—which is a human condition that can't be helped—constitutes child abuse. That's to equate fundamental conditions of life with abuse. The equation being: suffering equals abuse. Which is a weird, inside-out version of the worst Pollyanna fantasy, because what "suffering equals abuse" *really* means is, "Life equals, or is supposed to equal, happiness and perfection, and anything that is not happiness and perfection is unnatural and abusive."

That woman's no doubt on the extreme end, but the fundamental attitude that suffering equals abuse is pervasive, and it's infecting therapy on many levels.

PASSY: Hades, the underworld of the imagination, is now the wounded child of the imagination. That's the substitution. The realm of Hades has become the realm of childhood.

HILLMAN: The attention to child abuse in the culture is serving the culture's puritanism. You can't give candies to a child, you can't cuddle with children in the morning in bed, you can't feel erotic joy, physical erotic joy at their presence. Any kind of spanking is regarded already as a kind of reentry into perversion. Nudity, bathing. You've got a whole set of extraordinary trepidations about the relation to children. So the children grow up in a kind of new fear of their own. It protects the American notion of innocence and virginity. It serves that, and the repression of sexuality.

PASSY: This is all part of the way therapy thinks about it, which seems to be damaging, deeply damaging.

HILLMAN: We did a book at Spring Publications called *The Cult of Childhood*. It shows how this fantasy about childhood, this worship of the child that we were talking about, goes back prior to Freudian theory and developmental psychology, back to the Romantics and Rousseau, to German education, which set up kindergartens, and so on. Then the idea infected the arts: artists produce wonderful things because the artist becomes like a child filled with spontaneity and creativity.

VENTURA: That's such bullshit. Art is hard work. Van Gogh said, "An artist is a man with his work to do."

HILLMAN: So even our theory, the commonly accepted theory, of art is affected by our fantasy of the child. I think the worship of the child and the cult of childhood are substitutes for really worshiping the imagination. That's what we really want, but it's been misplaced.

VENTURA: And worship isn't love.

HILLMAN: Actually, I don't think Americans love their children, particularly.

VENTURA: America has systematized the abuse of children now—it doesn't educate them. Which is an enormous abuse.

PASSY: It poisons them with bad food—potato chips, soda pop.

VENTURA: Hypnotizes them with an electronic substitute for activity.

HILLMAN: And a substitute for their own access to imagination.

PASSY: The government finds any excuse it can to cut off aid to them, and much of our business is for products and services that are bad and dangerous for them.

VENTURA: And so the American *system* is child abusive. Could it be that the country's obsession with child abuse is a projection, the shadow of America not taking care of its children?

HILLMAN: The obsession, as you call it, is saying, "The child in America is abused." And, as we inevitably do in a Christian culture, we locate the abuse always in a sexual place. When we're talking about anything in a Christian culture, the shadow is always sexual in one way or another. So it immediately gets focused on the sexual aspect, which isn't where the basic American abuse of the child is going on, according to you.

Yes, the American abuse of the child is going on in education, and in the deeper question of, "What do you want to have a child for? What is a child for?"

VENTURA: What *is* a child for?

HILLMAN: "Do you know what a child costs nowadays? Do you know what it costs me to educate you? Do you know what it costs me to keep giving you all that crap you want?" The anger about what children cost is amazing. And then comes the teenager, and the child is just a constant worry, an agony around the house. The anger, the deep feeling of, "What do I want this child for unless it's going to do just what I want it to do like a mini me?"

VENTURA: Then there's the type of professional who decides to have a child and right away goes back to being an executive or whatever, and the actual time spent with the child is very little. Really minimal.

HILLMAN: "She's an amazing woman, a consummate professional, and she has a child!" See, what does that have to do with the *child?* This is the child as achievement—

VENTURA: —as something one *should* be doing with one's life, something on one's cosmic résumé—

HILLMAN: —rather than the child as the community, as the future of our ritual, the future of our religion, the future of our culture. And as the carrier of joy and pleasure. The child is joy. Now if joy and pleasure are not desirables, if a child's joy and pleasure are not really beautiful and psychologically valuable—which they're not in a puritan world—that's going to be hated in the child because you don't have it in your world.

VENTURA: In tribal culture, which is the culture of the shamans after all, children are cared for deeply but they're not taken so seriously, not until they're old enough to become adults. That initiation is taken very seriously, but the child as child is just kind of an enjoyable nuisance. As you've said before, Jim, tribal people don't search out the problems of adults in their childhood.

HILLMAN: And as you've said, incest isn't new. Fairy tales and myths show us it's been going on forever, which doesn't excuse or justify it. Still, that incest and violence to children are mythical, archetypal, does suggest that these things belong to human heritage, and so are profoundly significant. Just getting panicked and morally shocked or legalistic are not the right responses. We have to *think* about it deeply. We have to ask why has this particular syndrome, when there are so many other cruelties and injustices around, seized our white bread American culture just now at the end of the millennium?

VENTURA: So why in our time do we *need* this attention, this focus, on real and/or imagined incest and abuse?

PASSY: I'll tell you *who* needs it: the Christian imagination.

HILLMAN: Oh, yes.

PASSY: It's a question of Hell. We've lost the place of Hell in our culture. The Judeo-Christian mythology lost Hell, they really lost it, they go, "Where's our Hell today? Where is it? Where can we find our Hell, what are we gonna do, we're desperate, we have to have a Hell! We have to have some place where all our monsters can reside, where our doubles and our shadows can act out!" Most people today don't believe, as they did in the medieval world, in a real, geographical, topological Hell in which they imagine their monsters. We are desperate to rediscover it, and I'm convinced that in modern culture the rediscovery of Hell emerges as:

Childhood!

Our childhood.

HILLMAN: That's a great thought. That's good.

PASSY: So psychotherapy today becomes—

HILLMAN: We're delivering people from their childhood.

PASSY: With a messianic exuberance! This is why we're all priests, we're no longer psychologists. We're delivering them from the maw of Hell. Because let's call a spade a spade here, this is *not* childhood, you're delivering them from Hell itself.

HILLMAN: That's why it's so gripping—so gripping to therapists, and why therapists become so blind, because when you have a mission you can see nothing, you can only see that mission. This poor person needs deliverance.

PASSY: Let me just add: How could it be, how could childhood become Hell?

VENTURA: Maybe on accounta it *is?*

PASSY: The idea prevalent now is that we enter the world a blank slate, we're born to the world as innocent, we come into the world as Christ nature. To be a blank slate is to be the innocent Christ child. So if we have a conceptual child born innocent—

HILLMAN: Alice Miller. Alice Miller's therapy would say, "Hell is what happens to you, it's not your original nature."

PASSY: Exactly Alice Miller! Then it is an inevitable next step that anything that will rob us of our innocence—and there is no childhood that can't do this—anything that will corrupt us from that original nature—

HILLMAN: —is Hell, is sent from the devil in Hell.

PASSY: This is your Jungian colleague, Edward Edinger, too, this is exactly how he views it: we start out and then we lose our Self-nature.

HILLMAN: He's a tremendous Christian, Edinger.

PASSY: It can't be overstated—

VENTURA: Try. We like that here.

PASSY: It can't be overstated that the only way that childhood could *become* Hell would be if we imagine the child as a Christ-innocent nature. If there's a thing called a child that comes out of the womb perfectly pure and innocent, then we see the end result twenty years later as a screwed-up mess.

HILLMAN: Pure and innocent even *before* it comes out of the womb. That's why we shouldn't kill it, we're told. It's not a fetus, it's a "preborn child."

PASSY: That explains the grip of psychotherapy, because the new religion is, "Purge me from Hell, recover my original Christ-nature, deliver me from my childhood." And then it becomes a socialization process. So we have a new Hell in modern times called childhood and a priest cult, a craft, designed to save you from that Hell, all with the aim of recovering one's lost innocence.

VENTURA: But if people are born with something like destiny, with what Jim calls the acorns and the nubs, and with the voices of their ancestors—

PASSY: —they're already corrupted.

VENTURA: Let's forget that Christian word, let's say instead that you're born with *stuff,* born with places to go and things to do, not predetermined and predefined but with a momentum toward places to go and things to do, then—

PASSY: This is very important, this is the big difference. If you're born corrupt, then: who's corrupting whom in childhood?

VENTURA: *Forget* the word *corrupt!* Because if you use that word, *original sin* is not far behind and you're just moving from one Christian conundrum to another. Say, instead, we're born with a destiny, a momentum. Say, we hit the ground running. Then the child draws others into his destiny; his momentum affects the momentums of others—and that's not corrupting anybody. A dog running across a playing field isn't corrupting anybody, but it's disrupting the game.

In other words, the child *isn't* Alice Miller's child, isn't blankly innocent and passive, isn't passive at all, is disruptive in a profound sense, a far more profound sense than just screaming in the middle of the night. The disruption people feel at the entrance of a child into their lives is that they're feeling the pull and influence of its own momentum, its own destiny, which may in the long run have very little to do with theirs.

The fantasy of a child's blank slate, of innocence, is an attempt to ignore, minimize, and/or *control* that momentum.

PASSY: The scary part for me is that we literalize the Hell. Because when you try to make childhood the Hell, and it really isn't, the shadow of that will be the creation of new Hell, everything you both spoke of—the denial of education, the poverty, the violence, the literal Hell that we're creating for American children.

HILLMAN: And therapy isn't trying to redeem anybody from *that* Hell.

PASSY: Right! That's the rejection of the world. Today

we have this convenient way of doing this kind of cultural, romantic Hell called "redemption from childhood"—

HILLMAN: —which is wholly imaginary—

VENTURA: —imaginary as in "a thing made of images, of psyche"—

PASSY: —that really ignores the *real* Hell.

HILLMAN: If the consulting room is to become a cell of revolution it cannot ignore the real Hell.

VENTURA: Hmmmm.

HILLMAN: What?

VENTURA: God says to Abraham, "Go and kill your child." Abraham says, "Sure." Goes out there, sharpens his knife, takes the kid, they go for a ride, Abraham pulls out his knife, just when he's about to kill his kid God says, "Uh, you don't have to *really* kill him." It begins with: You have to be willing to kill the child if you're going to make a covenant with me.

Abraham is asked to kill his child, which is also the child within; you have to be willing to leave that behind to make a covenant with the eternal. God says, "If you're not willing to kill the child, then forget about this covenant."

PASSY: That's an interesting God that would say something like that. Let's say he has all these different figures to pick on; it's a curious choice to pick on the child to sacrifice. So what is that in the imagination? A figure that is obsessed with killing the child?

HILLMAN: You're killing the next generation, which, within language, is the second meaning. It's metaphorical, the next generation, the next way of seeing something. So by killing the child you keep the linearism. In other words, killing the child is the maintenance of literalism—is the equivalent of literalism—on the language level. That's why you have to kill the son, because the son is the second interpretation, he generates it further, so you've gotta kill that, if you're a literalist, a "fundy."

VENTURA: So when God says to Abraham, "You don't have to kill the son after all," he's saying: "Hey—don't take me so literally!"

HILLMAN: He's also showing that the compelling insistence to kill has its own inhibition.

VENTURA: At the same time there's the demand: "I'm not going to tell you 'Don't take me literally' until you've traveled three days with this intent and you're on the mountain and you're holding the knife." You have to live with this intent for as long as Jesus was in the tomb, you have to *really know what it means* to take God literally, before he turns around and says, "Don't take me so literally."

Jesus never turned around and said, "Don't take me so literally." The mistake Jesus made as a teacher was saying take it even *more* literally. "If you *think* you're committing adultery, you're committing it." That destroys the imagination. That's what's made Christian culture terrified of its own imagination for two thousand years.

Here's a thought: in history, the God of the last eon becomes the devil of the next. The serpent of the pagans became the devil of Judeo-Christianism.

HILLMAN: Pan—

VENTURA: —becomes Satan.

HILLMAN: The Jews get seen as satanic in the Christian world.

VENTURA: So is Jesus going to be the devil of the era to come?

HILLMAN: Let's not even ask the question "Is he going to be?" Let's imagine it that way. In that case, we see the fundamentalist world as a satanic cult.

VENTURA: And they're projecting their satanic cults on other people, but their cult is not about Jesus, it's about Satan.

HILLMAN: I would say it a little differently. They are projecting satanism on everyone else, and they're seeing satanism everywhere. Which means that their mindset is already satanic. You can only see what your eyes allow you to see, so if you're seeing satanism your mindset has got satanism in it. Also, as we know, the amount of strange satanic cults going on in America is remarkable and is tied in with the multiple personality disorders that are appearing everywhere.

So if that's the case, that Christian fundamentalism is actually a satanic cult, then—the inner child, which was Jesus, is kicked out of Christianity, so the inner child is lost now.

VENTURA: All these lost inner children running around the books of Bradshaw and Miller.

HILLMAN: Pick up your original theme: the new religion always demonizes the old religion. In that case as we move into the twenty-first century after two thousand years of Christianity, Jesus will become demonized, is becoming demonized, becomes the new Satan, the new devil. In that case the holy child, which was associated with Jesus for two thousand years, the bambino, can no longer be associated there, is lost, is an archetypal figure without a symbolic representation.

So where is that lost child, lost baby? That lost child becomes the thing in all Western psyches now, the central figure of the therapy cult. Then therapy, which started as a revolution against Christianity, will have become a kind of sublimated Christianity.

VENTURA: A sublimated Christianity in which childhood serves as the new Hell.

PASSY: Why is incest being discovered at such a fast pace in psychotherapy? That's a very important question. And incidentally, as a therapist hearing this stuff I'm not convinced that all of the incest being reported has literally occurred.

VENTURA: It's hard to tell one way or the other.

PASSY: Okay, let's say rather that incest is part of today's imagination, not twenty years ago.

VENTURA: The incest is and was there, but today dealing with it is more important to our imaginations, and you're asking?

PASSY: Why did our culture today, at this very moment, require incest—in its imagination? My hunch is that we've lost the ability for different figures of the imagination, the psyche, even to talk to one another. Our inner selves are so isolated!

HILLMAN: From each other.

PASSY: And what would be a psychic necessity under a circumstance like that? What would serve to inseminate?

HILLMAN: Incest. They fuck each other.

PASSY: Our psychic figures fuck each other, and we imagine that as incest.

HILLMAN: To connect they have to invade, transgress boundaries.

PASSY: Exactly. And what is so frustrating is *that's* what's really going on in the consulting room with this incest concern; it's being read in the wrong way.

HILLMAN: It's being read in terms of a further separation. And that produces more incest.

PASSY: The more the imagination is thwarted, the more the acted-out incest comes to even further break down that boundary.

It's really exciting when you work that way, because then you can say—I'm thinking of a typical incest fantasy, a common one that comes up in therapy, Grandpa. Why is Grandpa in this girl's imagination now wanting to fuck her? What happened or failed to happen between the two of them that *now,* in her imagination, they need to fertilize one another, need to make contact with one another?

HILLMAN: Fucking isn't the crucial thing, it's being in touch.

PASSY: They lost touch with each other. Grandpa and granddaughter, in life, in the selves, in the imagination—they lost touch with each other, and now they need to be brought back in touch.

VENTURA: And then people stay in therapy and incest groups for years talking about it as a way of continuing it, so that those figures can, in imagination, continue to fertilize each other?

PASSY: Exactly! And—

VENTURA: A lot of this incest has happened, for a long time, but I think what you're saying is both the reason it has happened and the reason it is, as we've talked about, remembered traumatically—instead of being remembered some other way.

PASSY: In a culture that doesn't allow those different figures to be in touch with each other, you're gonna have incest. Our culture is so separatist. It doesn't allow.

And that's what I called to say. So. I think I'm through interrupting you.

HILLMAN: Thanks, Stan.

VENTURA: 'Night, Stan.

PASSY: Good night.

A pause.

VENTURA: When Stan's on a tear, he just gets hold of an idea and shoves it in your face till you deal with it, and he won't be put off.

HILLMAN: That's how thinking used to get done—communities of people like that. That's how the concepts of school and university started.

A pause.

HILLMAN: The compulsion to innocence. What is it about America? Why this dominant theme going all the way back to our first novels in the eighteenth century—the loss of innocence? It's been written of again and again. That's the major theme of American literature. Why are we a culture that doesn't want to lose its innocence?

VENTURA: Doesn't want to lose its virginity. And constantly manufactures new versions of virginity.

HILLMAN: What is the moral superiority of being innocent? And why are sophistication and culture somehow corruption?

VENTURA: It goes back to the Puritans, where any sort of imagination was doubt or deviation and considered the work of Satan.

HILLMAN: What does puritanism have to do with therapy?

VENTURA: I think puritanism is the root of why a lot of people go to therapy. In the sense of, "Why do I go to therapy? I don't know how to be monogamous, I have all these terrible thoughts, I don't know how to live the straight and narrow like I'm supposed to, it's driving me crazy, I go to therapy to—"

HILLMAN: "—get straightened out."

VENTURA: "Yes. So I can live in this confined place that my puritanism tells me I should live in. I should be a good husband and love only my wife, and a good father and sacrifice everything for my kids, and I should go to work and love going to work, and I should go to church on Sunday but not let the Gods and spirits into my daily life where they're too disruptive, and if only I could do that I'd be fine, but I have moods, I have tempers, I have fears, they all get in the way, they throw me off the good path."

HILLMAN: "And I know I should keep my body under control. But instead I eat too much and I drink too much, and I eat chocolate at night before I go to bed and I really shouldn't be doing that anymore, and I still smoke, and my body is full of appetites and lusts and perversions and peculiarities and—"

VENTURA: "—and I want therapy to cure me of all this." In other words: *"I want therapy to cure me of having a psyche."*

Because that's what puritanism says: "If you do this and that and practice such and so and believe that and this, you won't have to worry about having a psyche. Your psyche won't matter, it won't be a factor."

HILLMAN: "You won't have to worry about having a body, either."

VENTURA: "And anything that intrudes on the 'normal,' the straight and narrow, is evil. Which is an insidious way of saying: the psyche is evil. And if the psyche is trying to put some curves in your 'straight' and widen your 'narrow,' if your imagination is coaxing you, goading you, seducing you, prodding you—"

HILLMAN: "Yes, my imagination is *filled* with extraordinary things that I shouldn't be doing—"

VENTURA: "If your psyche and your body are trying to keep you from living as we, the Puritans, would have you live, then they are evil."

You have this thing in psychology where you're going to therapy to be cured of having a psyche!

HILLMAN: That's right. That's extraordinary.

VENTURA: So it's not too goddamn surprising that the thing often doesn't work. Or you're going to a therapist for years—the therapist is the most stable and certainly the most expensive relationship in your life, and you keep that relationship so that therapy can act like a cattle prod on your psyche and keep it in the corral.

HILLMAN: Well, now, wait a minute, there are two kinds —we have to divide psychology a little bit. The kind of psychology that would support the puritanism, is what I would call ego psychology: behavior psychology, behavior therapy, cognitive therapy—the kinds that try to bring things under control.

VENTURA: Plus all those estian pseudotherapies.

HILLMAN: Right. Then there's another kind of therapy, and one I think we ought to remember, which is expressive therapy, and this would include Perls and Jung and some of the movement things, to name a few. Their idea is to let that stuff appear but not to bring it under control—I don't think controlling it is their ultimate theory.

VENTURA: It's not the theoretical aim, but even in the expressive therapies it usually becomes the aim in practice. It's only the really excellent, highly developed therapists who don't have that aim. The person, the client, the paying customer, comes in and the aim becomes: Bring your life under control.

HILLMAN: Cope.

VENTURA: Cope. And there's something to be said for coping, god knows.

HILLMAN: But, my god, coping can't be the end, the goal, of life!

VENTURA: Many people would disagree with you. And most therapists would disagree with you, not in theory but in practice. Now, most therapists would argue, "They're troubled when they come in, you've got to get them into a position to cope before you can do the rest." And that's where therapists start to sound like the Defense Department and the White House talking about national security. "Once we handle national security we'll have time for the real life, the psyche, of the nation." But in therapy and in government, everything goes into coping and/or national security, and the real life of the psyche or the nation is barely addressed. Regardless of their theories, many therapists don't see one inch beyond getting their clients functional.

HILLMAN: Functional defined as "in control." "You are out of control," "I am out of control," are big sentences now in this culture. And the important thing is to be able to control your behavior, get your shit together. I think *control* is one of the most dangerous words we've got right now in our vocabulary. First of all, it's a word that belongs with Honeywell, it's a "control systems" idea—that the *controls* (not the psyche or the Gods) are what run everything, run the ship, run the air conditioner, run the factory. Second of all, it's a word that belongs in the police world. So it's a combination of technological and bureaucratic or oligarchic or fascist. And it's become an ideal of therapy!

VENTURA: And yet when your life is out of control—

HILLMAN: When *is* your life out of control? Tell me about it.

VENTURA: When you're falling in love your life's out of control. And when you're falling out of love.

HILLMAN: Your life is *very* out of control! Out of control.

VENTURA: You get fired or let go or have an accident, your life's out of control.

HILLMAN: When you have a breakdown of any kind—bankruptcy, a death, a big illness—your life's out of control.

Do you realize the conditions we've just described are the great dramatic moments of life?

VENTURA: Which we're supposedly living for!

HILLMAN: That's what we're living for. Falling in love, being heartbroken by love—

VENTURA: —revelations that turn you inside out—

HILLMAN: —mourning and grief—

VENTURA: —victory, defeat—because when you get a big victory you're often as out of control as when you're badly defeated—

HILLMAN: —losing it, finding it—

What is all that emphasis on control? Isn't that what they call secular humanism, to ban the Gods?

VENTURA: We're banning the Gods—

HILLMAN: —with that control system.

VENTURA: We want to control all those things you supposedly live for—all those things that, if you get to be an old person, and you have not had them, you go, "What was my life about?"

HILLMAN: All the times you drove through the storm, all the times that bastard broke your heart.

VENTURA: And the old-timers smile and cry when they tell the stories. So on one level what you want is to be out of control, and on another level you're fighting that. That's your dialectic.

That's called, being around on the planet.

HILLMAN *(laughing)***:** That's called being around on the planet.

VENTURA: But a therapy that forgets the dialectic and weighs in so heavily, in practice if not in theory, on coping and control—

HILLMAN: Then in that sense therapy becomes a servant of the state. I've said that for a long time, and so have Ivan Illich, Ronnie Laing, Tom Szasz, and others. But what the republic—as opposed to the state—requires is not coping, adjustive functionaries; the republic requires active citizens. Individually thinking citizens—and loyal to, or part of, their community.

Maybe therapy hasn't been able to distinguish enough between the adjusted coper and the intelligent, sensitive citizen. 'Cause the sensitive citizen, if the society is dysfunctional, will not be able to cope.

VENTURA: You can't lead a sane life in an insane society. Function is going to clash with dysfunction. There can be no "successful conclusion" to a therapy that ignores this.

But what happens to the poor bastards who, for the best of reasons, cannot cope?

HILLMAN: Well, they go back to another therapist is what tends to happen.

VENTURA: They also get eaten alive, is what tends to happen.

HILLMAN: That's also what happens. You lose economic position, you lose status, you *lose* it. You don't get appointed to the academic chairs, you don't get the perks, you get low fees, and all the rest, because you're an outsider. You become marginalized.

VENTURA: And those dues can be pretty heavy. That's very real. I'm marginalized, you're marginalized. We've been very lucky, but it's the luck of the outer margins, outer-fucking-space as far as this society is concerned. I mean, there's the society, out this window and eight stories down. It's a dangerous place at best and a *really* dangerous place to be marginal in. A lot of people don't wanna pay those dues, take those risks, and you can hardly blame 'em.

But I do blame them.

I mean, really, what's being said here, what we're really saying, is an invitation to the hard life on the margins.

HILLMAN: I don't believe the hard life on the margins is worse, in many different ways, than coping in the middle.

VENTURA: I wouldn't take the life of coping in the middle for even a minute! I'd ten times rather have life on the margins than the *impossible* life of coping. Because coping in the middle—the psyche doesn't go away, the contradictions don't go away, the *conscience* doesn't go away. The lost dreams haunt. Coping in the middle every day drains a little more of your spirit until—until not only aren't you happy, 'cause coping is an impossibility—

HILLMAN: Coping with the dysfunctional suggests that you become more and more dysfunctional as you become more and more adjusted.

VENTURA: Not only does that happen, but the one thing that didn't have to happen has also happened: you've betrayed yourself. There are all these parts of you that you thought, once, were important, and that you don't pay any attention to any longer, because with coping in the middle you can't.

HILLMAN: I presented something like that at a meeting in Washington and a woman stood up and said from the floor, "I agree with what you say and this has been my life and my philosophy. And I have now an M.A.—" maybe it was even a Ph.D., but the point is, she had been so marginalized that she was down to earning $4.50 an hour putting cloth into some machine on a production line. She'd had an endless number of jobs, was constantly going down scale. Okay, we can say *she* was at fault. Her point was, "Yes, I'm fucked up, yes I am hysterical, neurotic,

I've had a lot of troubles, but there is no way I can live in the society truly following the beliefs I have." The beliefs we've been talking about.

VENTURA: Right. Unless you're very, very lucky, there isn't.

HILLMAN: Then you agree with her.

VENTURA: Absolutely. You and I have been lucky.

HILLMAN: I'll say we have, my goodness! But also, I've compromised, you've compromised. I wouldn't use either of us as an example of the heroic marginal person. I don't think I am.

VENTURA: It's not a question of "heroic marginal." Now *we're* getting puritan: "If you're on the margin, you have to be heroic." No. But there's a difference between compromising and selling out. Sometimes you're gonna maneuver, you're gonna give a little, you're gonna dance, you're gonna duck, to stay alive; you don't wanna be a dead or even penniless hero without a *very* good reason. But selling out means accepting the goals and the tactics of the society as your own, as a way of life, when privately you don't agree with that way of life at all. Going along with stuff that you know contributes to the greater dysfunction. Living off the dysfunction. *That's* selling out.

If you share the commercial, "me first" values of this society, survival's hard enough. If you don't, survival *with your values* is a great deal harder, because the society doesn't support any of it. *Any* of it.

I wonder how many therapists deal with their clients' relationship to this issue. And I don't see how the consulting room can become a cell of revolution if this issue isn't discussed in the consulting room.

A pall seems to rise in the room. There's total silence except for the noises outside. It's extraordinary how through all the traffic, brake squeals, honking, and sirens, fragments of human voices drift up eight stories through a closed window. They can't make out the words, but they can hear the voices.

And the snug, orderly, colorful apartment seems to hover above it all like a dirigible.

VENTURA: You know, the changes we want are *so* radical; we are scratching at the beginnings of a huge new conceptual framework. For therapy to be a cell of revolution—

HILLMAN: I've been lecturing about one direction for the revolution: let's begin with support and recovery groups. "Monday night I'm at an AA meeting, and Wednesday night I'm with the fat people, and Thursday night I'm with the child-abused and abusers, Friday night I'm with sex addicts, and over the weekend I'm recovering from another catastrophe. Hell, I don't even have time to go to the movies, there's just so much going on in my psychic life."

Now these support groups are symptomatic of therapy today. They're all over the country. Millions of people are meeting every night of the week in the United States. The people in each support group are all joined by a single symptom. They become very much like single-issue politics. Instead of joining to be pro- or antiabortion or to take on schoolbook censorship, they're focused on the fact that I'm overweight, that I drink too much or smoke too much.

Now, what's wrong with them and why I call them symptoms—

VENTURA: You're calling the support groups symptoms?

HILLMAN: I'm calling the support groups a symptom of our time because they further the individualism.

VENTURA: How do they do that? Isn't each group a kind of community?

HILLMAN: It isn't community. I'm there, everybody is there, in order to support *me.* "I have a terrible time with my smoking. And you do, too. And each of us is there to deal with *my* smoking problem. And I'll help you with your smoking problem—"

VENTURA: "—my drinking problem, my abuse problems, my problem that my parents drank—"

HILLMAN: "I'm an exhibitionist, that's my problem, and the court has sent me into this group, and I meet every Friday night with other exhibitionists, and we're trying to work, each of us, on *my* problem."

Now, a *possibility* of community does arise. The loyalty to that group is a very strong thing. People are really, as they say, bonded. People don't miss their groups. They stay in them. There is a deep affection. But the focus of this "community" is still not on any communal activity.

My point is—let's use food as an example. Instead of being there because I'm part of an eating disorder, let's say I'm there because of a food disorder.

VENTURA: Eating is something *you* do, but food is an issue out there in the world. I like the distinction. So you have "food disorder" and?

HILLMAN: And in my group from now on we must talk not only about my personal habits but also about agribusiness, fertilizers, pesticides, packaging, advertising, school lunches, fast foods, diets. We have to talk about the entire thing, because an obese person, a person with an eating disorder, is already in the food business. So there's a conversion of the group from being me-focused to being food-focused. And that leads you into the world. Political awareness. Political action.

That could be done for the alcohol people. That could be done for the wife batterers.

VENTURA: How?

HILLMAN: Let's take battered women. "What we need to do here is not only talk about why I submit and I can't let go of this guy. I've been hit by him four times now, he threatens me and I'm terrified, and that reminds me of the fact that my father used to do that and I was always trying to make up with my father to keep him calm and peaceful. And I really love this guy. Besides, *maybe* I get certain kicks out of being beaten. Maybe. I don't want to admit that, but hell, we're all in this group together—" and so forth.

Now, suppose we move that conversation a little bit, to violence on TV. And further, to the ultimate way of discipline: the final step of discipline in our culture is to hit someone. Hit the kid. The hitting is kind of a crude form of keeping something in order. The breakdown of language, of communication.

VENTURA: Hitting as communication. Hitting as the only way to touch, because of the roles and pressures put on males at all levels of this society. "I can't fuck you, I can't get it up, I can't talk to you, I can hit you, I love you. After I hit you I can break down and say I love you, I can't do it before then."

HILLMAN: "And my weeping, and being excused, is terribly important to me. Because I'm *never* excused, I walk around with such a load of guilt you can't imagine—"

VENTURA: "I need to be forgiven so bad that I'll do this so you can forgive me for it, and I'll keep hitting you so you can keep on forgiving me, because I need forgiveness over and over—"

HILLMAN: Okay, but we're still into "you and me." I want to get this into the society. It's got to be political. "Why is it that I'm unable to be forgiven, to get forgiveness? Why do I carry such a load of guilt? Why can't I break down and cry? I know what the group leader says, I even have a therapist and I know what he says and we've investigated my family background, and it doesn't seem to change this tremendous load, why do I feel so bad and need to be forgiven so?"

VENTURA: The discussion could be moved like so, the man could be made aware that maybe it's: "Because there's no place for me in the world. Because I feel so unimportant. The voting system tells me I'm unimportant, only the ones with the most money win, my vote doesn't count. The television tells me I'm unimportant. I watch the television, it doesn't watch me, it doesn't talk about me, it doesn't show anything about my life. "Cosby" is not my life, "Dallas" and "Roseanne" are not my life. I am so unimportant that this huge media world doesn't care about depicting anything like my life—"

HILLMAN: "And where I work I get shit on all day long. I have no importance there at all."

VENTURA: "So I am worthless. I feel worthless because the whole society is structured to say it can do without me."

HILLMAN: "I can be replaced at any moment. You—my wife, my home—are the only place where I'm not replaceable."

VENTURA: "Home is the only place where I can exert any sort of power. But, I'm not educated to speak. It's not just that I *can't,* it's that I've been educated to be stupid."

HILLMAN: "I've been educated to be psychologically stupid too. Inarticulate. I've been educated to be inarticulate. There's no elocution in school, and all they tell you there is to shut up, they don't teach you how to talk. They told me to shut up for twelve years. Talking's not in my education. I'm never allowed to stand up and rap, which is one of my ways of talking. Or curse, which is another way."

VENTURA: "I can't use black English," which is a legitimate and beautiful language.

HILLMAN: It's not only black English. "If I'm Appalachian, if I'm blue collar, I've got an enormous language that I can't bring to school."

VENTURA: "So the school says I'm worthless. And I can't speak to you because I'm in a society that does not speak. Its version of a conversation is Johnny Carson and Arsenio Hall, innuendos and one-liners that mean nothing. And I can't touch you because I'm in a society where there are more guns than people and all touching is threatening. Growing up male, to be touched is to be threatened—you have to be ready to fight. Hitting, fighting, soldiering, being tough—that's what's been expected of me as a man, by my family, by my street, by my friends, by my country, by my TV. I am not *really* a man unless I can hit.

"So how in the hell am I supposed to get it up? If I touch you I'm harming you. If you touch me, that's a threat. All touching is threatening, all touching is bad, and to break through all those inhibitions I have to get angry, let my anger out, and you get hit."

HILLMAN: Well now, listen, it goes even deeper. We have to deal with touching not only between people but in the entire way of one's work. "I hardly touch a fucking thing in my work. There's very little touching that has any kind of sensitivity, where my fingers actually feel anything. And the stuff that I touch, the surfaces I touch all day, are plastic, styrofoam, cold metal, so in a way there's a slow anesthetizing, my hands have become brutal."

VENTURA: "There's nothing subtle that I touch, there's no texture in my life. And then the lights go out and I'm supposed to touch you. I don't know how to do that. And that makes me even more humiliated and afraid. And *angry*."

The psyche is saying this all the goddamn time. Some of the more extreme results are battering and rape, but, as most women will tell you, there's an epidemic of impotency out there, and that's related to all of this.

HILLMAN: *This* stuff, now, *is* political. This has to do with architecture and design, and who makes those decisions, which are so important for the community at large, and how those people get to make the decisions and why. This has to do with surfaces, the quality of the world, an untouchable world.

Your angle about "I can't get it up" is very important, because it's deep in the male psyche to get it up. And "If I'm in a system, in an office, a warehouse, or any place where I am impotent all day long in my social, physical, architectural life, then the value of potency becomes tremendous. I have no potency anywhere out there. Only in my home. And if she doesn't deliver, or if I can't—it's the one place where the society gives me the 'right' to be potent, and the humiliation of not being able to or being denied is insupportable to me."

VENTURA: "When I'm degraded in my situation, I also feel very guilty and very ashamed. Because something in me is saying that even though the whole world is constructed this way, my failure is purely and simply *my fault.* And what passes for individualism in this society agrees and points the finger at me: 'It's *your fault.*'"

HILLMAN: And therapy chimes in with, "And it's *your mother's* fault and *your father's* fault. You should be ashamed and angry with your whole damn family."

VENTURA: And you can't be ashamed of your family without being ashamed of something in yourself.

HILLMAN: "Therefore I'm carrying around such a self-hatred that you can't imagine. I've internalized the fact that I'm low man everywhere. So I need forgiveness more than you can imagine. So I beat you so that you'll forgive me."

So we're saying that, in order for the group to be a community and for the group and the consulting hour to be a cell of revolution, therapy has to talk about the person's physical and work environment, and about what goes on in the person's day.

The sex addict needs to talk about pornography, about advertising, everything that is designed to turn you on.

VENTURA: *And* everything designed to keep you repressed. The churches, Miss Manners—

HILLMAN: —and therapy's ideas of "relationship." In the sex addict, what kind of political awareness can you have about that? You wouldn't be for restrictions. My solution would be—

A long pause.

Prostitution.

VENTURA: Your credibility just took a very long walk on a very short pier. Prostitution so that—

HILLMAN: —so that the fantasy life would be freed.

VENTURA: Heavy-duty bordellos. As in Genet's *The Balcony,* or in the Marquis de Sade. Yes. Yes!

HILLMAN: The classical bordellos that have been with us throughout history as part of high culture.

VENTURA: I hear a chorus of, "Throughout the history of the *patriarchy,* you mean!" But prostitution appears to have started in the temples and rituals of what were still matriarchal religions. It was about fucking in ritual space—

HILLMAN: —as a sacred experience.

VENTURA: And that's what a lot of so-called sex addiction is about—the search for fucking in ritual space. People will risk an enormous amount—their reputations, their marriages, their jobs—to fuck in ritual space every now and again. Or you could put that a little harsher, as the puritan culture would, and say: people often take enormous risks to exercise their perversion.

HILLMAN: The only way you can understand some marriages, or why certain people stay together, is they've finally found someone they can share their perversion with.

VENTURA: I like that. That's a reasonable reason to get married and a reasonable reason to stay married. Because what the society is calling perversion you're feeling as a transcendent experience.

HILLMAN: That's where to go with dilemmas of sex. Fucking in ritual space. It's not pictures of pussy or dick.

VENTURA: Fucking in the temple. "I call thee in the Goddess's name" was the ancient phrase.

HILLMAN: In the old-fashioned bordello the *imagination* of a person was cared for. Same for de Sade, which is a storybook of images. When the imagination of a person is not cared for we're left not only with what they now call sex addiction and sex therapy (which is a technology of sex and not the art of sex), but we're also left with the grandfather and the uncle who finger the little girls. Again, sex molestation and all that is partly a function of the repression of prostitution and of all sexuality not considered "normal."

VENTURA: And with the repression of prostitution, as with the repression of drugs, you instigate and even foster its worst abuses: pimping, violence, illness, slavery.

HILLMAN: So it's the RITUALIZATION of sexuality we're talking about. It would be what we would call the improvement of prostitution.

VENTURA: Taking prostitution back where it began, as ritual, so the prostitute isn't an outcast but is honored. Sex is an art too, and prostitutes would become regarded as highly sophisticated performance artists.

HILLMAN: Instead of sex therapy we should have sex artists.

VENTURA: People judge prostitution now in relation to what? In relation to their fantasy of normality. But what about people who don't feel "normal"? And they exist.

HILLMAN: In droves. Through telephone sex we already have this imaginal sex going on at a tremendous rate.

VENTURA: And we're talking about male as well as female prostitutes, old as well as young, fat, bony, one breasted, no breasted.

HILLMAN: A guy comes to a therapist or a sex addiction group, and he says he masturbates in front of a mirror and he feels that he's a God. And this is one of the *complaints* that he brings to therapy and to his support group, because this exalted feeling makes him a sex addict, a weirdo, abnormal. Now of course he's out of control. But the moments of being out of control are the divine moments.

VENTURA: What did Blake say? "The road of excess leads to the palace of wisdom." The most antipuritan idea there is.

HILLMAN: Freud's revolution was an attempt to deal with nineteenth-century European puritanism. Then Jung and Reich did the same thing. That *is* the root, psychotherapy *is* a revolutionary movement against puritanism. And puritanism has reappeared in our time in all these recovery groups. What you're recovering from is excess, an idea of excess, and from desire—desire for drink, desire for smoke, desire for sex, desire for work.

VENTURA: The assumption is that the desire is wrong and the social structure is right. And in that sense the Twelve-Step programs, unconsciously but at their very core, support not only the state but the state of *affairs* that causes so many of the problems that they're attempting to deal with.

We're back to vicious circles.

A silence.

Do therapists ever ask their patients how they vote?

HILLMAN: I asked that at a conference of therapists, and their answer was shock at the question.

VENTURA: That would be something. Or dealing with how the policies of who they're voting for relate to the things they're angry about, the things they feel belittled by in the world.

HILLMAN: And what they think about the new referendum on taxes or car insurance, where to put the new prison or hazardous waste dump. Do we ever talk about the actual political issues of that day?

When the patient talks about being angry about something—"The goddamn developers, they're putting up this building that's gonna cut the sun off for the afternoon just down my block, no more afternoon sun"—does that come into the hour, and if it comes into the hour, how is it talked about? Is it talked about as a personal problem? Is it talked about symbolically, about being "cut off from the sun" as though the guy were dreaming it? Is it talked about in terms of aggression and hostility and why you have an authority problem and that you always somehow are rebelling and coming in and bitching about what's wrong with the world? *Or is it taken up as a vital part of the citizen's life?*

That would be the cell of revolution—when the therapist gives to every single hour a lot of attention to what's going on in the client's actual emotional life in the world. How does he feel about the subway? How does she feel about the way her workplace is organized? What do clients feel and think and desire about these kinds of things, and how do they impinge on and influence their lives with family and friends?

VENTURA: How does that become a cell of revolution?

HILLMAN: Clients begin to have to relate their psychological lives to the world's problems. And they cannot duck out of positions in the world by referring to victimization and weakness and "I'm only one person," and scoot back into an internal life or personal relationships.

VENTURA: But, man, if it's the therapy of revolution we're after, we have to be responsible for that word *revolution.* 'Cause revolution is a pretty heavy word, a pretty heavy situation.

HILLMAN: Why don't we just call it "the therapy of revolt"? No, it's not enough.

VENTURA: *Revolution* just *feels* better.

They laugh.

VENTURA: We have had, in the last several years, concrete examples of revolutions, extraordinary revolutions—Eastern Europe, China, Palestine, the Soviet Union. You hear people saying about Europe and about Russia, "Well, they're in this big mess now," as though everything was supposed to be all hunky-dory right away. But they tore down a whole *system* in months, sometimes in days, in many places without firing a shot. Of course they're confused and troubled about where to go next, but they definitely have been through a revolution, and most of it was nonviolent.

HILLMAN: Utterly unpredictable and amazing.

VENTURA: They tore that whole structure down, and it's going to take them ten or twenty years to build another, twenty or thirty messy years, and there will be a lot to criticize about that new structure, but it will be *their* fucking structure.

HILLMAN: They put themselves in a position where they are having to imagine how to do new things. That is revolution.

VENTURA: So what are we talking about when we say "revolution" here in the United States of America, where, among other things, there are more guns than people? See, I feel that fact strongly. I don't wanna get caught in anybody's cross fire, and I don't want to inspire people to get caught in a cross fire. They're caught in enough cross fires as it is. At the same time, we have seen that one of the strongest forces in the twentieth century has been people, unarmed people, getting out into the street in a common cause—sometimes spontaneously, sometimes organized; sometimes with a charismatic leader, sometimes without.

HILLMAN: But it begins with the realization that things are not right and an analysis of how they are not right—that's the first step. *And that is the job of therapy.* Because therapy deals with things that are not right. It's called dysfunction. And instead of imagining that I am dysfunctional, my family is dysfunctional, you realize what R.D. Laing said long ago and Freud, of course, too: it is the civilization that is dysfunctional. The society is dysfunctional. The political process is dysfunctional. And we have to work on cures that are beyond *my* cure. That's revolution. That's realizing that things out there are dysfunctional. That's the therapeutic task. It's not to tell a person how to fight or where to fight, but the *awareness* of dysfunction in society, in the outer world.

VENTURA: It's not just your parents, your childhood—

HILLMAN: —or my relationship with my marriage. There is a dysfunction in the society that is affecting us. And the second step is: I cannot repair it in myself in my own relationships alone, because my problem is social dysfunctions. So how is settling things with my wife going to repair the dysfunction of the general situation? That's a romantic delusion—that if we could just get our sex right, our conversations right, "if I could just find the right relationship—"

VENTURA: "If my little home could be perfect, could be safe—if I could find balance in my home I'd be happy. Talk to my kid, talk to my wife, quit drinking, get laid decently a couple of times a week, get on a decent diet, get exercise, make a little more money, then I would really be okay." Except you won't. Because you still live in this crazy world of dysfunction that impinges on you and influences you and yours twenty-four hours a day.

HILLMAN: "Where the school isn't right for my kids, where the food I eat is not right, where the air I breathe is not right, where the architecture in which I spend my time assaults me, the lighting and the chairs and the smells and the plastic are not right. Where the words that I hear on TV and are printed in the newspaper are lies, where the people who are in charge of things are not right because they are hypocritical and hiding what they are really doing—so how can I ever get it right within my home and within my marriage?"

VENTURA: One of the things we are saying is: You can't make a separate peace. You can't sign a peace treaty with society through therapy.

HILLMAN: And you can't use your therapist as solace and as retreat.

And your therapist can't use you. The three big diagnostic terms that you hear thrown around now are *codependency, addiction,* and *narcissism.* We know from the new literary criticism, deconstruction, that any descriptions you use are always descriptions of the reader, not of the text. They are readers' self-descriptions. In the same way, those diagnostic terms are analysts talking about *their* conditions: that *they* are codependent, in therapy; that *they* are addicted and can't stop; and that they are involved in a narcissistic activity, which is called countertransference—they keep examining themselves about how they're feeling about their patients.

VENTURA: An element comes in here, and that is: time. Because the problems we are speaking of are *enormous* problems.

HILLMAN: You don't think communism in Poland wasn't an enormous problem? Or in East Germany? Or the Soviet Union? They weren't enormous problems?

VENTURA: But it's as though Eastern Europe had to get rid of those relatively enormous problems in order to start to cope with the *really* enormous problems that face us. Communism in Eastern Europe wasn't as enormous a problem as an entire world sustaining itself through self-destructive and planet-destructive work. Because with *that* problem, you have to change the means of production, and even more you have to change the *goals* of production. You have to change what you use, how you live, what you expect.

So what therapy would be saying, then, if it's really going to be a cell of revolution, is what Rilke claimed was the fundamental meaning of art: "You must change your life." But it's not defining your life simply as who you are at home.

HILLMAN: As who I am in myself, in my room, when I'm thinking about myself.

VENTURA: It's defining your life as you at work, you as a citizen, you with a history that is not only the history of your family but of your country and your civilization. It's making you aware of all that.

HILLMAN: The history of the way you live and not only the history of you.

VENTURA: To see your story as yours alone is to repress the community—and repress the Other World. And this devastates the imagination.

HILLMAN: I think it is very important to recognize that the imagination is not "mine."

VENTURA: Whose is it?

HILLMAN: Better to ask, where is it?

VENTURA: Where is it, then?

HILLMAN: We're in it. We're *in* it. It's the medium in which we live.

VENTURA: There's something else that should come in when you include, in your case history, the history of the way we live, which is that the way we live, or the way we've tried to live, is ending. Western civilization is ending.

The phone rings.
The message plays, and then:

A WOMAN'S VOICE: Michael? Pick up if you're there.

VENTURA: *That's* one of the sentences of our time.

HILLMAN: It certainly is.

VENTURA: And what's that *mean?*

WOMAN'S VOICE: Are you there? If you are, pick up.

VENTURA: In rooms all across the country, the phone rings, the person is there, the caller sort of feels or suspects the person is there because they do the same thing—

HILLMAN: Are you going to pick up?

WOMAN'S VOICE: Okay, later for you.

The woman hangs up.

VENTURA: Too late now. This happens in millions of rooms all over the country every day. Constantly. People there and not there. There but not answering. Sorta there, but—

HILLMAN: "Pick up if you're there" isn't even a question. It's a request phrased as a command, and it's an assumption—historically, it's an extraordinary assumption—

VENTURA: —that the person might very well be there but is ignoring you for whatever reason. And there's a kind of acceptance in the assumption—

HILLMAN: That they have the right to do this?

VENTURA: More like: that's just how it is now. That you can't call somebody and expect an answer. And you know, in turn, that you don't always answer when you're called, so it's not a question of blame, it's just—it's not that kind of a world anymore, not an *answering* world.

HILLMAN: We have answering machines in order not to answer.

VENTURA: The call of one person to another doesn't have the authority it used to have. That authority of the human call has been subverted, undermined. And it's twisted, distorted, as in: someone calls you but then, while you're speaking, their call-waiting beeps and even though *they've* made the call to you they put *you* on hold—an incredibly rude, crude behavior. But it's become accepted, first in the business world and now in personal calls. It's disgusting, when you think about it—the degradation of the human call.

HILLMAN: I refuse to get call waiting.

VENTURA: Yeah, that's where I draw the line too. I believe in busy signals.

HILLMAN: What you just did with that woman is acceptable behavior?

VENTURA: In an equally disgusting sort of way, yeah. When you really sit down and look at it, it's shameful. It's shameful not to answer a human call. And we most of us do it. What comes to mind for me is part of a poem by Yannis Ristos, where he compresses the ancient Greek ethic into:

> Never refuse fire and water to anyone.
> Never mislead anyone who asks for the way.

All of that has fallen to pieces so completely—

HILLMAN: —that we live with the sentence "Pick up if you're there."

VENTURA: It's hard for the therapist to bring "the history of the way we live" to people who behave as we behave. And I think you've touched on why, but we haven't gone far enough with it and it's been haunting me—what I was talking about when the phone rang. I think the reason is that, collectively, we are denying the tragedy of this historical moment in which we live: the fact that our civilization is ending.

HILLMAN: Does it have to end? Maybe the decline can be halted.

VENTURA: But it's more than a decline, it's a total transformation. The very technology we're inventing dooms the civilization we had. Our Caucasian-dominated, Euro-American civilization has less and less authority every day precisely because its technology has joined the world in such a way that *all* cultures are rushing together at a dizzying rate and not one of them is strong enough, philosophically or economically, to dominate the others. So all are losing power in various ways and are in varying states of hysteria, whether it takes the form of Islamic fundamentalism or an America in which the average person watches six to eight hours of TV a day. That's all hysterical behavior.

Even what appear to be victories aren't victories for the traditional civilizations. The technological superiority of the Japanese is destroying that culture's traditions. In the so-called victory of America over communism, the countries of Europe and the world don't need the American military anymore, so America loses its central position in world policy. Civilizations, and the paradigms they were based on, are disintegrating all over the earth, all at once. And the very technology we cling to increases the disintegration, so it's another vicious circle, nothing can stop it.

No, let me go on.

The night we saw *Dances with Wolves,* watching that story of the death of the Sioux culture I thought: We too are experiencing the death of a culture. (Which is the secret, I think, of why that movie was so popular.) Collectively we're sharing the experience of the end of Western civilization—a great and tragic moment. It's tragic not because Western civilization is better than other civilizations, but because there's a ground note of tragedy when anything passes from the world forever. And this *is* a great thing, an incredible event, the death of Western civilization—an epic moment in the life of the human race. And, like the Sioux, we should savor and sing the beauty of this death.

HILLMAN: That's very Latin—a Latin or Latin American or Eastern European vision. We should savor and sing and grieve the beauty of the death instead of wallowing in nostalgia and sentimentality for the good old days.

VENTURA: And instead of giving into, being possessed

by, terror. Not that you don't feel terror—you can't help it—you *can't* get used to hearing sirens all through the night, not really, not deep down. But this *is* the historical moment we're in. A great culture, Western culture, is dying. Or, to put it a little less darkly, it's transforming such that you won't be able to call it Western civilization anymore. Nobody knows what's going to come. The New Agers think a marvelous period is about to dawn; the right and left each live in fear of the other "winning" the transformation; while the technocrats think they're going to reprogram humanity. In reality, it's out of everyone's control, and the very grasping to control it just increases the momentum and cost of the decline.

HILLMAN: And the American government tries to maintain the old political culture by indulging in things like the Gulf War, doing the same old thing again to keep the same system going. It is simply a diversion from the great descent we're now involved in and prevents us from recognizing and experiencing the beauty of the decline or of treating it realistically. The Gulf War puts the whole culture in a hyper state, praising the use of power, when that isn't the issue.

VENTURA: The issue is: our culture is over—

HILLMAN: —and how do we go through the rituals of the dying of the culture?

VENTURA: This is part of the therapy of revolution, as in "the wheel revolves." The wheel of human history is revolving.

HILLMAN: So this implies that individual suffering—

VENTURA: Any individual's grief and panic is, at this moment in history, in part a grief and panic at the dying of our culture. And if psychotherapy doesn't deal with that, it's in a state of denial of one of the root causes of our pain.

HILLMAN: That involves our panic at the concept, and the fact, of death. It's part of the notion in Western culture that we die alone. It's the background of existentialism, of

Heidegger and Sartre, the background of Western religion—you meet your maker, you're all alone with your maker or the void. *No!* We do not live alone, we do not die alone. You die—other cultures say you join your ancestors. That's what you're doing when you're dying, you're joining your ancestors. It's a joint event, as the funeral is a joint event. The whole thing of dying is really a big communal event for the dead and the living. It is not dying alone in an existential trapped-ego consciousness.

VENTURA: Or having to be judged.

HILLMAN: Or going into a white light, where Saint Peter meets you personally. Or Jesus, your *personal* lord and savior. No, you meet your ancestors, other cultures say—you meet your loved ones. It's a very important, different notion of death. We concretize our dying alone into the hospital bed with the tubes up the nose. See, we've literalized the fantasy.

VENTURA: So we in the West don't have a vision of this dying civilization joining the collective memory and heritage of the race, where it would feed the human heritage long after its time, as other civilizations have done. Instead we see the death of Western civilization as an absolute ending in which we have to justify all our history—so we fake and lie a lot and wave flags—and which will probably (so we tend to think) bring the end of the entire world.

HILLMAN: After us, the deluge.

VENTURA: Many people are, without being aware of it, taking this moment in history as a *personal* thing—personal grief and panic as a victim of all this. And there's probably even a thing about it somehow being "my" fault: "If I were a better person the civilization wouldn't be collapsing all around me! I could control that collapse, at least as far as what's right around me is concerned." It's pathetic when you think about it, though we've all felt it.

HILLMAN: Not only taken as a personal thing, but what

do you do as the ship hits the rocks? People hold each other's arms and say, "You know, I really love you." Watch every movie, what do they do as the plane begins to go down?

VENTURA: Not just movies. All those black box cockpit tapes of the last moments of an airplane crew, somebody's always saying, "I love you, Mom," "I love you, Mabel."

HILLMAN: Now this is a very important way of reading the search for the significant other.

VENTURA: It's part of the whole emphasis on relationships, in therapy and everywhere.

HILLMAN: You want somebody to hold in your arms as the plane goes down.

VENTURA: As the civilization goes down. That's "love" as we approach the year 2000!

HILLMAN: Now I can hear voices say, "You guys are so morbid. Jesus, are you morbid!"

VENTURA: *I'm* morbid?! Children are being *shot to death* in America at the rate of several a day, hundreds a year, and *I'm* morbid? Kids in East L.A. and South Central L.A., when a car comes down the street a little too slowly they take cover, they hit the dirt—no shit, they do, it's part of their daily life. And tonight, in Manhattan, which fancies itself the capital of the twentieth century, we've barely had a moment without the sound of sirens. That's the America we're living in. *I'm* morbid?

We've been talking about "what story are you in, as a person in therapy." We are in the story now, collectively as a culture, of the death of the dominant culture. And if you see *that* as the backdrop of any personal story, then it's a whole other vision. For one thing, then you're not a victim, you're a character in an epic story, and the story contains all the characters. And *meaning,* itself, as in any great epic, is not in the individual characters but in the story as a whole.

We're living the story of—

HILLMAN: —the shipwreck—

VENTURA: —of a culture.

HILLMAN: The world is going down.

VENTURA: And we seem to have no metaphor for that but the metaphor in the Bible's book of Revelation: Apocalypse. And if we're not careful, we're going to enact that because it's our only metaphor.

HILLMAN: It's fundamental to our Western myth.

VENTURA: But it *can't* be the only metaphor. Cultures and civilizations have died again and again and again, maybe more than we know.

HILLMAN: Now what are you getting to?

VENTURA: That if we look at the death of the culture as an epic story that we are in the middle of, then that is not as fearsome a thing, because the story in a way gets resolved by its ending—by the fact that it, the culture, ends.

HILLMAN: I wonder about that.

VENTURA: I don't mean this makes anything all right or easy, I mean—

HILLMAN: You're saying the *story* is not shipwrecked.

VENTURA: Right. The *story* is not shipwrecked, and the story is there to tell, to be told, to be lived—and the whole culture is in the story.

HILLMAN: That's important. Yes. Shipwreck is going on but the story is not shipwrecked. You're saying—

VENTURA: —you can't negotiate with an avalanche. Nothing, nothing, nothing is going to stop the shipwreck of this civilization. The forces, the momentum, are too great. The wheel is revolving. That revolution—not in the political sense but in the sense of a change in everything we know—that revolution is inexorable. But it is part of a larger story that is even greater than the event.

HILLMAN: But my approach is, the world is getting worse and that's correlated with therapy's concerns, and if we were less concerned with ourselves and paid more attention to the world, the world wouldn't be getting worse. So, in your view, I'm still doing a therapy.

VENTURA: You're still doing a therapy. You're trying to turn the story, or trying to give a tragic story a happy ending. And that can't be done.

HILLMAN: You're saying, "The world is getting worse, *that's* the story, and you won't accept the story, Hillman, you won't accept the story."

VENTURA: But accepting the story, accepting that this civilization is ending, doesn't mean you don't fight for what you believe. You take part in the story. You do the portion of the story that is given you.

HILLMAN: Krishna and Arjuna.

VENTURA: See, we get such hubris about, "Well if the world is getting so bad then I shouldn't do anything. If that's the story then fuck the story." Which is like saying, "If I'm gonna die why should I live?"

HILLMAN: How do you live in a time of decline, and what role does therapy have in a time of decline?

VENTURA: You do the work of the soul. You don't fuck around. You don't waste your life trying to find a secure place in the avalanche, 'cause there ain't no such animal. You do the work of your soul.

HILLMAN: You don't depend on the culture, the culture will not carry you.

VENTURA: Right. But the story will, the story of the fall and rise of civilizations. That story's larger than the culture. It's *about* the culture, so it's outside the culture.

HILLMAN: Some people would say the story is a product of the culture, that only a declining culture would create a story that says it is a declining culture.

VENTURA: And other people would say the story begins outside the culture with, "Once upon a time, there was a culture." A story told, perhaps, by the Gods.

HILLMAN: The role of therapy, then, is to awaken the patient to the fact that, not only is the society dysfunctional, but—

VENTURA: —it's going through an absolutely fundamental change. The concept "dysfunctional society" itself may be palliative, because it assumes something else is possible during a change like this. What is clearly not possible is to find your own little psychologically safe and stable place.

But bringing in the community, the Gods, the history of the country, and the end of civilization as we know it—

HILLMAN *(laughing)*: The poor client!

VENTURA: The poor bastard's groaning, "All you're gonna tell me about is one more fucked thing. And I've heard all the fucked things I want to hear. I can't do nuthin' about the fucked things I already know about, and you're bringing all this shit in."

Why isn't that depressing beyond belief?

HILLMAN: It's only depressing if you are in the posture of the child and feeling powerless and then there's still another big thing out there to blame and you can't do anything about it. But for me it doesn't feel depressing, it feels relieving, immensely relieving to know that it's not me that's at fault and I don't have to own and be the cause of all my misery. There's something fundamentally wrong in the society and this relieves me of the blame, first of all; and second of all, it relieves me of the guilt; and third, it excites me, draws my attention outside to more than myself. That's not depressing.

Depression tends to make you focus on yourself. The very focus on oneself that we do in therapy is, per se, a depressive move. Therapy could be causing depression as much as curing it, because the classic symptoms of depression are remorse, a concentration on oneself, repetition—"What's wrong with me? How did it get this way? I shouldn't have done that." Feeling poor and broke and without energy—in other words, a withdrawal of libido from the world. The moment you're focusing back on the world as dysfunctional, you're drawing attention to the world. That's not depressing.

VENTURA: But it could be incredibly overwhelming. "What can I do about the collapse of a civilization, f'crissake?!"

HILLMAN: That's why it's so important to focus on pieces. Now this is where you and I don't agree. I'm a Ralph Naderite: let's get this little thing fixed, then this, then this—this ridiculously small fixing of the social order. Your vision is, it's an avalanche, it's an entire mindset, it's inexorable, you can't really do anything about it—

VENTURA: —and anything you try to do, no matter how well motivated, will only speed the avalanche along a little. (Which, in my view, isn't a bad thing.)

HILLMAN: So I could be very stupid with my Ralph Naderism.

VENTURA: But I could be very stupid with my avalanche, I could be draining myself and others of power. But all this dysfunction doesn't personally depress *me* because it gives me a lot of room to maneuver in, an awful lot of room to maneuver in.

HILLMAN: Right. It says, off the bat, "I'm not neurotic." That's a huge relief.

VENTURA: "I'm not neurotic, this is not my fault, and it's not my family's fault either."

HILLMAN: "The world-soul's sickness is announcing its despair through me."

VENTURA: "*But* I'm not a victim, because this is the sweep of history and I'm a participant."

HILLMAN: Which also means, "I'm also not the healer."

VENTURA: "Putting it all right is not my job"—which is another lightening of the weight, more room to manuever in.

HILLMAN: That also came up in regard to feminism and the mens' movement. "I am not responsible for two thousand years of what you call patriarchy. I'm responsible for the fact that I've left all the dishes on the counter, and I've done that night after night and I've not cleaned up after myself, but don't tell me about the patriarchy 'cause *I'm* not responsible for two thousand years of what happened."

So the dysfunction around you—is it possible to deal with things piecemeal?

VENTURA: I.e., if putting it all right is not your job, what *is* your job? Well, it's obviously possible to deal with some things piecemeal. You and your community in Thompson, Connecticut, have kept your village from turning into a 7–11. That's a big thing.

HILLMAN: And to fight over trees as Gary Snyder does.

VENTURA: So it's definitely possible, there are definite things you can accomplish.

HILLMAN: People who've fought for the dolphins, so that there are now labels on tuna cans—I think those things are important! I'm still a therapist. As the ship goes down, you do the little jobs of caulking and trying to keep the plumbing running, even if the whole ship is going down. *Do* you stand there and keep the hot water system going in a shipwreck?

It's a great question, a lovely question.

VENTURA: I think you do, and you know why? Because we don't know anything. In spite of all the evidence of decline and catastrophe, we don't know *anything*. Remember what I said before about the fundamental wildness of the universe? Life is beyond anyone's power to predict or control. As Laing said, "Who are we to decide that it is hopeless?"

It's not like the negative, destructive forces have all the power. They don't.

HILLMAN: Look at the Berlin wall. Look at Eastern Europe.

VENTURA: Something I've thought for a long time is that this negativity, the official negativity, if you like, the destructive acts that just seem to pour out of Washington, D.C., and the corporate decisions—they enlist such enormous power. The things I am for and love have virtually no obvious power, so how strong must they be, to be able to do what they have done! How innately strong must, if you like, *beauty* be to do what it has done and save what it has managed to save with no power and resources against a destructive system that has immense power and resources.

HILLMAN: My friends talk about decency. Isn't it extraordinary how the world goes on working with decency, in spite of it all? Somebody falls, somebody tries to help them. There's just an immense reservoir of human decency around. It's a great power in the world, for keeping things going, in spite of all the corruption.

Therefore we can't predict, we can't say the world is going to hell in a basket, it's too easy. You run the risk of being caught in an archetypal fantasy.

VENTURA: That's the danger I always run into.

HILLMAN: Any one of the archetypal fantasies, whether it's "the world is getting better" or "the world is going to hell in a basket"—these are myths that seize us and are comforting, because any single one you get into is comforting.

VENTURA: Whoa, how is "it's all going to hell in a basket" comforting?

HILLMAN: If your nature is dark, you may find the darker fantasy comforting. Another friend of mine's fantasy that comforts him is that everything is senseless and all our systems are attempts to make sense of what is essentially senseless. Therefore you're always in a valley, you can never get out of the valley, no matter which system you set up. I find that a despairing notion, but for him it's a mythological fantasy that gives comfort and safety. And when you say to him, "Look, you're just hiding in that one," he says, "No, don't you see how despairing it is, there's no safety?" But he's safe inside a fantasy of no safety.

VENTURA: If you say it's all beyond prediction or control—that in fact your fantasies don't fulfill themselves in the long run, they contradict themselves in the long run—then you can't control it with your systems, because life is beyond what we can think about it. Life is going to fool us all.

HILLMAN: Life is beyond what you can think about it. We need, nonetheless, to think about it.

VENTURA: We have to, because that's how human beings are made.

HILLMAN: That's part of life, to think about it.

VENTURA: But it's beyond any system we can concoct, so if we say, as I've been saying, that it's an avalanche—it clearly is an avalanche, but it's more. And if we say, as you've been saying, that it can be treated, well clearly it can—but it can't. And if we say that the continual denial of the Bill of Rights by the

Supreme Court, the government, and most of the population —if we say that's the end of the American republic, clearly it is. But it isn't.

HILLMAN: How isn't it?

VENTURA: Because the idea "all men are created equal and endowed by their creator with inalienable rights" is larger than America and larger than Western civilization. The statement that "government of the people, by the people, and for the people shall not perish from the earth" transcends America.

HILLMAN: Regardless of how hard some Americans are trying to make it disappear from the earth.

VENTURA: The idea is larger than America. It's an idea America gave the world, but our republic being finished doesn't mean the idea is finished.

HILLMAN: Yes. If you are for the American republic, the Bill of Rights, the Declaration of Independence, if you are for these things you are against the American empire. The task of the consulting room is in part to keep the pores open to what goes on in the empire. The job of psychotherapy is to keep one *suffering* the decline of the republic.

By suffering I mean acutely aware of the pain of this loss. That you are afraid, politically afraid. That you and the patient are unconsciously making little moves that adjust and adapt you to the new empire. That you *are* using sports as the Romans used gladiators. That you are watching victory parades as the Romans watched Triumphs. Again, as I've said, the job of therapy, in part, becomes one of keeping you acutely conscious of the dysfunctional society.

VENTURA: Because when you keep the pain of the loss of the republic alive, when you keep the pain of the death of the civilization alive, then you keep *possibility* alive.

HILLMAN: What do you mean by *possibility?*

VENTURA: Okay. My feeling is that this worldwide disintegration is going to play itself out no matter what, and it's going to take a while, a century or two—a century or two of a kind of chaos, possibly a corporate nightmare, I don't know, but call it a Dark Age. We had a technologically primitive Dark Age, now we're going to have a technologically extraordinary Dark Age. But you remember what philosopher Miguel de Unamuno said: "We die of cold and not of darkness."

Just around when he was turning thirteen my kid came home one night, after dark, sat on the couch, and in a kind of fury suddenly burst out with, "It's *fucked,* it so *fucked,* man, the whole thing is fucking *fucked.* What do you *do* in this world, man?" What could I say to him, that things are gonna be all right, when they're not? That it'll be okay when he grows up and gets a job, when it won't? I got a little crazy and impassioned and I said something like this:

That we are living in a Dark Age. And we are not going to see the end of it, nor are our children, nor probably our children's children. And our job, every single one of us, is to cherish whatever in the human heritage we love and to feed it and keep it going and pass it on, because this Dark Age isn't going to go on forever, and when it stops those people are gonna need the pieces that we pass on. They're not going to be able to build a new world without us passing on whatever we can—ideas, art, knowledge, skills, or just plain old fragile love, how we treat people, how we help people: *that's* something to be passed on.

HILLMAN: Passing on what you love can also mean taking action—political action, civil disobedience, *even if you know you're going to lose.* Because the memory of actions taken is an important way that things get passed on from generation to generation.

VENTURA: Remember the Alamo.

HILLMAN: You bet. And John Brown, Nat Turner, Birmingham, Tiananmen Square, and the brutal suppression of Solidarity only a decade ago—and now they're in charge.

VENTURA: And all of this passing things on, in all its

forms, may not cure the world now—curing the world now may not be a human possibility—but it keeps the great things alive. And we have to do this because, as Laing said, who are we to decide that it is hopeless? And I said to my son, if you wanted to volunteer for fascinating, dangerous, necessary work, this would be a great job to volunteer for—trying to be a wide-awake human during a Dark Age and keeping alive what you think is beautiful and important.

HILLMAN: Keep the memory alive.

And an important part of that memory is the memory of our political ancestors. See, I don't think Jefferson and Madison are just political ancestors. They're psychological ancestors; they're ancestors of the American soul. So we want to keep Lincoln alive, and Jefferson alive, because they represent why we are Americans. To think of them as psychological, as ancestors of the American soul—that's very important.

VENTURA: Our republic, which is dying politically and culturally, has to live within us psychologically—yes, that's a wonderful idea. We are responsible for the republic now. We always were, but now it's critical. We are responsible for the republic. If the republic doesn't live in *us* it doesn't live, because the American government and much of the population have denied it so thoroughly.

It's still as Wilhelm Reich said: "Work, knowledge, and love are the wellsprings of life."

HILLMAN: Whether the ship is going down or not.

VENTURA: It's *so* difficult, because when the ship is not going down then work, knowledge, and love have a resonance in the community. You don't feel that depth of resonance in an era of panic. The word *Panic* comes from the great God Pan, the Disruptive One, the divine energy gone mad, the Pan who suddenly appears screaming and everybody goes crazy and runs away. That's the "ic" of Pan-ic.

And it's not just that the civilization is dying. Nature as we know it seems to be dying too—seems to be dying *because* the civilization is dying, which is an extraordinary thing.

HILLMAN: We usually get it reversed. We tend to think the culture is dying because nature is dying, but, no, nature is dying because the culture is dying. The culture does not support the nature.

VENTURA: And the culture got powerful enough for that to matter. When Rome fell, nature didn't give a damn. The tribal cultures fell, nature didn't seem to blink.

HILLMAN: When the French monarchy fell—

VENTURA: —nature didn't care.

HILLMAN: I think when Hitler fell nature didn't care either.

VENTURA: But we're falling and there's a dialectic with nature involved, though I think nature's too strong to die. It *is* changing drastically, it will never again be the nature of our mythology.

HILLMAN: Well, I don't agree. I think Mother Nature is on dialysis. And we have to keep nature going with technology, for a long time, till it's in another balance—technology in the service of nature.

VENTURA: It'll get to another balance without us just fine, but it depends on what you're defining as nature.

HILLMAN: I'm defining nature as songbirds and the ocean and the water supplies—the whole rhythm of the climate.

VENTURA: But we're nature too. So this decimation is something that nature is doing to itself. We're not these nature aliens fucking up nature, we are something that's happening—

HILLMAN: —*in* nature.

VENTURA: Yes. Between nature and nature. The phenomenon of the ecological disaster as a whole is natural in that it is something nature as a whole is doing. It's as though nature used a flood to change everything in one era, ice in another, and humanity in this era. To nature as a whole there's no big difference if the catastrophic changes come through ice or an asteroid or humanity. What seems to be important, if you look at *the long-term behavior of nature,* is that the catastrophic changes come now and then to wipe the species slate fairly clean to make room for new varieties.

How do you do therapy on *that?* With that as a backdrop?

HILLMAN: Don't look at me, kid. That's *your* backdrop.

VENTURA: I'm back to the concept of the avalanche—that we are in the midst of inexorable processes not susceptible to acts of will.

And it raises the question: In the context of the avalanche, of the ship going down, the death of cultures, what is the difference between madness and insanity?

HILLMAN: You made a move and said that the *story* doesn't end—the story is the mythical imagination. It's only if you forget that the ship going down is a story and take the end of the culture literally—

VENTURA: —as the end of the human race, the end of all history and all nature—

HILLMAN: —that would be insane.

VENTURA: It's when you mistake the end of the culture for the end of the story that you get incredibly depressed. "Everything is ending." But everything *isn't* ending, it's just this civilization that's ending. Nature isn't ending either. Even in a worst-case scenario, nature is changing one balance for another, and it's unlikely that balance won't include humanity.

HILLMAN: The Apocalypse is the myth of our culture, it's *the* book of our culture, it's the last chapter of the holy book, of the writ. And what it is is the destruction of the entire world. If you take that literally you get that book called *The Late Great Planet Earth,* which is one of the only books Ronald Reagan ever read, and which was the largest-selling book in the United States in the 1970s. That's a literal interpretation of the Apocalypse.

But suppose you take it not literally but imaginatively. Then it is just the last chapter, the last chapter of the Bible. It is the Apocalypse of the *Bible.*

VENTURA: Not of the world.

HILLMAN: It's the end of the story!

VENTURA: The end of—

HILLMAN: —*that* story.

VENTURA: *That* story. The end—of the Bible. The Bible is over, and the civilization based on the Bible is over, but not the world.

HILLMAN: Exactly. The Bible is over, not the world.

The phone rings.
The message plays.

THE WOMAN'S VOICE: Hey, baby. It's me. Pick up if you're there.

Coda: Several Weeks Later

Hillman and Ventura are in Ventura's Chevy on Highway 101 near Santa Barbara. It's late at night, they've had a good meal and maybe a little too much wine. Ventura has already missed his exit once. The tape recorder is on as usual.

HILLMAN: Why can't therapy be interested in each hour as it appears and not try to thread those hours together into what's called a process, a journey, developmental growth?

VENTURA: The thread makes for the linear model, and the linear model is based on the idea of progress: this moment has to be better than the last moment or you're failing. There is this constant comparison between the present and the past and a constant anxiety at the comparison.

HILLMAN: Improvement. A big idea in clinical work is the word *improvement*.

The next right, the man said, which would be—shit, I hope that exit wasn't it. I think it was.

VENTURA: What, Sheffield?

HILLMAN: No, San Ysidro, that was it.

VENTURA: I missed it *again?!*

HILLMAN: Yeah.

VENTURA: Well, good! I didn't wanna miss it once. Better I miss it twice.

HILLMAN: That's really missing it, man.

VENTURA: That's *really* missing it.

HILLMAN: Anybody can miss it once.

VENTURA: Any asshole—

VENTURA AND HILLMAN: —can miss it once.